ew **Books**

PHONE (310) 253-2233 OR 254-0200 X361

D1010939

Defying the Crowd

Cultivating Creativity
in a Culture
of Conformity

Robert J. Sternberg

Todd I. Lubart

THE FREE PRESS

New York   London   Toronto   Sydney   Tokyo   Singapore

We dedicate this book to our wives,
Alejandra Campos and Sylvie Tordjman-Lubart

The Free Press
A Division of Simon & Schuster Inc.
866 Third Avenue, New York, N.Y. 10022

Printed in the United States of America

printing number

1 2 3 4 5 6 7 8 9 0

Library of Congress Cataloging-in-Publication Data

Sternberg, Robert J.

    Defying the crowd: cultivating creativity in a culture of confomity/
Robert J. Sternberg, Todd I. Lubart.
      p. cm.
    Includes bibliographical references and index.
    ISBN 0-02-931475-5
    1. Creative ability. 2. Originality. I. Lubart, Todd I. II. Title.
BF408.S76 1995   94-41129
153.3'5—dc20   CIP

Contents

Preface

People often speak of creativity as though it were a prized possession of only a few. We view this restriction as a sin—of which psychologists especially have been guilty—because many people with the potential for creativity probably never realize it: They believe that creativity is a quality they could never have. We found out the hard way the degree to which psychologists participate in this conspiracy: A research grant proposal we had written was dismissed with the comment that whereas we proposed to study creativity in ordinary people, it was worth studying only in the exceptionally gifted—a Picasso, a Cervantes, an Einstein, and the like.

We reject this point of view. We believe that creativity, like intelligence, is something that everyone possesses in some amount. Moreover, creativity is not a fixed attribute: A person's level of creativity is not carved in stone at birth, and like any talent, it is something virtually anyone can develop in varying degrees. This book tries to present a cohesive discussion of creativity. And although it is not a "how-to" book, it does contain many suggestions for ways in which people can develop their own and their children's creativity.

We find creativity in everyday life when people see new ways of accomplishing different tasks in their work, when they try daring new ways of relating to one another, and when they strive to turn their lives around. This is the kind of creativity available to all of us to confront the challenges in our lives. Although the contributions of people like Van Gogh, Milton, or Beethoven are of great interest, the study of creativity has to be made relevant to everyone, and that's what we are trying to do in this book.

As we approach the turn of the century, intelligence is not enough. There are plenty of "smart" people around, and many of them are failing to realize their life goals because they can't keep up with a rapidly changing world. Thus we cannot emphasize enough the importance of creativity. In such a world it may be *the* key to both survival and success.

Having begun our research on creativity by looking for commonalities among many creative individuals, some famous and others not, we came to the conclusion that there was something shared by all of them. This shared quality, however, was not what we had been reading about in the psychological literature on creativity, but instead the willingness to go against the crowd in effective ways—to "buy low and sell high," as we came to call it, drawing an analogy to successful investors who defy others in the stock market. We recognized that if few people had the guts to defy the crowd, it was probably because doing so requires a confluence of six resources, whose nature we will discuss in this book. These resources are available in varying degrees to everyone; by tapping into them, everyone can more fully utilize and develop his or her resources for creativity.

We hope to see and contribute to such a change coming to pass. In general this book is about creativity, both as it applies to the "greats" and, more importantly, as it applies in everyday life to all of us. We will discuss what creativity is, how it can be understood, how it can be measured, and how it can be enhanced in each of us. We have written a book that we hope will be of interest to all readers—young and old, professionals and laypeople, people who believe themselves to be creative and people who don't. For those of you who believe that you are not creative, we hope to show you that it is within your power to develop your creativity. For those of you who believe that you show creative gifts, we hope to show you how you can develop them further.

We have not attempted to review the entire literature on creativity to represent every viewpoint equally. For those who are interested in reviews of current and past literature, we suggest either *The Nature of Creativity* (Sternberg, 1988b) or *Before the Gates of Excellence* (Ochse, 1990). For those particularly interested in creative insight, we recommend *The Nature of Insight* (Sternberg & Davidson, 1995). There are many other fine treatments of creativity as well. In our book we emphasize our own point of view and discuss other points of view as they relate to our own. Toward that end we discuss the concept of creativity in chapter 2, present in detail our investment concept in chapter 3, and in subsequent chapters present the role this concept can play in fostering both the generation and the appreciation of creativity.

Acknowledgments

We are grateful to a number of people who have assisted us in the writing of the book. Susan Milmoe and then Susan Arellano, our editors at The Free Press, helped us shape the book. Jonathan Lovins helped to compile information. Melanie Grimes helped in editing the manuscript. Lana Edwards helped with tables, figures, and boxes. Sai Durvasula and Douglas Rau helped in producing the manuscript. Vicky Griggs helped compile references. And the members of our research group at Yale gave us comments on our ideas as we developed them. Some of our work on creativity has been supported under the Javits Act Program (grant No. R206R00001) as administered by the Office of Educational Research and Improvement (OERI), U.S. Department of Education. Grantees undertaking such projects are encouraged to express freely their professional judgment. Our book, therefore, does not necessarily represent positions or policies of the U.S. government, and no official endorsement should be inferred.

We give special thanks to our families for encouraging and supporting our creative efforts.

The Nature of Creativity

"They didn't want to hear it."

That's the straightforward, succinct explanation by an unhappy former employee of a high-tech firm, fired after suggesting a new consumer protection plan for purchasers of the company's products.

Or was it just a case of sour grapes?

Several years ago one of the authors was a consultant for a well-known and highly regarded firm facing an onslaught from competitors. Losing business, the firm wanted suggestions on how to improve its products in order to make them more viable. Troubleshooters outlined a plan that won the interest of the entrenched management hierarchy, which in turn asked the consultant for his approval, suggestions for improvement, or ideas for a new plan altogether. On evaluation the proposal was neither innovative nor competitive. The consultant therefore took them at their word and suggested a more revolutionary and forward-looking plan. His contract was terminated shortly thereafter.

They didn't want to hear it.

These are oft-told tales. It is probably safe to say that each year thousands of workers are victims of what might be called the "let a thousand flowers bloom" maneuver, formulated by Mao Tse-tung when he controlled the world's most populous country. After years of suppressing practically all new ideas, Mao suddenly appeared to do an about-face, encouraging the Chinese people to speak their minds. Some did, and having thus succeeded in identifying his formerly hidden "enemies" by encouraging them to "bloom," Mao imprisoned or executed many of them. Similarly, many times employees or students have heard that creative ideas are welcome, only to be ignored or punished by supervisors, instructors, and even peers for actually presenting such ideas. The others just don't want to hear it.

Does this mean that creativity is not desirable? Not at all! What is creative is new and often brings about positive change. But what is new is also strange, and what is strange can be scary, even threatening—which is why "they" don't want to hear it. But they are unwise not to listen, for the creative person with original ideas is the one who, with support, will advance and improve the milieu to the benefit of all.

What exactly is a creative person? Psychologists generally agree that to be creative, one needs to generate ideas that are relatively novel, appropriate, and of high quality (Sternberg, 1988b). But how does one do this?

In order to be creative, people need to act like good investors: They must "buy low and sell high." An investor who buys low in the stock market or in any other, buys investment vehicles that are not well regarded or well rewarded at the time. In the realm of ideas, a person who buys low, metaphorically, is willing to generate and promote ideas that are novel and even strange and out of fashion. This is not necessarily easy to do. Other people react to the creative person the way they react to the investor who swims against the tide: "What's the matter with you?" Others often see him or her as irrational or even stupid: If the investment or idea were any good, other people would already be using it, right?

Wrong.

Is our view of creativity idiosyncratic? Apparently not. In 1985 we did a study asking laypeople: "What are the essential attributes of the person who is highly creative?" (Sternberg, 1985b). Consider some of the core attributes listed:

"Tries to do what others think is impossible."

"Is a nonconformist."

"Is unorthodox."

"Questions societal norms, truisms, and assumptions."

"Is willing to take a stand."

The subjects who gave these descriptions were nonprofessionals—ordinary people. But would experts in various disciplines have said the same? As it happens, yes. Artists said that the creative artist is a risk taker who persists in following through on the consequences of risks. Businesspeople said that the creative individual in business tries to escape the traps of conventional thinking. Philosophers emphasized that creative thinkers never automatically accept the "accepted." Physicists highlighted the importance of questioning the basic principles to which everyone subscribes.

In other words all sorts of people agree: Metaphorically the creative person "buys low" by rejecting currently popular, conventional ideas that others are readily buying into, instead coming up with and championing fresh ideas. He or she then "sells high" when the idea "purchased" for a "low price" achieves societal value, as others finally recognize its worth and jump on the bandwagon. Analogous to stock market investment success, sometimes creativity fails to occur because a person puts forth ("sells") an idea prematurely, or holds an idea for so long that it becomes common or obsolete. We propose that selling high is important for creative success on an individual project and for a career of creative work. This book is about "buying low and selling high," about the resources one needs in order to do so, and about the people who are willing to follow this difficult path.

If we again consult our subjects, we get a very good sense of the kinds of resources that are needed to be creative—to be a good investor in the marketplace of ideas. In this introductory look at our investment theory and its components, we take the remarks of our panel of ordinary people as emphasizing that our theory is, in large part, consistent with common sense. It is built on our research findings and focuses on what people commonly mean by creativity, rather than on some highflying, psychologized sense of the word. Furthermore, it is also extremely important to note that in our view of creativity, a distinction exists between creative potential and creative performance. We focus on the latter—overtly manifested creativity. Some people may have creative potential, but it remains latent unless they manifest it in some observable form, by using the creative resources available to them. Our research and the remarks of our subjects point to six personal resources that are needed for buying low, selling high, and producing creative work:

Intelligence

Intelligence serves three key roles in creativity: synthetic, analytic, and practical. The first role of intelligence is to help see a problem in a new way, or to redefine a problem altogether. This is part of the synthetic, or formative, aspect of intelligence, which also involves insightful information processes. The participants in the study mentioned above noted the importance to creativity of being "able to put old information, theories, and so forth together in a new way," of being able to use "the materials around him or her and make something unique out of them," and of having the "ability to change directions and use another procedure." These statements express in different ways the need to see problems in a new light. In terms of the investment metaphor, one needs to form or recognize the idea that others probably do not yet see as valuable.

Consider, for example, the Post-its on which many people jot reminders of things they need to get done. These "stick-ums" were created when an engineer at the 3M Company ended up doing the opposite of what he was supposed to. He created a weak adhesive, rather than the strong one that was the goal of his working division. But instead of throwing out the weak adhesive, he redefined the problem he was trying to solve: namely, to find the best use for a very weak adhesive. The rest is history—not to mention increased convenience for consumers and fine profits for the company. Some of the greatest discoveries and inventions happen when people do just the opposite of what they have been told to do!

The second role of intelligence is to recognize which new idea is also a good idea, to allocate resources effectively, and accomplish other problem-solving basics. Here intelligence must serve an analytical role. For example, just because an idea is new doesn't mean it is good. It might be a new idea to build a house out of tissue paper, but it probably isn't a very good one. In the investment world any number of stocks sell at low price-to-earnings ratios, meaning that they are viewed unfavorably by the market. The creative investor needs to spot which ones have the potential to rise. In the world of ideas the creative person needs to distinguish those that have the potential not only to be accepted but ultimately widely valued.

An employee one of us has known in the creative department of an advertising agency illustrates the importance of this ability to be critical of ideas. Constantly coming up with new ideas, many of them good, the employee was extraordinary in the first, synthetic aspect of intelligence. In fact, he was intimidating to his coworkers for this reason. But this man had a problem: He wasn't able to tell his good ideas from his bad ones; he lacked the analytic perspicacity to know which ideas were worth following up and which weren't. Moreover, he had trouble making the ideas concrete—they tended to remain will-o'-the-wisps, half formed. The result was that, despite his synthetic intelligence, this man was not very successful at his job. In contrast, a coworker with fewer original ideas but more ability to analyze and realize the promising ones was rewarded with promotions and recognition.

The third aspect of intelligence is the practical one—the ability effectively to present one's work to an audience. Usually there is a critically important phase of bringing a new idea to fruition that involves "selling" the idea to others. The skill with which an idea is packaged can enhance it or disguise its quality. Also, a person will inevitably receive feedback on his or her work. Knowing how to react to this feedback is a practical skill. Is the criticism worth considering? Should one change the product? What changes will be optimal to meet the critiques?

To summarize, then, synthetic, analytic, and practical intelligence—the ability to see things in new or nonentrenched ways, redefine problems, and turn things on their heads; to structure problems, allocate resources, and evaluate ideas; and to promote an idea and use feedback from others—are essential for doing creative work. But in order to do original work one has to go beyond the status quo in one's field; and to do that one has to know what the status quo is. And this leads us to our second resource.

Knowledge

Financiers say that there is no substitute for knowledge when it comes to investment success. To know which low-valued companies are genuinely undervalued, one has to know a lot about them to distinguish the future winners from the perennial losers. In the world of ideas, similarly, one needs to know a fair amount about the field in which one hopes to be creative. To go beyond the contributions of the past, one needs to know what they are. Otherwise one risks reinventing the wheel.

Again, our study of people's conceptions of creativity supports the importance of knowledge to creativity. People mentioned "the ability for high achievement." To toy imaginatively with notions and combinations of ideas, one needs to know what the ideas are. Never to accept the accepted, one has to know what the accepted is. To question basic principles, one needs to know them. Creativity does not exist in a vacuum. Even when it consists of utterly rejecting conventional notions, it still requires knowing what those notions are.

We see the effects of lack of knowledge on creative performance every day, when people come up with ideas that are original for them but that nevertheless have been thought of before. A strikingly poignant case of this phenomenon is that of the Indian mathematician Srinivasa Ramanujan, considered one of the most brilliant mathematical thinkers ever. Because of his lack of contact with the outside world, he unwittingly spent much of his lifetime singlehandedly "rediscovering" much of what was already known in Western mathematics. Had he first gained a broad perspective of his field, he could have avoided this amazing yet futile career and instead turned his considerable talents to advancing, not rehashing, the mathematical knowledge base.

But how do we reconcile the need for knowledge with the importance of nonconformity and unorthodoxy? Might there come a point at which too much knowledge becomes a dangerous thing, at which one becomes so inured to a knowledge framework that it is difficult to see beyond it? We suspect this to be the case. Simonton (1984) has suggested that the most creative individuals historically have been those who are moderately educated in their disciplines—those with neither the most nor the least background. In the same vein, our view is that large amounts of knowledge can lead to entrenched thinking and the inability to go beyond the established bounds of a field. In effect one becomes the slave rather than the master of one's knowledge or point of view.

For example, in one case a group of mainframe computer designers was in charge of installing and updating files from diskettes to hard-disk storage. These specialists were approaching the update operation with a standard serial method, which involved reading and writing from diskette each file and directory individually. The standard procedure for a system update took twenty-one hours, and, if there was an error during the process, it had to be started over. A consultant who at that time specialized in a somewhat different area of computer design was able to look at the problem from a fresh viewpoint. He made use of the physical attributes of the diskette and hard drive to read and write efficiently whole sections of a disk rather than file by file. The system-update time was reduced to only forty-two minutes and could be restarted in the middle if an error occurred along the way. As this case illustrates, people can become used to looking at things in one way and have trouble seeing them in another. Thus not only knowledge, but also a willingness to see past it, is needed for creative vision.

Thinking Styles

Thinking styles are how one utilizes or exploits one's intelligence. They are not abilities but rather ways in which one chooses to engage and use those abilities. In the study of conceptions of creativity (Sternberg, 1985b), people mentioned that the creative person likes to "make up rules as he or she goes along" and "questions societal norms, truisms, and assumptions." These are styles with which people approach particular problems, and even life in general. Preferring to make up rules rather than follow established ones and questioning rather than simply accepting the consensual norms constitute what we call a "legislative style" (Sternberg, 1988a), which is a hallmark of a creative person. (See chapter 7 for further discussion of the legislative and other relevant styles.)

It is important to distinguish style from ability. A person may have the ability to buy low and sell high but not enjoy using his or her abilities in this way. The investor who can spot the winners among stocks currently considered to be dogs isn't necessarily going to use that ability if he or she is not naturally inquisitive and willing to question conventional wisdom. Similarly, a person who can devise new ways of seeing problems may do so rarely if he or she has developed a preference for problem situations that require executing well-defined instructions.

We have seen this ourselves in workers who have the ability to forge their own paths but simply prefer not to. Although they are wired for creativity, the juice is never turned on. On the other hand, we have also seen workers who want to come up with new ideas—who have the legislative style—but who don't have the intellectual ability to do so effectively. Although their switches are turned on, the wiring is incomplete. Style, then, is not ability—it is whether and how one uses that ability. And style is a key ingredient in creativity, as it is needed to help complete the circuit; to "switch on" abilities that otherwise might lie dormant.

Personality

It takes a certain kind of person to buy low and sell high in the financial markets, not just in terms of intellectual ability and style but in terms of general personality. Similarly, we would argue, a creative person tends to show a particular set of personality attributes. If we return to our study, we also find that people recognize creativity to be more than just a cognitive, or mental, trait: Creativity involves overall personality traits as well.

For example, our participants described the creative person as someone who "takes chances." We believe that this is an aspect of personality that is a main key to creativity. It is one thing to know that one should buy low and sell high but quite another actually to do it. It is hard to buy a "loser," just as it is hard to let go of a "winner." Moreover, someone who buys low in the financial markets inevitably takes the risk that the investment will never go up. In creative endeavors as well, it is difficult to convince other people that they are wrong and should see things another way. The pressure for conformity is usually strong, and the possibility of making a colossal fool of oneself by disagreeing with the crowd always lurks. Yet, to be creative, one needs to take that risk.

We cannot emphasize enough another personality attribute mentioned by participants in our study: A person must be willing to take a stand. One needs not only the desire and persistance to overcome the obstacles that others are likely to put in the way but also the courage to stand up for beliefs, even in the face of objections and ridicule. In fact the participants in our study also indicated the importance of a sense of humor to creativity, because a wry take on life or an ironical point of view may be a big help in pulling oneself through difficult moments of self-doubt and ostracism.

The hardest ideas to get accepted by others are the brilliant ones, just because they are creative and fly in the face of what everyone else seems to "know" is true. Galileo faced the Inquisition for his beliefs about the relation of the earth to the sun. In the nineteenth century, Ignaz Semmelweiss, a Hungarian physician-researcher, committed suicide, so despondent was he over the professional reaction to his suggestion that obstetrical patients might be dying because of germs on the unwashed hands of surgeons. Mozart died a pauper and was buried in a common grave. Each in his own way, however, was great; each left his mark. Still, one who is creative truly needs to show courage, even to laugh, when facing all those for whom conventions are a way of life.

Motivation

Investors who buy low and sell high are motivated to make the very best investments they can, regardless of what others think. The analogy holds for highly creative people. To go beyond mere potential and actually be creative, one needs to be motivated, as our panel of participants recognized in describing highly creative persons. They required that innovators be "energetic," "productive," and "motivated by goals." These goals may be extrinsic (for example, money, power, fame) or intrinsic (for example, self-expression, personal challenge). In financial markets the monetary goals are most salient. We will argue that for creative work both extrinsic and intrinsic motivators are useful, to the extent that they lead a person to concentrate on the task at hand.

Creative people are indeed high-energy, task-focused people, and Simonton's (1984) studies have shown them to be far more productive than ordinary people. In the scholarly professions they publish much more, and in the realm of technology they invent much more. As observed by Gruber (1986), they have a sequence of interrelated projects that unfold throughout their lives. At times their goals may be clearer and at other less so, but they are always intensely motivated to achieve objectives that they themselves set. Although, as our participants noted, creative persons "like to be complimented on their work," they are strongly motivated intrinsically by an attachment to this work. Creative people are almost always doing something they love. Likewise, distinctive work will rarely come from someone who hates the task at hand.

Environmental Context

Some environments nurture creativity and others squelch it. Consider the case of a student who was studying the planets of our solar system in her third-grade class. The teacher had a good idea—that the students dress up like astronauts and simulate visiting Mars. As psychologists we liked this teaching technique: What better way to understand the problems astronauts would confront on another planet than by pretending to be actual astronauts? Then one student suggested carrying the simulation a step further: She would dress up like a Martian and meet the astronauts when they arrived. The teacher immediately rejected the plan: "We all know that there are no Martians on Mars," she said.

This clearly was not an environment that nurtured offbeat ideas. Creativity is in part the product of an interaction between a person and his or her context. A setting that stimulates creative ideas, encourages them when presented, and rewards a broad range of ideas and behaviors will surely foster original and nonconformist thinking.

Maybe the teacher really didn't like the idea of the student dressing up as a Martian, or maybe she was preoccupied with other things that day, or maybe there was only a limited amount of time in which to prepare the lesson and she couldn't make last-minute changes. But the lesson for this student (and, sadly, for many schoolchildren in many classrooms) was not about astronauts or Martians: It was about what to do with one's creative ideas—namely, keep them to oneself.

And so we return to the theme of this chapter. In coming up with creative ideas—in buying low and selling high—one risks offending, scaring, and even threatening others and their beliefs. In some cases one risks one's very career, friends, or reputation. So who needs creativity? Our answer is that everyone does—for creativity is the spring that propels technological, cultural, financial, intellectual, and certainly personal leaps. How much more creativity might we see in the world if only those who *should* support creativity really *did*—if they *truly* wanted to hear it?

What Is Creativity and Who Needs It?

Glance at a newspaper; talk to your friends and colleagues: You will find many diverse problems calling for creative solutions and many cases in which individuals or companies exercise creativity. In a newspaper story we read of two chefs who concocted a recipe for tapioca smothered in a blackened caramel sauce to fulfill the premise of a *Saturday Night Live* sketch calling for 150 gallons of faux caviar. In a project to raise funds for a school, students learned to market a line of health food products and the school shared in the profits from the sales. In a courtroom a judge awarded temporary custody of two children to a church as part of a solution to the mandatory waiting period for adoption. The minister and members of his congregation shared responsibility for the children. Finally, a construction company needed to provide flexible day care for working mothers, who made up an important part of their labor force. Because the job required schedule adjustments due to weather, working late without notice, and working weekends, traditional child care was not always available. The solution was a company-run child-care facility built from mobile homes that could be set up at each construction site.

What Is Creativity?

What do we mean by creativity? We describe a product as creative when it is (*a*) novel and (*b*) appropriate. These two elements are necessary for creativity. A novel product is one that is statistically unusual—it's different

11

from the products that other people tend to produce. A novel product is original, not predictable, and can provoke surprise in the viewer because it is more than the next logical step. A product can be novel to different degrees. Some products involve a minor deviation from prior work, whereas others involve a major leap. The highest levels of creativity involve a large step from preceding work. The perceived novelty of a product also depends on the audience's prior experience.

A product must also serve some function—it must be an appropriate answer to some question—it must be useful. There is a range of appropriateness from minimally satisfactory to extremely good fulfillment of problem constraints. Something that is novel but doesn't fit the constraints of the problem at hand is not creative—it's just bizarre (and irrelevant).

In addition to novelty and appropriateness, which we view as necessary features of a creative product, there are quality and importance. These are additive features of creativity because the higher the quality and the importance of a product, the more creative it tends to be. However, these aspects of a product are not required components of creative work.

A high-quality product is one that is judged to show a high level of technical skill and to be well executed in one or more ways. If a novel, appropriate idea is not skillfully turned into a full-fledged product, the work may be viewed as less creative because the audience does not fully appreciate or see the novelty and appropriateness.

The importance of a product can also serve to enhance or diminish judgments of creativity. Sometimes an idea can be novel and useful but rather limited. An example is finding an innovative way to attach a rearview mirror to a car in an automobile manufacturing plant. In contrast, sometimes an idea can have wide scope and lead people to even further ideas. Conceiving of a whole new mode of transportation is an example that takes our point to the extreme. Thus, the bigger the concept and the more the product stimulates further work and ideas, the more the product is a creative one.

We describe a person as creative when he or she regularly produces creative products. We differ from some psychologists who would require as evidence of creativity not necessarily creative products but some indication of the potential for producing them. In our view it is one thing to have the *potential* to be creative, and quite another to *be* creative. We suggest that everyone has at least some potential to be creative—and people differ widely in the extent to which they realize that potential, for reasons to be discussed in this book.

Why Creativity Is Important

If you were interested enough to pick up this book, you may find it absurd to question the importance of creativity. However, the importance of creativity is not obvious to everyone. One of the authors, in a colloquium with undergraduates at one of the national military academies, was asked by a student: "Why is creativity important, anyway?" This question does not arise only from elite undergraduates. We have met many professionals, including psychologists and educators, who view creativity as a somewhat secondary and insignificant psychological phenomenon. Others aren't even sure that creativity exists as a separate attribute, for example, or that it is different from intelligence. Consider a story that speaks to these issues.

Two boys were walking in a forest when they encountered a problem. A huge, ferocious, obviously angry grizzly bear was charging at them. In order to understand the reactions of the two boys, you need to know something about each one. The first had a high IQ, excellent grades in school, and superior commendations from his teachers. His teachers thought he was smart, his parents thought he was smart, and, perhaps unsurprisingly, he thought he was smart too. The second boy didn't have such a high IQ, such good grades, or particularly strong commendations from his teachers. Some people thought he was offbeat; others just found him strange.

As the grizzly bear approached, the first boy calculated the approximate speed of the bear and the approximate distance it would have to run to reach them, figuring that the bear would reach them in 17.9 seconds. Clearly the boy was smart! He was smart, perhaps, in the same way as Spock in the first Star Trek series or Data in The Next Generation. The boy looked at his companion and, to his amazement, saw him taking off his hiking boots and putting on his jogging shoes.

"You really must be stupid," said the first boy. "We'll never outrun that grizzly."

"That's true," said the second boy. "But all I have to do is outrun you."

The first boy was eaten alive, while the second one jogged off to safety. The first boy was smart, but the second boy was creative.

Of course the importance of creativity, and its difference from intelligence, can be demonstrated in ways that do not involve apocryphal stories. Consider a number of different occupations and what is important for success in each of them.

In science there can be little doubt that success requires a heavy dose of creativity. Studies of the sociology of science (for example, Zuckerman, 1983) show that creative scientists are those who deal with large and important problems rather than small and trivial ones. They are people who come up with new ways of seeing scientific phenomena rather than merely confirming the ways others see them. The most creative scientists come up with their own paradigms for scientific research, which often differ from the paradigms others in the field are using (Kuhn, 1970). Creative scientists are leaders in their field, and indeed, as Simonton (1984) has noted, it is often difficult to distinguish genuine leadership from creativity.

Although you may think that everyone knows these facts about scientific creativity, they are often not reflected in schooling. For example, in most schools, a good grade in science is a result not of creative work but of memorizing a textbook and successfully solving problems at the end of each chapter. Indeed, in our own field, psychology, most introductory courses require little more than memorizing the main "facts" presented in an introductory book.

The senior author's own introductory psychology course—back in 1968 when he studied psychology formally for the first time as a college freshman—was certainly of this kind. He got a C in the course. The grade was enough to convince him to change his intended major—from psychology to mathematics. Perhaps it is fortunate that he switched to mathematics, because he quickly discovered that he was even worse in it than in psychology! He promptly switched back to psychology and stayed with it. But how many potential majors in psychology, or other sciences, have left the field as college freshmen or sophomores because they didn't like to memorize or because they weren't particularly good at doing so? In the case of the senior author, he has been a professional psychologist for almost twenty years, and not once in those years has he had to memorize a book or solve end-of-chapter problems. What you need to do well in elementary and secondary school, and even in university science, often has nothing to do with the kind of creative endeavor that is required of scientists. The result may well be that some of our most potentially creative scientists are derailed early from studying science, whereas some students who specialize in memorizing books and solving problems at the backs of chapters may continue in the field, only to discover later that what they are cut out for is taking science courses but not actually doing science.

Perhaps you are thinking that of course science requires creativity, but science is not a typical profession. How many of our children will eventually become scientists? Then take writing, whether as a reporter, novelist, poet, playwright, or whatever. It is one thing to write an essay on an assigned theme and quite another to come up with a topic on your own and then to write a creative work, whether fact or fiction. The person who is able competently to produce an essay on an assigned topic is not necessarily the same person who is able competently to come up with his or her own ideas.

Consider the case of Arthur, a college student. Arthur had received excellent grades throughout secondary school and even in his first three years of college. But then, in his fourth year, he needed to do an independent project. For the first time he was not in his element at all: He had to come up with his own topic, his own thesis, his own organization. He received a low grade on the paper. Arthur was a good example of someone who was smart, in a manner of speaking (he had in fact had sky-high SAT scores), but definitely lacking in creativity.

Or take another example: art. There is a difference between being able to draw well and drawing creatively. One has only to go to a museum and see the people, their easels next to great works of art, copying them in minute detail, to realize that their ability to reproduce existing work does not imply an ability to produce new and creative work.

Several years ago one of us gave a talk in an elementary school and passed a typical first-grade classroom. On a bulletin board outside the classroom were roughly twenty pictures, under a sign, MY HOUSE. Each picture was of the child's own house. And many of the pictures were indeed fine renditions of the houses in which the various children lived. But whatever skills the teacher may have been trying to develop, she certainly was not doing her utmost to develop creative ones. Obviously she had told the children to draw their houses, rather than allowing them to have some choice of topic. The teacher had thus deprived the children of one of the most creative aspects of the artistic enterprise. That's not to say, however, that teachers should never give children a topic. Nor is it to say that there's no possibility for creativity when one is given a topic. Rather, what's important is to give the children a choice at least some of the time.

This lack of choice is not limited to art, or to first grade. One of us once visited a school that was holding an exhibition of sixth-grade social studies projects. (Parents had been invited to the school to see their children's projects.) What were the projects? "Minnesota," "New Mexico," "Florida," and so on. Probably the teacher thought he was giving the children choice by allowing them to choose which state they would study. How little things change! Again, there is nothing wrong with sometimes recommending topics to children, and there are degrees to which children can be given choice in any project. The problem arises when teachers rarely give children any meaningful choice, a situation that is rather common in many of our schools and at all levels of schooling.

Science, writing, and art may all seem like specialized and even high-falutin' professions to some readers. How many of the nation's children will ever go into these somewhat rarefied fields? But if we look at one of the more popular and perhaps everyday fields, such as business, we see the same need for creativity.

Every year *Business Week* does an annual survey of business schools. Some of the other business magazines have similar surveys. And every year the results are the same: When business executives are asked to state their number one complaint about the training students receive in business schools, it is that the business schools don't prepare students for the real world of business. The schools may teach them sophisticated quantitative techniques for solving inventory problems, or may even teach them by a case-study method. But the executives complain that when it comes to what business really needs—new ideas about how to stay competitive in a rapidly changing marketplace, compete with companies abroad, and get more shelf space for their products or new ideas for innovative and useful products and services—the graduates of business schools often fall short. In other words what they are not learning is how to be creative in a rapidly changing world.

The need to be creative in a rapidly changing world applies to many other fields of endeavor as well. One of the best examples is politics. In the 1950s certain "truths" were accepted without question by many U.S. citizens. One was that Americans were the good guys, and that the principal enemy of our country was and probably always would be the Soviets. Children learned that American products were the best in the world, and that Japanese products were nothing better than cheap imitations. And in economics they may have learned that you could invest as you wished in stocks and bonds, but you could certainly not invest in gold, even speculatively, because gold ownership was illegal. Of course, all these things (and many of the others that children learned to take for granted) no longer hold true. As citizens of any country, we, and politicians as leaders, need to be flexible and creative in the face of a world that seems to change on an almost daily basis. To the extent that we cannot go beyond our old and pat ways of looking at things, we risk the future. Indeed—as we write this book—we are seeing many of the largest and formerly most successful companies facing failure and in some cases utter collapse.

A good example of the importance of creativity in teaching derives from an experience one of the authors had several years ago when delivering a lecture on creativity to a group of education professors at the University of Puerto Rico. For some reason the talk wasn't going over well at all. Maybe it was the heat; maybe it was the content or the delivery. But the audience couldn't have been more bored, and they didn't hesitate to show it. They were walking in and out of the room and up and down the aisles, talking and otherwise seeking distractions—and distracting the speaker. In desperation the speaker finally decided to try some of the time-honored strategies for classroom management that one learns in an education course. These strategies may not be creative, but they're supposed to work.

First the speaker tried lowering his voice. The idea is that if you speak quietly, people in the room will have to quiet down to be able to hear you. (Of course, you are assuming they *want* to hear you.) No one quieted down.

Next the speaker politely asked the members of the audience to be quiet so that those who wanted to hear would be able to. The problem with this request was that it assumed once again that there were actually people in the audience who wanted to hear. If there were, they were in hiding, because the request had no effect whatsoever.

The speaker lost his patience and told the people in the audience, "Shut up!" No dice. People ignored him. Is there any noisier audience than a bunch of people who teach strategies for getting people not to be so noisy?

At that point the speaker pretty much gave up. What the hell—he would be on a plane back to the mainland the next day. But just seconds after he gave up, a member of the audience stood up and said something in rapid-fire Spanish. Her behavior may have been unusual, but it worked. After she said it you could have heard a pin drop for the rest of the talk. That's what we mean by creativity in education. She figured out a very unconventional way to get her own group to quiet down and to stay quiet.

You may be wondering what she said. She was creative, that teacher, and also a good judge of human nature. She recognized that the lecturer's efforts to quiet people down appealed to guilt. This strategy is a common one in U.S. and other Western cultures, where we often appeal to guilt to achieve behavioral compliance. From the time children are young, parents and others make them feel guilty if they do certain things that are considered wrong. The hope is that they will eventually internalize the guilt so that they will do the right thing. Freud even gave a name to this internalized watchdog—the superego.

The teacher knew, however, that in many Hispanic cultures, people are ruled more by shame than by guilt. You are more likely to gain compliance by making someone feel ashamed of him- or herself than by making the person feel guilty. What the teacher said was that the people in the audience ought to be ashamed of themselves. If they continued to make noise, the speaker would go back to the mainland and say bad things about the University of Puerto Rico. And whether or not they liked the talk, they had no right to put the university to shame, even if they shamed themselves. (Other people in the audience may also have known that Puerto Rico is more a shame-based than a guilt-based culture, but what they perhaps wouldn't have recognized is how to use the knowledge in a creative way, given a formal lecture situation, to get people to quiet down. That's creativity, and it worked like a charm.)

You should not think that the use of creative strategies is necessarily limited to teachers at the college level. Consider a strategy used by a kindergarten teacher in Mexico to find out who had stolen a book. None of the students in the class was willing to admit to having stolen it. So the teacher gave each of them a thin stick of equal size and told them that the stick of the student who was lying would grow larger overnight, so that when the teacher demanded the next day to see the sticks, she would know who had stolen the book. What stratagem did the teacher use?

Of course, the child who was guilty was consumed by fear. Her stick would grow, and the next day the teacher would know she was the culprit. So what did she do? She broke off the end of the stick so that the next day, when it had grown, it would be about the same size as the sticks of the rest of the students. The teacher would never know it was she. Of course, the little girl did exactly what the teacher had anticipated, and the next day the teacher found out who had stolen the book—the student with the shorter stick. Who says there aren't creative teachers out there?

The need for creativity is not limited to desk jobs. Sylvia Scribner (1984) showed that men who worked in a milk-packing plant—placing milk bottles in cartons all day—would come up with complex and creative strategies for speeding up their work and thereby getting out of work faster. Thus, even a job that would seem to be among the most routine in the world can sometimes be rendered creative if people set their minds to it.

The Importance of Creativity Is Underappreciated

We strongly believe that the importance of creativity is underappreciated both by the society, in general, and by particular institutions within the society, such as schools. The evidence and reasons for this are everywhere.

All Talk–No Show: Debasing the Notion of Creativity

Business executives talk about the need for creativity and innovation. But once again change is more conspicuous in talk than in action. Many people who have worked in or consulted with businesses are more impressed by how slowly things change than by how rapidly. Organizational cultures and ways of doing things have a life that seems to extend beyond the particular people who inhabit the organization, just as the culture of a country is passed on even when all members of a given generation die. Creativity is as hard to find in the business world as anywhere else, perhaps because—much as executives recognize the need for it—at some level they may be afraid of it.

People Fear Change

Despite the fact that many people claim to value novel ideas, there is solid evidence that they don't much like exactly what they supposedly value.

One of the most solid findings in psychology is the "mere-exposure effect" (Zajonc, 1968); people most like what is familiar. The more they hear rap music or study cubist art, the more comfortable they become with it, and the more they like it. Thus research indicates that although people may value creativity because it will bring progress, they are often uncomfortable with it, and hence may initially react negatively to creative work.

Some years ago we did a study investigating conceptions of creativity, wisdom, and intelligence in different groups, including experts in philosophy, physics, art, and business, as well as laypeople. There was one particularly striking finding with respect to the experts in business. In most groups the correlation between the behaviors believed to characterize the creative person in a given field and the behaviors believed to characterize the wise person in a given field was about zero. In other words there just wasn't any particular relation between the two sets of behaviors. But in the business group the correlation was actually negative: People believed to show creativity and those believed to show wisdom were viewed as being at opposite ends of the spectrum. You could be one or the other, but not both. In fact, our experience suggests that the most creative people in an organization are often viewed as oddballs and even as outcasts. The question is whether the business recognizes the need for such people, or whether it decides to discharge them as not fitting in with the rest of the organization.

Undervaluing Creativity

Perhaps the most flagrant examples of the undervaluing of creativity are found in the schools. Of course, you'd be unlikely to find even one teacher in a typical school who would say that he or she does not value creativity. But again there is often a notable gap between what is said and what is done. Consider some examples:

A physics teacher asked his students to describe how they could measure the height of a tall building with a barometer. One student proposed taking the barometer to the top of the building, using a rope to lower the barometer to the street, and then measuring the length of the rope. Needless to say, this answer received no credit (LeBoeuf, 1980).

Sometimes teachers are so focused on one goal that creativity gets lost in the shuffle. In the above example, the teacher wanted to see that students had learned the material presented in class. Other times teachers just want to maintain the class's attention. For example, Matt Groening, famous for creating *The Simpsons*, was punished for drawing and doodling in school. Teachers would rip up and throw away the drawings. Groening says, "Some of the stuff was senseless and immature, but other stuff was really creative, and I was amazed that there was no differentiation between the good stuff and the bad stuff, or very little" (Morgenstern, 1990, p. 12). Ideally Groening's teachers would have thought about how they might encourage him to channel his artistic talents into his schoolwork.

Elementary school is often supposed to be the time when creativity is most encouraged in children. But if you have children, examine their report cards someday, as one of the authors of this book did over a period of a number of years. Although the author's two children went to two different schools over the course of their elementary school careers, and although these schools were supposed to be among the better public schools in the state, in no year was there—among the many check-off boxes that appeared on their report cards—even one box that mentioned creativity. There were many boxes representing various forms of good behavior (most of which could be read as referring to "conforming behavior"), and there were many boxes that evaluated various forms of knowledge and other accomplishments. But creative accomplishments were not among them. You can tell what an institution values by how it evaluates its members, and creativity just never appeared on the lists.

Consider a specific example of a kindergartener in a situation that recurs for many children in various forms and in various ways. The child drew a pink lion and a purple giraffe. The teacher dutifully informed the child (and later the parents) that lions aren't pink and giraffes aren't purple, and that she should redraw them. Well, you get the picture. The teacher was just trying to be helpful. And without even realizing it, she, like tens of thousands of other teachers, was showing what she valued and what she didn't.

Obviously we're not saying that no teachers anywhere ever value creativity. Many do. The problem isn't so much with individual teachers as it is with their training and socialization as teachers. For example, student teaching with an established teacher is an important part of teacher training. But the odds are that this "model" teacher was trained in a way that will perpetuate views on education that do not promote creativity. Perhaps creative teachers should be identified and become central resources for teacher training. Then, too, many teachers are so restrained by mandated curricular guidelines that they don't have the flexibility for creativity. For example, many states mandate that a series of topics be covered each year at the high school level. Teachers have to follow these guidelines or their students will not be prepared for the statewide exams. As a result teachers can spend only a limited time on each lesson and do not have time creatively to enhance a chosen topic without causing another topic to suffer. Furthermore, students' test results form an important measure of teacher performance, which creates a vicious circle of teaching *for* test results. This impact of tests on creativity is discussed in greater detail in the next section.

The Tyranny of Testing

The problem of the undervaluing of creativity in the schools is augmented by the nature of standardized tests. Our complaints are that an industry has grown up around standardized testing and that, perhaps inadvertently, these tests have served to squelch creativity as much as any institution in our society. The kinds of test items used—"Define 'loquacious'"; "What number comes next in the series 8, 27, 64, 125?"; "What is the capital city of Italy?"—don't encourage the least bit of creative thinking. Ironically, few industries are less creative than the testing industry. Even people in the industry admit that the standardized tests our children take aren't much different from the tests that children took near the beginning of the century. This chapter is being written on a three-and-half-pound laptop computer with more processing power and storage capacity than those found in computers thousands of times its weight just a few generations ago. Indeed, the first of the modern computers, UNIVAC, was built in 1939, some years after the introduction of a widely used test of intelligence, the Wechsler-Bellevue Adult Intelligence Scales (see Wechsler, 1944). But you know what's sad? The computers of today are thousands of times more powerful and cheaper than were their predecessors of the 1950s, whereas the tests that we use today are, except for cosmetic changes, the same. That's what we mean by a not very creative and even stagnant industry. The problem isn't with tests per se but with the glacial pace of innovation. New kinds of tests are now on the horizon, but only time will tell whether they will catch on. In these tests children are asked to write a creative essay, design a science project, solve a social problem, and otherwise engage in creative thinking.

Again we wish to emphasize that we are not quibbling with what standardized tests reward. They reward memory and analytic abilities, which are, after all, one-third of the senior author's triarchic theory of intelligence (Sternberg, 1985a, 1988e). But there are two other parts to the theory: practical abilities and the focus of this book—creative abilities (often as applied in practical settings). What we are emphasizing is what these tests *don't* reward.

Some years back, one of the authors of this book was director of graduate studies in the Department of Psychology at Yale, and he was particularly interested in the application of a particular applicant we'll call Barbara. She was a real test case for the tests. In fact, her test scores (on the Graduate Record Examination, or GRE) were abysmal by Yale standards. Yet her letters of recommendation were glowing and described Barbara as insightful, creative, and a gem of a person as well. These letters were written by people we knew and respected, among them a distinguished graduate of our own graduate psychology department who had gone on to achieve considerable renown in the field. Moreover, the letters said that if we had any doubts, we should look at Barbara's work. Barbara had in fact included a portfolio of work, which contained even published articles, a rare commodity among applicants to graduate school. Anyone who took the trouble to read the work, as the author did, would have been impressed by the creativity and imagination shown there.

When it came time for the admissions-committee meeting, the author expected Barbara's case to go without a hitch, because even though the scores were low, the work spoke for itself. After all, what better predictor of creative work in the future can there be than creative work in the past? The graduate faculty members had always talked about how they were desperately seeking creative students, and here was their chance to make good on their talk. In fact Barbara's case was discussed in detail. The vote was five-to-one against her admission, with only the author voting in her favor.

The story of Barbara is true, not just for this Barbara but for tens of thousands of Barbaras. At the end of the day, when all the candidates' credentials are considered, there are often more than enough students with good test scores to fill an undergraduate or graduate or professional school class, so why take a chance on someone who doesn't test well? The result, we believe, is that tens of thousands of potentially creative individuals are derailed from first-rate higher educational opportunities because they don't test well. In Barbara's case this derailment was particularly ironic, because her problem wasn't even a lack of memory or analytical skills but rather test anxiety. The test-anxious individual pays a tremendous price in U.S. society, because such important outcomes depend on the results of tests. Moreover, individuals who don't test well are cut off not only from admission to one prestigious undergraduate or graduate program, but from admission to other comparable programs as well, because they use the same tests in the same way in making their admissions decisions.

Even if students with low scores gain entry, or are students in schools in which admission is noncompetitive, low scores can haunt them. In our own case, one of us, like Barbara, suffered from debilitating test anxiety when he was very young. He did horribly on IQ tests. The result was that his teachers expected very little from him during his first three years of elementary school. And, being eager to please his teachers, he gave them very little—exactly what they expected and wanted. So the teachers were pleased, and the young author-to-be was pleased that his teachers were pleased. It wasn't until the fourth grade that he had a teacher who expected much more of him, and he wanted to please her, too. So for the first time, he produced A-level work, and no one was more surprised than he himself. He had never believed himself capable of it. From then on he was an A student. But suppose he hadn't had that teacher! He might have been relegated to the bottom of the educational system, a place reserved for those who don't perform at high levels.

Thus, potentially creative individuals may never be recognized as such, and may even encounter the low expectations reserved for the weakest of students. Moreover, if students express their creativity, especially in the context of classes for the academically weak, they are often labeled problem children rather than creative kids. And ultimately, as they are frustrated again and again in their attempts to realize their abilities, they may in fact *become* problem children.

In Barbara's case, she was perhaps luckier than all but a small fraction of the creative students who don't test well. The author hired her as a research associate. She came to Yale, did marvelous work, and two years later was admitted as the top pick to the graduate program. Has the admissions system changed? Judge for yourself: We're still using the GRE, and we're still reluctant to take the Barbaras of the world.

How have tests become such an ingrained part of our system of evaluating and sorting students? Why are these tests, which weigh memory and analytic abilities (plus knowing how to take tests) 100 percent and creative (and practical) abilities 0 percent, so heavily used in a system that so badly needs to recognize and foster creative potentials? We believe that at least five reasons work together to preserve the status quo.

We call the first one the "pseudoquantitative precision" reason. The basic idea is that people tend to be infatuated with the aura of precision that surrounds test scores. An IQ of 121, an SAT score of 570, an achievement test score in the thirty-ninth percentile—these ring true. Obviously the test companies emphasize the scores more than they do the error of measurement in the scores. But even the error of measurement in the scores is only with respect to what they actually measure, not with respect to either what they are supposed to measure or with respect to what they are not supposed to measure—and don't—such as creativity.

We label the second the "similarity" reason. Ask yourself who is writing the test questions and who is making the decisions in the educational system. Obviously, people who score high on the tests. You don't get a job writing test questions for a major test publisher if you have lousy test scores. And you don't get a job as an admissions officer at a prestigious college or a graduate or professional school if you didn't have test scores good enough to get you into the school or a comparable one in the first place. Because people tend to value in others what they have in abundance themselves, each generation looks for members of the next generation who look pretty much like the elite members of their own. So we pass on a set of values and place in our elite people who excel in the same way as does the current elite—namely, in memory and analytic skills.

Third is the "culpability" reason. Put yourself in the place of an admissions officer making a decision about a college applicant, or even a personnel officer making a decision about a potential clerical or technical hire. You've got an applicant with some interesting credentials suggesting creative abilities but also with bargain-basement test scores. At the same time you have plenty of other applicants who don't have the creative credentials but whose test scores range from good to sky-high. Why take the risk on the low test scorer? Suppose the person doesn't work out in the college or on the job. People may go back to the files and discover the person's low test scores and that you recommended the admission or hire. Then who will get blamed? The person who was selected? No—you. In contrast, if the test scores were high and the person flubs his work, no one can blame you: You did what any reasonable person would have done in your place. The result is that you go for the high scorer in order to cover your flanks (and other parts as well).

Fourth is what we refer to as the "publication" reason. More and more, schools and school districts are publishing average test scores. For example, you can easily buy a college guidebook to find out the average SAT scores for colleges that require the SAT. The same goes for the comparable ACT, which is used more in the Midwest of the United States. Similarly, you can find out average Secondary School Admission Test (SSAT) scores for private secondary schools, and average GRE scores for graduate schools. Many states now have statewide mastery tests in the public schools, and our own state, Connecticut, publishes scores on a district-by-district basis. These scores have become, in our opinion, one of the most powerful determinants of real estate values around. Who wants to pay a premium for property in a district with third-rate test scores, or even second-rate ones, for that matter? The result of all this publication is that schools are doing everything they can to maintain their competitive edge (read "image"), and hence are stressing high test scores. No one is publishing test scores comparing Squeedunk High with Podunk High on creativity, so who has time to worry about it?

We refer to the fifth reason that test scores have become so intrusive in our lives as the "rain-dance" reason, and we believe it is ultimately the most powerful one.

From time to time we give presentations in various places, but we rarely have time to stay in the really nice places long enough to enjoy them. We thus often wish that we'd get invited back, although such invitations are scarcer than we'd like—after all, they've already heard us. So suppose that we decide that we need some other way to get ourselves invited back to one of these interesting spots, perhaps in the Middle East. What might we do?

One possibility would be to guarantee that rain will follow if we are invited. After all, these areas are desperate for rain, and it's not easy to turn down an invitation to people who can guarantee rain, especially when we offer a double-your-money-back guarantee!

So we go to the Middle Eastern country that is clever enough to invite us, and the first morning we are there, we do a rain dance. The question arises: Does it then rain? You are probably thinking: Of course not. And you are right. It doesn't rain. The country asks for double its money back, and we say, "You must be crazy. There's no way that a rain dance will work after just one day! Besides, this is the Middle East, and nothing ever gets done here in just one day. Has the Arab-Israeli conflict really been resolved? No. And a lot more than a day has passed. Besides, you've had a drought condition here for thousands of years—you can't expect rain overnight."

So each morning we do a fifteen-minute rain dance, and of course we go touring and sightseeing for the rest of the day. Eventually, of course, it rains, and at that point we say: "Thanks a lot for your confidence in us. It's been a pleasure doing business with you, and we hope to do business again with you in the future."

You may be thinking, as would most people, that it wasn't actually the rain dance that caused the rain. But think about it. What makes a superstition so hard to get rid of is that it is almost impossible to disconfirm. If you keep doing rain dances, eventually it will rain; any medicine man knows that. You may be thinking that this is all silly. After all, you don't have superstitions; you have beliefs. But all you have to do is stand in front of a busy elevator in an office building or hotel and watch the people as they arrive. Someone will come and press the button; it will light up. Then someone else will come. The button is already lit, but the new person presses it anyway. Then perhaps someone else in a hurry will come along and press again and again. Why does he or she do this? After all, the button is already lit. Well, you'll soon see why. The elevator comes. In fact, if you keep pressing the elevator button, the elevator will *always* come! Is it any wonder that even intelligent people keep doing so? It's very hard to shake a superstition.

We're not claiming to be immune. One of us wears a gold chain around his neck. Why? Because his parents gave him the gold chain when he was an adolescent. They told him it would bring him luck. Does it bring him luck? Who knows? But the fact is that he believes that his luck has been pretty good since he started wearing the gold chain. Maybe his luck would remain good if he took off the gold chain, but why take the risk? There is no real cost to wearing the chain, so the author keeps wearing it rather than risk the bad luck that might follow if he took it off. (Actually, the only time he takes it off is for chest X-rays, and everyone knows that chest X-rays in large doses can cause cancer!)

This kind of illogical thinking promotes superstitions, and we believe that our society's fervent reliance on tests is among its most entrenched superstitions. Once people believe that the tests will work, in a sense they will, not because of the tests but rather because of people's reactions to them. We already spoke of self-fulfilling prophecies, and of how a belief that something will come to be (poor school performance) can cause that thing to come to be. But the insidiousness of test overuse has another manifestation as well.

Suppose that you admit to your Advanced Basket Weaving program only students with SAT scores above six hundred. Any student with a score below six hundred is instantly rejected. Many schools may not publish or even believe they have such a cutoff, but often they do, even if it is implicit. Now put yourself in the place of faculty members in the Advanced Basket Weaving program. How many students have they seen succeed in their program with scores below six hundred? Zero—they've never seen one. And how many students with scores above six hundred have ever failed? Well, maybe a few. But they had emotional problems, or were unmotivated, or whatever. Get the point? Once the test is in place, you've got the rain-dance phenomenon, also known as the elevator phenomenon. It becomes practically impossible to prove that the test isn't working. Because students with scores below six hundred are never admitted, you never really get the chance to see whether they would have succeeded. So you go on believing that students need a score of six hundred in order to succeed.

You don't believe that educated people can be so superstitious? Let's try to persuade you one more time. Sternberg and his colleague Wendy Williams decided that the time had come to put their money (and their time) where their mouths had been. After years of complaining about the GRE, they decided to do a validation study for the graduate psychology program at Yale. So they acquired the records of all graduate students matriculating in the Yale psychology program over the past ten years. For each of these students, they obtained his or her GRE Verbal, Quantitative, and

Analytic scores, and for those students who had taken it, scores in the Advanced Test in Psychology. Sternberg and Williams also obtained the first- and second-year grades in the graduate program, as well as dissertation advisers' ratings of the students' analytic, creative, practical, research, and teaching abilities. They further obtained dissertation readers' ratings of the quality of the dissertation. (These readers are faculty in the psychology department but do not include the main adviser.) Finally Sternberg and Williams looked at students' gender as well as some other variables.

The results were simple. GREs predicted first-year grades in the graduate program, and that was about it. The scores did not predict second-year grades and did not predict any of the faculty members' ratings, except for a modest correlation of the GRE Analytical with the ratings, but only for men. Thus, if you were interested in anything other than first-year grades, you would get little or nothing out of GRE scores. You certainly wouldn't get predictions of creativity. Is the department still using the test? You bet. Sure, the study didn't answer every question about the GRE that one might wish. But we now doubt that any study would convince certain people that the test just doesn't predict important criteria. Press those elevator buttons, friends—the elevator is guaranteed to come!

We have nothing against high scores. Again, we believe that the memory and analytical abilities measured by conventional tests are important. But we also believe that the institution of testing is distracting attention from the use of creativity as a basis for admission and selection decisions. And our reliance on tests may be squandering what is arguably our most precious human resource.

But Can We Test for Creativity?

It's one thing to criticize others for not taking creativity into account; it's another to take it into account yourself and, moreover, to find a way to measure it.

We are not enamored of typical creativity tests that ask people to perform very brief, content-limited tasks that emphasize divergent thinking. For example, people might be asked to think of unusual uses for a paper clip (for example, Guilford, 1950). Real-life creativity occurs in real-life domains. The domains may be academic or they may be everyday, but the kind of creativity that we care about is nontrivial creativity, and to us, thinking of unusual uses for a paper clip is rather limited.

We use a product-centered approach, as have Amabile (1983) and many other researchers—including those who study creative greats. Tangible products are at the center of assessment in many fields. For example, have you heard of "The Louis," named after Louis Prang, the father of American greeting cards? This award is given to the most imaginative, artistic, sendable greeting cards of the year at the annual international greeting card show. Product-based awards for creativity are common and can be found in many diverse fields, including teaching. In our research we have tested creativity in the domains of writing, drawing, advertising, and science. We do not claim that these domains are representative of all possible domains, and obviously they are not exhaustive. But the four, taken together, give at least a sampling of the kinds of creative performances a person can produce. The tasks have a parallel form across the four domains and include topic selection as an integral part of the creative process. In each domain subjects are asked to be as imaginative as they can be. Ideally subjects should be given as much time as possible to produce their work.

In the domain of writing, people are asked to pick two titles from a list and to write a brief short story for each. We purposely chose titles that people were unlikely to have thought about before, such as: "Beyond the Edge," "A Fifth Chance," "Saved," "Under the Table," "Between the Lines," "Not Enough Time," "The Keyhole," "The Octopus's Sneakers," "2983," or "It's Moving Backwards." These titles are ones that can lead to a wide diversity of stories.

In the domain of art, people are given art materials and are asked to produce a drawing for two of several suggested topics. Again, we chose topics they were not likely to have drawn or even to have thought about before as themes for artistic compositions: "A Dream," "A Quark," "Hope," "Rage," "Pleasure," "Earth from an Insect's Point of View," "Contrast," "Tension," "Motion," and "Beginning of Time."

In the domain of advertising, people are asked to come up with a TV commercial for two products. We tried to select products that are as boring as possible and for which the people were not likely to have seen commercials. Topics included "Double-Pane Windows," "Brussels Sprouts," "The Internal Revenue Service" (presenting a positive image), "Broom," "Iron," "Cuff Links," "Bow Ties," "Doorknobs," and "Sugar Substitute."

Finally, in the domain of science, people are asked to solve two science problems that are rather different in kind from those they are likely to have encountered. The science problems included: "How can we find out if extraterrestrial aliens are living among us?", "How might we determine if someone has been on the moon in the past month?", and "How could we solve the problem of decoys in a Star Wars defense system?"

In the study, forty-eight individuals from New Haven, Connecticut— twenty-four males and twenty-four females, ranging in age from eighteen to sixty-five, with an average age of thirty-three—completed two products in each of the four domains. People were recruited through an ad in a local newspaper and were paid to participate. The only requirement for participation, other than a minimum age of eighteen, was that the candidate be a high school graduate.

A second, new group of fifteen people from New Haven rated for creativity the products of the members of the first group using a 1 (low) to 7 (high) numerical scale. Each judge used his or her own view of creativity when rating the products. The judges' ratings were averaged to form a creativity score for each product.

The first question that needs to be raised is whether judges can even reliably rate creativity. Some of the makers and users of conventional standardized tests argue that at least, with their tests, there is agreement as to the right answer, whereas with problems that require creative or other skills, there will be no consensus as to what is good and what is not. On the contrary, however, we found an interrater reliability (consistency across judges) among our raters of .92, on a 0 to 1 scale where 0 would indicate no consistency at all and 1 would indicate perfect consistency. This interrater agreement is high by any standard, and indicates that people do show considerable (although not perfect) agreement as to what they judge as creative and what they judge as uncreative. In several other studies, including the extensive work by Amabile (1983), judges (peer or expert) have been used, and similar good interjudge reliability has been found. If you'd like to see some examples of products in each of the domains judged as creative and as uncreative, see figure 2.1 (pp. 32–35).

In general the story and art products were judged to be significantly more creative than the advertising and scientific products. This difference probably results from the fact that people have more experience writing

FIGURE 2.1

Items Judged as More or Less Creative

Writing: Write an Essay Based on the Title "2983"

MORE CREATIVE

"Take a number!" Everywhere I go it's "Take a number!" So, again I'm standing in line waiting my turn. My number is 2983! They just announced number 145! This should give me plenty of time to learn about the others in line. Who will be patient enough to wait? Who will give up and leave? Will the man ahead of me in his striped Bermuda shorts lose his temper waiting? He looks like a high-blood-pressure type. Will the frazzled-looking young woman holding the toddler by one hand and an infant in the other arm bear up under the wait? Will anyone offer to help her when the little ones fuss? Will I? Perhaps.

The line has moved an inch or two. What number was that they just called? I couldn't quite hear them. Oh well, I'm fairly sure it's not mine yet.

The line is building behind me. Does everyone need to be here as much as I?

"Bermuda Shorts" couldn't take the pressure of patience; he's given up and left. One less person in front of me.

"1492!" Oh great. Halfway there!

Why am I in this line? What am I waiting for? Why are all these people waiting? It's another day, another line, another reason to wait. Why am I in line? Does it matter?

LESS CREATIVE

The scientists manning the machines that receive sound waves from outer space are perplexed. They are receiving some type of communication that they are unable to understand. They communicate with other scientists in different parts of the world, who are also experiencing the same difficulties.

After going through a process of elimination and discarding several impractical theories, they come to the conclusion that they are being approached by some unknown beings. A spaceship is outfitted, manned, and sent out to seek the source. After traveling 2,983 million miles, the spaceship arrives at its destination—an unknown galaxy. The inhabitants of this galaxy, however, are suspicious of their visitors. The space travelers are kept prisoners and their spaceship is destroyed.

Art: Draw a Picture Illustrating "Earth from an Insect's Point of View"

MORE CREATIVE

This drawing uses the idea that insects have multifaceted eyes. Through its representation of objects hazardous to insects—a can of Raid, an Italian shoe, a bird, a fly swatter, an electric bug zapper, and an oncoming truck—the drawing suggests that insects may have a rather anxious view of their world.

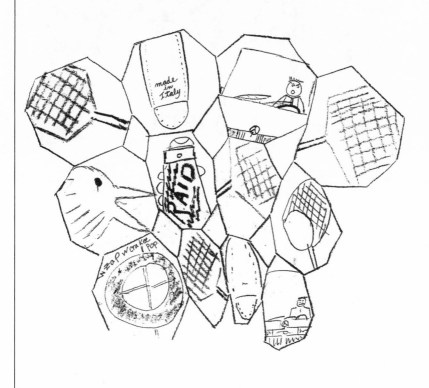

This drawing is representative of many that depicted the insect as seeing everything in the world as very large.

Advertising: Design a Commercial Promoting IRS Services

MORE CREATIVE

This commercial would show positive government agencies in action: Social Security, VA hospitals, U.S. Mail, DEA, FBI, U.S. Park Service (park rangers like in Yellowstone), NASA, U.S. Armed Forces. Show how all these government agencies benefit the country. After you show each government agency, then show the clips again. But this time start slowing down the film until it finally stops. Voice over that this is what will happen to these agencies if taxes aren't collected.

LESS CREATIVE

This commercial would show that the IRS works for the people personally, and the IRS is not out to get us so we would work with them to make tax collecting as pleasurable as possible for both parties.

This basic idea can be conveyed by showing IRS employees helping people with their taxes. During the advertisement they can also show new tax forms that people can look at and rate at their local IRS or government office. An IRS employee can be shown making up a new tax form by asking a person he or she is helping what gives them the most difficulty.

Science: How Could We Find Out If Extraterrestrial Aliens Were Living Among Us?

MORE CREATIVE

I would try to spend lots of time with the potential alien in his or her living situation and bombard him/her/it with lots of questions about history, literature, world events, etc., as well as ask more personal information.

I would also take him/her/it to see movies like *Alien* and *Brother from Another Planet*, and then observe its reaction to such films in detail. In contrast I would also take the alien to see classic American films like *It's a Wonderful Life* and *Gone With the Wind* and compare reactions.

If that didn't tell me anything, I would insult and poke fun at all forms of alien life, ridiculing the notion of life existing anywhere beyond Earth. Maybe that would fluster and anger the alien, assuming that it had any emotions.

LESS CREATIVE

In the United States we would require a blood sample to be given in order to get a Social Security number or driver's license. Analysis would certainly show a different blood structure for creatures coming from another planet even if they looked like us externally. I think any aliens living on earth would tend to be blended into the society where they were living, and it would be difficult to survive in the United States without one of these forms of identification.

stories and drawing pictures than they do formulating TV advertisements and answers to scientific questions.

Now consider the question of whether there is a "general creative ability." In other words, are the people who are creative in one task necessarily creative in the others? This question can be addressed in several ways.

One way is to divide people in each domain on the basis of whether their products were judged as being above or below average. The question then becomes one of what percentage of people was above (or below) the average in the various domains. In the limiting case, if creativity were just a single ability, we would expect 50 percent of people to be above average in no domains, and 50 percent to be above average in all domains. On the other hand, if there were absolutely no general factor of creativity at all, we would expect roughly 6 percent to be above average in no domains, 23.5 percent to be above average in one domain, 41 percent to be above average in two domains, 23.5 percent to be above average in three domains, and 6 percent to be above average in all four domains.

We found that 19 percent of the subjects were above average in no domains (that is, all their products were judged as below average), 31 percent were above average in one domain, 17 percent above average in two domains, 15 percent above average in three domains, and 19 percent above average in all four domains. Obviously these results are intermediate between the two extremes. The results suggest that creativity is neither completely domain-general nor completely domain-specific, but if one were to say to which extreme it is closer, one would have to say that it is closer to domain-specificity than to domain-generality. In other words people tend to be creative in certain domains but not in others. Most people are above average in creativity in at least some domains but below average in others.

Another way of checking cross-domain generality is to look at statistical correlations of creativity ratings across domains. These scores, on a -1 to +1 scale, indicate the degree of consistency people show in creativity across domains. A correlation of 1 would indicate perfect consistency across domains, with the same people always creative or uncreative. A correlation of 0 would indicate absolutely no consistency whatever across domains. In this case creativity in one domain would not predict at all creativity in any other. A correlation of -1 would be strange, indicating that high creativity in one domain implies low creativity in another. The median correlation across domains was in fact .37. This number reinforces our analysis above. Creativity is neither completely domain-general nor domain-specific but tends more toward domain-specificity than toward domain-generality.

These results have important implications both for the way we think about creativity and for the way we act on the basis of these thoughts. In some schools we have "gifted" classrooms, in which we place the children who are identified as superior to others; other children remain in regular classes. Our results suggest that, with respect to creativity, there is no one group that can be properly identified as "gifted." Some people are gifted in one or several domains, others in other domains. One could, in fact, be very highly creatively gifted in one domain and not at all gifted in another. It would not make sense to have an overall "creatively gifted" group that is separated from all other children. Rather, we could possibly identify creatively gifted children, but the children (or adults, for that matter) so identified would vary across domains.

Similarly, if a business wished to select creative people for employment, its policy makers would have to ask themselves: Creative with respect to what? For example, the people who would be creative in the marketing department would not necessarily be those who would be creative in the finance department, and vice versa. Creativity is not just a single thing—it varies across domains.

But even if we were to identify people as creative in various domains, we would have to remember something else. Creativity within a domain can be developed, a point to which we will return throughout the book. So although we can measure creativity, we are measuring it in a given time and place.

We can see the effect of product within domain simply by correlating the ratings of creativity that subjects received for each of the two products they created in each of the four domains. If creativity were completely consistent within a domain, we would expect the correlation of rated creativity across products (for example, drawing 1 and drawing 2 for each participant) to approach 1. But if creativity were completely random within a domain, we would expect the correlation of rated creativity across products to be close to 0. In our data the average correlation between rated creativity for two products within a given domain was .58. Clearly people are more consistent within domain than they are between domains (where, you may remember, the average correlation was .36), but they are by no means perfectly consistent even within the domain. Thus we have to be very careful about generalizing across products.

We should emphasize that our correlations will be lower than they might have been if it were not for what is called "measurement error." That means that no measurement of any psychological attribute is perfect, and to the extent that our judges were less than perfect evaluators (which they certainly were), correlations would have been lower because of errors in their judgments.

We cannot emphasize enough the issue of error in judgment. Like others (for example, Hennessey & Amabile, 1988a), we have found that various judges are fairly consistent in what they find to be creative and uncreative. There is quite good agreement among them. Each judge brings a unique opinion, and the average judgment for each product reflects a central view of creativity. However, sometimes the set of judges may fail to see the value in a certain work, or they may see value where it hardly exists, when compared with another set of judges. There is no absolute standard for what constitutes creativity. What one society or culture or group considers creative another group may not consider creative.

Consider an example of a hazard in the measurement of creativity. In one of our studies forty-four participants were asked to produce creative products in the domains of story writing and art. In this particular study—for reasons that will become clear later—we predicted that people who were generally more willing to take risks would be judged as producing more creative products than would people who were not generally willing to take risks. As it turned out, the results were supportive of our thesis in the domain of art, but not in the domain of writing.

Out of curiosity we decided to inspect the written products of our subjects who were risk takers but who were not judged as creative in their writing. What we found was totally unexpected. We thought that the products of the risk takers were creative, although they had not been so evaluated by our judges. But the products had represented risks. For example, some of them were critical of such institutions as government or organized religion, and our judges had not reacted favorably to their content.

Our general point is that creativity ratings depend on the judges. One can have a group of judges agree that a product is not creative, and by their standards it may not be. But another group may find the product to be very creative. Creativity is not something that exists in the abstract—it is a sociocultural judgment of the novelty, appropriateness, quality, and importance of a product. Thus, when we look at assessments of creativity—or anything else for that matter—we should consider who's doing the judging.

Fans of conventional standardized tests may take these remarks as the stake through the heart of creativity measurement. They might argue that, at least with their measurements, we don't have to worry about subjectivity. But, in fact, the same limitations apply to *all* measurements. Consider an example of how a supposedly objective intelligence test with a clearly "correct" answer in one cultural setting can have a different answer in another cultural setting.

Joseph Glick, a psychologist at the City University of New York, was involved in a study to measure the cognitive skills of members of an African tribe called the Kpelle (Cole, Gay, Glick, & Sharp, 1971). He tested them with a sorting task. This task is a standard way of measuring cognitive skills. Suppose, for example, that people are asked to sort names of animals, such as "dog" and "cat"; names of trees, like "maple" and "oak"; and names of vehicles of conveyance, like "bus" and "bicycle." The idea is that more cognitively developed people will first sort taxonomically—for example, they will sort the names of the animals together and the names of the trees together. Then they will sort hierarchically, sorting both groups under a higher-order category, such as "living things." In contrast, less cognitively advanced people will sort things functionally. For example, they might sort "bus" with "gasoline," because a bus uses gas to move, or "bicycle" with "ride," because people ride bicycles.

The same assumption underlies much cognitive testing. For example, in the vocabulary section of a standard intelligence test such as the Stanford-Binet, if one is asked to define the word "automobile," one will receive more points for a definition of the word as a "vehicle of conveyance" than one will receive for a definition of the word as "something that uses gas." In other words a taxonomic definition receives more credit than does a functional one.

The Kpelle sort functionally, the way adults of inferior intelligence, or young children of average intelligence, would in our Western culture. Glick tried in various ways to get them to sort taxonomically, without success. Finally, as Glick was closing up shop, just for the hell of it he asked a Kpelle to sort the way a stupid person would. The man easily sorted the words taxonomically. For him the taxonomic sorting was stupid. Why? Well, in everyday life, we usually think functionally. For example, we think about eating apples, not about apples being members of the category "fruit," and fruits being members of the category "food." The Kpelle, therefore, were doing just what they would in ordinary life. Not being acculturated to a testing society, they had never learned that when you take tests, you are supposed to sort differently.

There are countless examples like this one. The very same behaviors that in one society or context are considered smart, in another are considered stupid. The point, though, is that the same problem that applies to the measurement of creativity applies to all measurements. There really is no such thing as wholly "objective" measurement. Measurement is always with respect to the norms and expectations of a particular group in a particular time and a particular place.

In this chapter we have introduced some of our thinking about creativity—what it is, why it is important but undervalued, and how it can be measured. In the next we go into more detail in elaborating some of the themes that have emerged here. You may have noticed that, in our view, people who are creative are people who don't just conform: They go their own way. In the next chapter we'll formalize this idea through our investment approach to creativity.

An Investment Perspective on Creativity

Great deeds are usually wrought at great risks.
—Herodotus

Buy Low and Sell High: Investment and Creativity

The standard advice given to an investor in the financial markets is to "buy low and sell high." What could be more obvious? Yet, even though everyone knows that one should follow the buy low–sell high strategy, few people do so (Dreman, 1982). Look at the New York Stock Exchange: When the market is low, there is relatively little buying or selling, whereas when the market is high, there is much more activity.

What Almost Everyone Knows and Almost No One Does

Of course, one might attribute this counterproductive trend only to the novices—to the small investors who don't know any better. But this would be incorrect. Even expert managers of mutual funds don't seem to heed their own advice. Consider a "piercing" demonstration of this fact. In June 1967 the editors of *Forbes* magazine threw darts at the *New York Times* stock market page. The twenty-eight stocks pierced by the darts became the basis for a simulated stock portfolio, with $1,000.00 invested in each stock. Seventeen years later, the $28,000.00 portfolio was worth $131,697.61, a 470 percent gain equal to a 9.5 percent annual compounded rate of return. Only a minuscule number of real mutual fund portfolios exceeded this rate of return during the same period (Malkiel, 1985). One might at-

41

tribute the success of the editors to sheer brazen luck. But the fact is that random selections of stocks via computer perform at about the level of the *Forbes* simulated portfolio, and surpass the performance of the large majority of mutual funds. Moreover, even mutual funds that do better than average in one year have only a 50 percent chance of doing so the next. Very few managed funds consistently perform better than would be expected by chance, and most perform worse (Malkiel, 1985). Whatever these managers may be doing, they are not buying low and selling high.

Why is it that even expert fund managers, who are often paid extraordinary amounts of money for their financial management expertise, do not buy low and sell high? Are they like overweight weight-reduction experts, addicted drug counselors, or divorced marriage therapists? Or is there something else going on here—something subtle that makes it difficult to follow the best advice, even if one wishes to?

Successful investors have to be bold, willing to take risks, and ready to act contrary to the behavior of other investors. They may have to take short-term losses for long-term gains. There is no guarantee when or even if one's stock will go up.

But it is difficult to be bold. When a professional fund manager buys out-of-favor stocks, she seems even more foolish than an individual amateur investor, who has only his own money to lose. The fund manager has the money of thousands or even tens of thousands of people in her hands. The pressure to produce favorable results is enormous.

Suppose, though, that the financial instrument bought by the individual investor or fund manager shows a gain and thus becomes widely recognized as a good investment. Its value will rise rapidly, and it will no longer be possible to buy it at a low share price. The investor who formerly seemed foolish will now seem prescient; she cornered the market when others didn't know how. All sorts of people will be clamoring for her financial acumen and advice.

A Key to Creativity

But what does all this talk about financial investment have to do with creativity? "Buying low and selling high" is the sine qua non of successful creative performance. Buying low means actively pursuing ideas that are unknown or out of favor but that have growth potential. Selling high involves moving on to new projects when an idea or product becomes valued and yields a significant return.

Take a person who jumps on a bandwagon, producing good work of a kind similar to what is already in vogue. He may be competent but not highly creative. In effect, the price of his work is already high, as with a stock that everyone else has already bought or is already buying. In contrast, an individual who generates and advances a new idea—an innovative sculpting style or a revolutionary mass-transit plan—may originally seem out of the mainstream. But once others recognize the value of his idea, he will be hailed as highly creative, and his ideas sought after hotly in the marketplace.

In the sciences, for example, Kuhn (1970) has observed that most researchers work within an established theoretical or methodological paradigm. Occasionally, however, revolutionary scientists shift the way others think about the world, resolve inconsistencies in earlier theories, and raise new questions to be addressed. Copernicus revolutionized astronomy with a heliocentric view of the solar system. But before Copernicus it would have seemed absurd to speak of the earth revolving around the sun, because all one had to do was to look up in the sky and "see" the sun revolving around the earth! Similarly Einstein shifted long-held theories of mass, energy, and light to a framework of relativity. But before Einstein, Newtonian views of these constructs seemed as obvious and certain as had Ptolemaic concepts of the geocentric universe. In general thinkers—scholars, business people, artists, inventors, anyone who can think innovatively—who cause paradigm shifts buy low, taking risks by advocating new and initially strange or unpopular ideas. As we will see throughout this book, the influence on such paradigm shifts of the six facets of creativity introduced in chapter 1—intelligence, knowledge, thinking styles, motivation, personality, and environment—cannot be ignored.

The Element of Risk

Why do people limit themselves when working on a problem or project? Why do they tend to "buy high," pursuing only ideas that are obvious, commonly chosen routes to a problem? As in financial investment, the key may be the *risks* that are inherent in buying low.

Risk, in general, is "the possibility of loss or injury" (*Webster's Ninth New Collegiate Dictionary*, 1983). In financial investments it is "the chance that expected security returns will not materialize and, in particular, that the securities you hold will fall in price" (Malkiel, 1985, p. 187). In practical terms most would agree that risk is the chance of a loss, and losses are indeed possible when one is taking gambles with either money or ideas.

Two Kinds of Risk

Furthermore, there are two types of risk to be considered: market risk and specific risk. Market risk depends on the financial health of a market (or creative area) as a whole. Specific risk depends on the trends of a specific security (or field of creative specialization) on top of the vagaries of general market trends. One can invest in "indexed" mutual funds, which are pegged to and reflect the activity of representative market stocks, hence taking market risk. One can also invest in a specific industry, such as pharmaceuticals. By doing so one assumes specific risk as well, because pharmaceuticals will perform partly as a result of the market as a whole, and partly as a result of what is occurring within that industry.

How do these risks apply to creativity? Quite directly. Buying low in any domain entails risk, for the field, product, or idea in which one invests may never catch fire. Just as not all stocks that are low will ever go up, not all fields or ideas that are untested will ever yield creative products. Indeed, one can expect that a majority will not. Hence contrarians who oppose trends always take the chance that what is out of the mainstream now will remain so. Here the roles of motivation and personality traits in fostering creativity certainly come into play. As stated by our panel, someone who buys low and sells high must be a maverick, ready to "take chances" and "take a stand."

Market and specific risks are an issue in creative as well as financial investment. Right now there is massive funding for AIDS research, and many people are specializing in this area. There is little market risk in this field, it seems. But a cure may be discovered, or the government may decide that cancer and heart disease claim many more victims and so are much more important, or the epidemic may slow because people take more precautions. Further research will then become a lower funding priority. What is now a fashionable field may become a dead one. When an investor takes a market risk, banking on what looks like a safe bet, he or she has to bear in mind that the market can still collapse.

Exploring out-of-fashion careers or techniques entails multiple nested risks, because one is subject not only to market but also to specific risk. If, for example, one takes a very unconventional approach to AIDS research, perhaps using natural herbal medicines, one is susceptible not only to the vagaries of the funding of AIDS research in general but also to whether herbal research in particular will be funded, even if traditional work on AIDS is being supported.

These nested risks are not limited to research. Working in the computer software field in today's computer age may seem like a decent market risk. Starting one's own software business, though, is chancier than going to work for a well-established company such as Microsoft. In turn, the amount of specific risk in starting one's own company will depend on the type of software produced. There is a certain market for business spreadsheet software, but it is already highly competitive. There is less competition for programming that determines home-gardening and shrub-planting schedules, but neither is there yet a readymade market for such software. Still, you might create the recognition of a need by supplying the software: Should you take the risk?

To buy low one must take the risk that what one buys at a low price will not in fact later go up in price. When selling high, one also takes the risk that what one sells at a high price may increase in value still more. One can never know for sure. It has been found that return increases, on the average, with risk, but not proportionately to the amount of risk taken (Malkiel, 1985). Still, those who do not take the chances will not reap the rewards—only those with the motivation and the right personality characteristics (discussed further in chapters 8 and 9) will do so.

Problem Framing

Besides motivation and personality, another factor that affects risk taking is the way in which a problem is framed. Framing effects arise when alternatives that are ultimately identical are evaluated in relation to different points of reference and so seem different (Kahneman & Tversky, 1982). Different framing of a scenario can lead a person to take greater or lesser investment risks. Kahneman and Tversky (1982) have found that most people are risk-averse when choosing between potential gains, but that they are risk-seeking when choosing between potential losses. For example, if someone has a 100 percent chance of winning eighty dollars versus an 85 percent chance of winning a hundred dollars, but also a 15 percent chance of winning nothing, he will probably pick the risk-averse sure shot and go for the 100 percent chance of getting eighty dollars. But now consider a bet with the odds framed in terms of losses. If a person has a 100 percent chance of losing eighty dollars versus an 85 percent chance of losing a hundred dollars and a 15 percent chance of losing nothing, he will probably choose the second bet, giving him the chance of losing nothing at all. Thus, whether one selects the riskier bet depends on whether gains or losses are involved.

How are these findings potentially relevant to the study of creativity? For the most part, creative work involves a potential gain, which, according to Kahneman and Tversky (1982), means that people will tend to be risk-averse. To the extent that we see less creativity than we would like, this risk aversion may be a cause. People's willingness to take creative risks may depend in part upon the way these risks are presented to them. For example, perhaps one is considering submitting an offbeat, original annual report to a superior, thereby risking either praise or condemnation. The individual could try to make the report chock full of creative ideas, but these ideas will defy conventional company thinking. Whether one dares to have the ideas in the first place and eventually hand them in may depend on whether one imagines the outcome in terms of potential gains (praise, a raise, perks) if it is favorably received or potential losses (disfavor, loss of supervisor's respect) if it is rejected. The same, of course, could be applied to consideration of whether to do a long-shot scientific project, compose an avant-garde poem, or write a nonstandard term paper in school.

Thus risk taking and the way one perceives it seem clearly related to financial gain and creative gain. Robert Gundlach, an inventor in the field of xerography and holder of more than 130 patents in the field, says, "If you want to invent, you have to be willing to risk. . . . Unless you're willing to risk something, you're really not going to try something new. And you're not going to be very creative unless you're willing to risk something" (quoted in Brown, 1988, pp. 109–110).

David McClelland (1953), a psychologist, agrees, stating that the person who does the safe thing is the high-fear-of-failure person. This person may make some contribution, but not a great one. At the same time Mc-Clelland notes that people who take crazy risks are not likely to contribute much either. The person who makes consistent contributions is the one who tempers his or her risk taking with prudence, using his intelligence and knowledge to balance his tendency to take chances.

Often a pattern of consistently buying low and selling high involves taking calculated risks and then persisting. Scott Rudin is a highly successful movie producer, whose films include *The Firm, Sister Act*, and *The Addams Family*. Rudin is a tactician when arranging a film—for example, avoiding directors after they've had a big hit; believing that good movies often come from bad books; and seeking actors who are either famous or unknown, avoiding the ones in the middle (Weiss, 1993). Once he commits to a movie, Rudin believes in himself and "bulls through" his project to keep it moving. By the time the film is at the box office, he is already on his next venture.

Like Rudin, creative individuals who do take risks, persevere, and eventually change existing views can later choose to sell high, moving on to another problem or perspective when others have bought into their point of view on the first. Some don't; some bank their entire careers on one exceptional idea. Those who are most influential, however, roll with the changes, finding a multiplicity of ways over the courses of their careers to express their creativity. These are the ones who sell high and thus are the most famous, most effective, and most rewarded. A good example of someone who bought low and sold high in the business world was Thomas Watson of IBM, who got into the data-processing business when others hardly knew what it was, and who managed for many years to stay ahead of the competition, moving on to new products when the old ones had reached a peak.

Risk Aversion

So why isn't everyone able to find a way to buy low? It is critical to realize that many people don't have the requisite personality traits. They are risk-averse, preferring to work with ideas that are already fairly well developed and accepted. They buy high into ideas that may have less "upside" potential, precisely because the ideas are already popular. This may seem odd, and yet anyone who has withstood the isolation and often ridicule of going against the trends knows just how difficult it is to blaze one's own trail. Approbation and rewards do come to those who break molds, but breaking molds is not for the faint of heart. That is why, for many, the short-term comfortable route is without question to follow the crowd, buying high.

Risk aversion may ultimately be traced to a low tolerance for failure. An interesting study by Clifford (1988) shows that failure tolerance declines as children progress through school, perhaps due to systematic rewards for good grades and punishments for bad ones. Clifford presented fourth, fifth, and sixth graders with math, spelling, and vocabulary problems that were marked as varying in difficulty from a second- to a ninth-grade level. Fourth graders, on average, chose problems rated as six to eight months below their ability level; fifth graders chose problems one year behind grade level; and sixth graders chose problems rated one and a half years below their difficulty level. We are particularly interested in the context of the school, because this is the child's workplace, supposedly in preparation for that of the adult. There are a number of reasons why students are reluctant to take risks, and more generally, to fail as a result of a risk that doesn't work out. First, failure is punished whereas good work is praised. Second, failure might lead to extra makeup work. Third, failure might be attributed to lack of motivation or even to stupidity. Perhaps most important, students are not given much opportunity to take risks in any case, so that they are unlikely to develop strategies that will lead them to take real risks.

Most of us don't need research studies to tell us that schools often discourage risk taking. Students overwhelmingly will take the safe courses and do the safe work in these courses so as not to jeopardize their future chances. Why take a challenging course if a low grade in it might mean that entrance to the college of one's choice is jeopardized? Why write a paper that a teacher might not like when there are plenty of ways to write it that are completely safe? At Yale students sometimes even switch between sections of a course like Introduction to Psychology if they discover that one teacher grades more easily than another. It doesn't matter how good the course is; they are concerned about getting high grades for future graduate school or employment. One of the problems with the culture of the schools, therefore, is that students never learn how to take sensible risks, a skill that will be needed if they are going to do genuinely creative work. If people are always being taught to "buy high," they may never even consider "buying low." We thus make the point now, as we will again, that creativity ought to start in the schools, but that it is often suppressed rather than encouraged. This suppression is not due to any kind of a plot against creativity or to teachers' loathing of creativity. It is due to a culture of the school that rewards safety rather than risk taking—a culture of which all of the participants in the school ultimately become a part.

The problem goes beyond just the schools. When they join the work force, the students will do the same thing. For fear of offending bosses, they will refuse to tell their superiors ideas the superiors don't want to hear. We can see this especially clearly in politics because of the intense press coverage of what happens.

In the early days of the Clinton administration, one misstep followed another in a breathtaking series of political follies: nominations for positions that were later withdrawn, a two-hundred-dollar haircut delivered while planes were circling over Los Angeles International Airport, a reversal of the president's stand on the admission of Haitian refugees to the United States, and a focus on the issue of gays in the military the very first week of the presidency—a time when economic issues were at the forefront in most people's minds.

It soon became clear that a large number of the mishaps were caused by the reluctance of members of Clinton's staff to tell Clinton what they really thought. To outsiders it appeared incredible that a political staff could be so bumbling. To insiders it appeared incredible that they would risk their jobs when they had just arrived in Washington with plans to live there for four years. These staff members had learned well the lesson that risk taking is unsafe—unfortunately, with sorry results for the administration.

We have spoken of how young people may avoid risks. But older people are even worse. Sometimes younger people recognize that the only way they are going to get anywhere is to take some risks, whereas older people who have gotten somewhere may forget it. As they grow older they become more cautious. Research suggests that older adults tend to opt out of risky situations when possible (Botwinick, 1984). In one study older people (ages sixty to seventy-six) chose problems that offered them a greater probability of success compared with the choices of younger people (ages eighteen to thirty). And even when the older participants did succeed in solving the problems, they tended to refuse to increase their risk level on other problems.

When it comes to careers, especially, it is not hard to see why older people would become cautious. Consider, for example, professional talks at various meetings, conventions, and conferences. If you ever go to one of these associations, you notice that although the big-name invited speakers may be older, a disproportionate number of those who have submitted papers for presentation are younger people. Indeed, as a young psychologist, one of the authors used to wonder why so many speakers at professional meetings were graduate students and young assistant professors rather than more established people in the field. Today, as an older professor, he knows.

When you are just starting out in your career, the risk factors argue very much in favor of your giving that talk. No one really knows who you are. So suppose you give a bad talk. Usually it will go practically unnoticed. No one knew your name before the talk, and people will have forgotten it (and you) by the time they walk out of your auditorium. On the other hand if you give a really good talk, people will stand up and take notice. Here, they will think, is a rising star, someone from whom they will be hearing a lot very soon. So they pay attention and watch for your star to rise. In essence the risk you take is that of staying as a professional nobody. But the possible gain is that, in your own field, you become a somebody.

The risk factors are quite different for someone more established in a given field. Before a presentation this person is a known quantity. People have come to expect a lot from him or her. When people enter the auditorium, they expect revelation. If they get an excellent presentation, big deal! Everyone knows that this person is a leader, and so it is no surprise when he or she gives an outstanding talk. Because that is what people expected, their impression of the senior person is not a whole lot different when they leave the auditorium from what it was when they entered.

But suppose instead that the person bombs, as everyone does once in awhile. Then the speaker immediately becomes the object of gossip and ridicule. One hears comments such as, "I can't believe what a piece of deadwood X has become," or, "How embarrassing that the Mighty X is now fallen," or, "X has really become pathetic in his old age—doesn't he know when it's time to retire?" In other words if the senior person gives a good talk, his reputation simply maintains itself at current levels, but it is ready to fall if he gives a bad one.

In a nutshell, when you are just starting out on your career, you have nowhere to go but up, whereas when you have advanced pretty far in your career, you may find yourself with nowhere to go but down. The result, if you are an older person, is that you may shy away from risks. At best you maintain your current standing, but at worst you lose it all. In general Adams (1986a) suggests that our culture is risk-averse. Even some of our most cherished proverbs—A bird in the hand is worth two in the bush, or A penny saved is a penny earned—imply risk aversion. If we wish to encourage creativity, we need to rethink our generalized cultural values and teach children from an early age to take the risks that can potentially lead to creative work.

Still, we believe that many people are not content to follow the crowd; they have both the desire and the ability to buy low. In our discussion and examples of creative investment, we want to stress that we are not speaking only of the Copernicuses and Einsteins of the world. Neither financial nor creative success is limited to well-heeled or high-stakes individuals. In the financial world there are both large- and small-scale investors; the same is true in creative investment. We often think of creativity in terms of the famous "greats": the medical discoveries of a Jonas Salk, the paintings of a Georgia O'Keeffe, or the novels of a William Faulkner. But, as the investment metaphor suggests, creativity is exhibited by more than the rarefied fraction of the population who engage in high-level or public pursuits. Creativity can be found in our daily lives—in cooking, in raising children, in remodeling or decorating a home. Furthermore it is not an all-or-nothing phenomenon. There is a continuum of creative effort and performance, just as there is a continuum of risks and profits across investments. An original and efficient filing system may not rock the world, but it'll go a long way toward improving one small corner of it.

Investment Strategies

So if one is willing to take some risks, how does one go about actually making an investment of time and energy in a creative endeavor? Strategies that are useful in selecting financial investments can also be employed in the creative domain. Many different kinds of guidelines exist for how to make investment decisions, but three stand out from among all others: technical analysis, fundamental analysis, and random-walk theory. Let's consider each strategy used to make investment decisions and their implications for sustained creativity.

Technical Analysis

Technical analysis is the study of past financial trends in order to predict future market behavior. It derives from the sound psychological principle that the best predictor of future behavior is past behavior of the same kind. By examining trends and especially cycles, technical analysts predict where things are going on the basis of where they have been. One is likely to find technical analysts poring over charts and tables of past trends in the search of indicators of future performance of the same securities. A technical analyst sees the market as largely psychological rather than logical, because people in general and investors in particular create markets that repeat past patterns of behavior. The use of technical analysis requires both knowledge and intelligence—the knowledge to know what trends to look for, and the intelligence to know how to interpret and extrapolate from them.

Technical analysis can be applied to creative work as well as to financial markets, because so many things go in cycles. One need not be a fashion designer to know that this is true of ties, which go from wide to narrow to wide and back again, conservative to flamboyant patterns and back again, and so on. In the scientific world much the same thing happens. In psychology models of how the mind works for many years were serial, implying that events are mentally processed in succession. Then parallel models were introduced, suggesting that mental events are processed all at once. Then it was shown that parallel and serial models seem to be pretty much indistinguishable, in that one can always mimic a parallel model with a serial one, or vice versa. So parallel models were out again. But now they are back—in force.

The implication for creative investment is that by studying trends in one's field, one can either consciously buck the trend or herald it just as the wave of interest is beginning to rise, hoping that the force of the cycle will propel one to the crest before others realize what is happening. Keep an eye on tie widths!

Fundamental Analysis

The basic idea of fundamental analysis is that one can best decide where to invest by focusing on the intrinsic properties of an investment vehicle (for example, a stock): its company earnings, dividends, growth, management, and so on. According to Malkiel (1985) the fundamental analyst believes markets to be 90 percent logical and perhaps 10 percent psychological. The fundamental analyst seeks to determine what a security should be worth in comparison to its current value. If the security's intrinsic value is estimated by the fundamental analyst to be above market value, he buys; if the security is estimated to be overvalued, he sells. As with technical analysis, use of fundamental analysis requires knowledge and intelligence. One must know what variables are important in predicting the future success of a security, and also have the intelligence to interpret the information about these variables.

By looking at available information and research trends, fundamental analysis provides another means for deciding in what areas of creative endeavor to invest one's energy. If a field, specialty, or problem within a field seems to be underrepresented at a given time, one has a "buy" signal; if it is overrepresented, one has a "sell" signal. If a domain lacks young blood or is casting about for leadership, that too may be a signal to jump into the fray.

Of course, the problem in the creative domain, as in the financial one, is that many people are doing fundamental analysis simultaneously and may come to similar conclusions. For example, as the AIDS epidemic became more and more threatening, a number of researchers saw an untapped gold mine, with little competition for increasingly generous funds. But the very fact that a number of investigators drew the same conclusion at the same time resulted in more and more researchers competing for the same gold. By the time they all invested, the vehicle had lost some of its attraction because the rational process of fundamental analysis had led so many to exactly the same conclusion.

This convergence on the same conclusion illustrates a problem with fundamental analysis that has been noted by random-walk theorists, among others (for example, Malkiel, 1985). If everyone, with the possible exception of a few inside traders, has access to pretty much the same information, then it will be difficult to use fundamental analysis to one's unique advantage. If everyone realizes at roughly the same time that a stock is undervalued, everyone will quickly buy it, immediately jacking up the price so that it is no longer undervalued. Similarly, simultaneous sell orders will drive down the price of a previously overvalued stock so rapidly that it will no longer be overvalued.

Random-Walk Theory

Random-walk models propose that because securities information is available to all serious investors at essentially the same time, securities will always be properly valued. Information about them will be immediately incorporated into prices so that there will be no gain from studying these data. Thus, there is simply no predicting what the market will do, because no one investing legally has an edge over anyone else. Given that the market is essentially "walking at random" (hence the name), the best thing to do is to diversify one's portfolio with securities that counterbalance one another, so that when one security is not doing well, another will be. Although one is encouraged to take risks in each of several areas, the specific risks will compensate for one another because they are not perfectly correlated, and moreover, including less risky investments will balance out the more risky ones.

Applied to creative work, the message of random-walk theory is that it is anyone's guess what the future will hold for a given field or specialization. People are likely to come to similar conclusions about things at a given time. This fact may account for the extraordinary incidence of "doubles" noted in scientific endeavors (Merton, 1973), as with the isolation of the HIV virus in France and the United States virtually simultaneously, and for the similarity of works within a field at a given time, as in architectural and automobile design. This is not to say that no one has any edge whatsoever. In the financial domain Malkiel (1985) has noted that a few select investors seem consistently to keep beating the odds, and it is true that elsewhere some people seem consistently to do more creative work than others. Thus the random-walk theory alone, like technical and fundamental analyses, does not adequately account for successes and failures in investments.

Our own view about how to choose to make a creative commitment, therefore, is something of a mixture. We believe, as do technical analysts, that in many fields trends are indeed cyclic. What is out of fashion today will come back, and what is in fashion will sooner or later be on the way out. Whether one can make precise enough predictions from the past to extrapolate to the future seems to us to be beyond the range of most, although perhaps not all, of those who try to predict future trends. Similarly we believe that fundamental analysis has some application to creative endeavor. A field that has been moribund for a long time can resurface if one or two genuinely creative ideas spark life in it again. The field of love research in psychology was dormant until Zick Rubin (1970) developed a scale on which to measure love. The presence of a few new good ideas can be a definite "buy" cue for an area of research.

Conversely, a heavily researched field in which new ideas are becoming fewer and farther between, like a heavily excavated gold mine, is probably a good candidate for exhaustion. It is difficult to imagine that any new plausible conjectures can be made about John F. Kennedy's assassination. Still, the cyclic approach suggests that eventually new theories may be proposed. With regard to random-walk theory, we would always advise that people "diversify" their portfolios, so that they are involved in a range of projects. If the risky ones work, success is theirs; if the risks don't pan out, they'll be left with something rather than nothing. The Washington Ballet is an artistic example of this balancing act. Its annual *Nutcracker* performances provide stable funding for the dance company's real passion—the performance of contemporary works that take creative risks, by up-and-coming choreographers. Many of the scientists we know do exactly the same thing, working on some sure-bet projects at the same time as they are investing time on more risky, creative work. People's creative interests are best served by "gambling" in this way. Jack Welch at General Electric is a good example of careful diversification. He has taken GE successfully into a range of financial services offerings that are far from GE's origins as an electric company, yet that have provided GE with the kind of diversification that has created a successful multifaceted business.

Investment Vehicles

Once an investor has selected a decision-making strategy, the choice of where to invest his or her resources still must be made. Again, intelligence, knowledge, and motivation are invaluable tools in good decision making. To make good decisions one needs to know what information to seek and to be smart enough to know how to use it. One also needs the sagacity to have sought out and used that knowledge in the first place. The kinds of stocks one can choose are illustrative of the kinds of domains and projects people can choose to pursue creatively.

Concept Stocks

Concept stocks represent industries or businesses that are highly favored at a given time. They exemplify some concept that is believed to be of key importance, such as biotechnology, computers, or aviation. Those who invest in these stocks often imagine themselves to have virtually no possibility of loss. After all, how could society exist any more without new drugs, information processing, or swift air travel? But the typical course of concept stocks includes some extremely good years, followed by some awful ones, and in some cases, good ones again. For example, biotechnology stocks soared until people began to despair that any truly usable products would emerge from the research. Many people feared it would just be an expensive flash in the pan. The stocks then sank, only to go up again when useful products indeed emerged, such as Genentech's tissue plasminogen activator (TPA), a protein that dissolves blood clots in the arteries after heart attacks. Computer stocks did extremely well for a number of years, until it became apparent that the market had become saturated. Those who were going to buy home computers had already bought them, and besides so many companies were producing cheap clones that it was not clear that consumers would go for name brands. The stocks sank. Similarly aviation is almost certainly a wave of the future, but changes in prices of gasoline and consumer willingness to travel, as well as competition among carriers, have had deadly effects, and some airlines have been forced into bankruptcy. Thus particular concept stocks come and go, although at a given time they seem like a sure bet.

Parallels to concept stocks can be found in areas of creative endeavor.

Self-help books were a hot concept during the selfless 1960s as well as the selfish and perhaps narcissistic 1980s. In each decade self-improvement was a primary goal, and people bought books telling them how to accomplish it. So far in the 1990s, however, such books have not been as successful. There may be any number of reasons—a recession, which has cut into the sales of most books; saturation of the market; a feeling that the effects of such books are minimal; or a feeling that when one needs to find extra work just to survive, self-help is a low priority. Maslow (1970) proposed a theory of motivation in which self-actualization needs are attended to only when basic needs for survival, such as food and shelter, have been met. And interestingly, with times being tough, voluntarism and personal acts of charity are on the rise.

The odd part is this: Even when one knows the up-and-down history of these fad concepts, it is difficult to convince oneself that today's fad is not the end of the line—that this trend, unlike the others, is here to stay. Stay it may—but the question always is, For how long? If one invests all one's financial, intellectual, or creative resources in a concept, one must be ready for the day when a once inviolable concept no longer seems sacred, or perhaps even worthwhile. Junk bonds, for example, have gone through periods of being viewed as a great investment, and through other periods of being viewed as—well—junk.

Blue-Chip Stocks

Blue-chip stocks, another investment option, are like concept stocks in that they are often focused on a particular industry or product, but a blue-chip's value inheres in the company rather than in the concept it represents. For example, the Goodyear Company makes an unexciting product—automobile tires—but it has been successful in that market for a long time, and there is no end in sight for the demand for tires, so it may be a blue-chip even if it is in no way a hot concept. Not usually at the top of the scale in terms of performance, blue-chips rather are solid buys that are expected to perform at least reasonably well, even in harder times. In almost any endeavor there are topics or paradigms that represent blue-chips of the field. For example, in psychology the study of perception—how people process visual, auditory, and other sensory information—can be considered a blue-chip. Perception has been a strong research area for the past fifty years, yielding a steady flow of insights into the phenomenon. In business there always seems to be a market for quality electronic products.

However, blue-chips don't represent a *permanent* haven of safety any more than concept stocks do. For example, AT&T was a blue-chip for many years before it became the defendant in an antitrust suit, which effectively broke up the company into a greatly shrunken version of its former self with many spinoff companies. Similarly the "Big Three" Detroit automobile manufacturers were also regarded as blue-chips in their time, only to see their sales and profits sag in the face of unexpected and still-undaunted foreign competitors. Today they have made a comeback.

In original work similar unexpected developments occur. Today's blue-chip may be tomorrow's failure. And one could argue that even if a blue-chip area is a good bet for creative work, it most likely will not lead a person to the highest levels of creative accomplishment—those associated with a third class of investment vehicles, called growth stocks.

Growth Stocks

"Growth stocks" is a generic term for stocks of usually small, fledgling companies that have not yet had an opportunity to prove themselves. Both the potential risk and the potential gain are great. The successes become oft-told tales—of how one could have become a millionaire, with no sweat, by investing in Xerox. The problem, of course, is that for every Xerox there are thousands of companies that do not do nearly as well, and many that go under completely. Yet growth companies offer a true opportunity for smart investing—if one selects the right companies. The tough job is to decide which ones are on their way up for the long haul; using one's intelligence and knowledge will help.

The same principles apply in creative endeavors. For example, in television advertising sound is emerging as a creative growth area. Some have begun to use 3-D sound to bring the viewer into the commercial, to use unnatural synthesized sounds to attract attention, or to use silence as a creative advertising tool. In general, when new starts emerge in a field or a new field arises altogether, it is difficult to say which will be lasting successes and which will soon be yesterday's bright lights and today's flickering ones. But much of the most creative and influential work of the future will undoubtedly come from the newest fields and from the newest people within those fields.

Selecting the right investment vehicle (field, problem, or approach to a problem) is a time-consuming process requiring the motivation, intelligence, and knowledge to work hard and effectively at analyzing data. The time, however, will be well spent when the investment decision pays off and paves the way for creative performance. People who invested in pharmaceuticals when there was a rapid increase in antibiotics did well. Now that many of these antibiotics have lost their effectiveness due to the proliferation of drug-resistant bacteria, this market may well be ready to open up again.

Capital

In investing, the types of investments made, and the particular choices made within those investments, depend in part on the capital available. A stock such as Berkshire Hathaway is out of range for those who cannot afford its price of more than $20,000 a share. Investments in real estate often involve substantial capital, and many mutual funds likewise require sizable minimum investments.

The concept of capital is also relevant to creative endeavors. Some theorists of creativity have taken seriously the concept of human capital as a determinant of potential and actualized creativity. What exactly is human capital, and what is its role in creativity?

Walberg (1988) notes that capital is an asset that gives rise to income, or more broadly, utility—including such nonmonetary benefits as tranquillity or honor. Human beings, according to Walberg, are themselves capital investments of a society. Rubenson and Runco (1992) define capital as "productive resources, such as land or tools, which can be used to transform raw materials into desired goods. Human capital refers to specific skills and knowledge which enter into the productive process" (p. 134). In their view part of human capital is the creative potential of the individual. They also use their notion of human capital to explain why younger people may be greater risk takers and hence more prone to major creative discoveries and invention.

According to these theorists one specific form of human capital is the accumulated knowledge a person has come to possess. Because older creators will, on the average, possess more of this knowledge, they will be able to produce minor contributions at lesser cost than can younger creators. And because the proportionate cost of minor contributions is greater for younger innovators, the latter have less incentive to make them. On the other hand their relative lack of human capital—specific knowledge and other resources—lowers the proportionate cost for them of more revolutionary contributions, because such contributions are likely to reduce the value of existing knowledge. Those who will be adversely affected by this reduction in value will be those with substantial investments in that (outdated) knowledge. In this vein Planck (1949) and others have proposed that older achievers in a discipline are less receptive to new ideas than are younger achievers. Hull, Tessner, and Diamond (1978) tested this hypothesis with historical records of British scientists who reacted to Darwin's theory of evolution in the decade after it was published. Scientists who accepted the theory were significantly younger (mean age = 41.7) than those who rejected it (mean age = 53.0). With less vested interest in the existing knowledge base, younger innovators can feel freer to try to change it than do their seniors.

At some level human capital is almost certainly self-perpetuating. Merton (1968) has referred to this self-perpetuation as the "Matthew effect," from the statement in Matthew 25:29 in the Bible that "unto every one that hath shall be given, and he shall have abundance." The basic notion, seen in our economy on a daily basis, is that the rich get richer and the poor, poorer. As one accumulates the trappings that aid a career—degrees, job experience, technical training, professional contacts, financial support, fame, and so on—these trappings tend to build on themselves. Investments tend to follow the mathematician Thomas Bayes's theorem (1763), interpreted in this case as meaning that they take into account past accomplishments. For example, in a government grant competition, someone with an established record is usually seen as a safer bet than someone with no track record at all. Likewise, some firms and universities hire only those from particular other firms or universities. Thus, although there is certainly upward mobility in the strata of creative endeavors, there can be little doubt that it is limited by the disproportionate bestowal of resources on those who have already benefited from them in the past.

In our view human capital that should be earmarked for innovative investment consists of synthetic and analytic intelligence, knowledge, motivation, a legislative thinking style, and a risk-taking, confident personality. Those who possess these qualities are ready to invest in creative endeavor. But their willingness and ability to invest in creativity will be affected by an aspect of the sixth resource for creativity, the environment.

Market Demands

How an individual decides to invest his or her "human capital" depends on another aspect of creativity, the environment. In general, societies may have different demands for creativity because the novel ideas will change the status quo, and some social environments value conformity to the status quo more than do others (Lubart, 1990; Mann, 1980). Also, the value of different sorts of creative work to society is anything but a constant. Sometimes certain kinds of creativity are in demand. For example, the Soviet launch of *Spuntnik I* in 1957 led to a call for American technological creativity. Recently, regarding the Supreme Court, there have been calls for the addition of a "creative" justice to balance the "technicians" on the court who tend to focus on detailed points of law. The social environment is a factor that cannot be ignored when making or evaluating investments, either financial or creative.

Any number of social factors can contribute to the value of creativity, just as social factors contribute to the value of an investment. Political instability, for example, tends to raise the value of some "necessary" investments (for example, precious metals or defense industries) and to lower the value of desirable but nonessential others (for example, tourism or fashion industries). According to Simonton (1984), political instability creates more demand for creativity because of a greater need to find imaginative solutions to serious problems. However, the resultant demand for creativity, like that for stocks, may be unequally distributed. Those in applied sciences will probably find more demand for their creative services than will those in basic sciences or the humanities. Furthermore, thinkers may find that their creative range is perhaps more circumscribed than in boom times. When money is tight, there may be more demand for ideas to cut costs on already existing products, or for less expensive alternatives, than for exciting new options.

Ironically, the person or idea seen as the most creative is not always the one that is most successful in the marketplace. Rubenson and Runco (1992) have suggested that the demand for creativity is driven by a "marginal utility curve." Up to a certain point those seeking creative solutions are willing to pay, monetarily or otherwise, for these solutions, but after that point the increased yield through additional creativity is not seen as justification for a further increase in price. When the cost of producing more creativity barely exceeds the benefit, increases in creativity will not be rewarded. For example, an advertising agency may hire the second-best job candidate because the executives do not believe that paying to get the very best talent will necessarily make that much difference. The extra revenue produced by the top applicant may not justify the additional cost. Similarly a university department may hire scholars who are not at the top of their field on the premise that the very best simply aren't worth what the university would have to pay to get them. This issue applies more generally. For example, some new drugs fail not for lack of effectiveness but because they are not sufficiently more effective than existing drugs to justify what can be a substantially greater cost.

John Maynard Keynes compared the psychological forces operating in markets to those in a newspaper competition offering a prize for picking out the six prettiest faces—"prettiest" as defined by the average of everyone who responds. In other words one will select not the faces most attractive to oneself but those one believes *others* will find most attractive. In investment markets the investor often tries to select what others will eventually value, regardless of what he himself values.

The psychology that applies to investments in the market applies to creativity as well. One can see it at work in the way many prestigious universities hire senior professors. Referees in other institutions are asked to comment on the quality of an applicant, either in isolation or in comparison with others. Even back in the 1950s, Caplow and McGee (1957) noted that in their survey of universities, the principal quality being sought was addition to the institutions' prestige. They wanted to make hires that other schools would envy. (Of course the worst fate was to make a hire that turned out to be publicly embarrassing.) Similarly, when acquisitions editors at publishing firms make decisions on which books to publish, the overriding consideration is not what they personally find to be fresh and exciting, but rather, what will appeal to a given audience. The same applies to new movies, new products, and new services.

Although the marketplace in which creativity will be competing cannot be ignored, neither should it be the sole motivator of activity. We have discussed six factors that contribute to creativity; environment is only one of them. Because the impetus toward innovation ultimately has to come from within, not without, the most creative work in any field is unlikely to come from attempts to be a crowd pleaser. One needs to think in ways that others simply may not like or understand, or to ask questions that others will find impertinent or irrelevant. As was stated by Garry Trudeau, creator of the controversial and influential Doonesbury political comic strip, when he received an honorary degree at Yale University in 1991:

> The impertinent question is the glory and engine of human inquiry. Copernicus asked it and shook the foundations of Renaissance Europe. Darwin asked it and redefined humankind's very sense of itself. Thomas Jefferson asked it and was so invigorated by it that he declared it an inalienable right. . . . Whether revered or reviled in their lifetimes, history's movers framed their questions in ways that were entirely disrespectful of conventional wisdom.

Leadership Skills

Once one has judged the market, found the right investment, and expended the capital, what next? Successful management of the investment is the next step—one some innovators are not ready for. A distinction is often made between entrepreneurial skills, which are most relevant in start-up companies, and managerial skills, which are most relevant once a business has gotten off the ground. These two kinds of leadership are sometimes viewed as antithetical, with people who are adept at one often seen as not particularly able at the other. Leadership tendencies and skills are fundamentally based in personality and thinking style.

Coming up with and marketing new creative products or ideas is essentially entrepreneurial in character, involving as it does starting a new business and persuading other people to support it. Entrepreneurship demands a willingness to take chances, stand alone, tolerate ambiguity, and overcome obstacles: all hallmarks of the creative personality.

But once a business takes off, good management is called for. Early success in the entrepreneurial mode often results in the establishment of a stable enterprise in which others start to work out the details of the "idea person's" ideas. This leaves the entrepreneur the choice of either finding someone else to supervise the business or else adapting him- or herself to the demands of doing it. Thus, as demands increase, the leadership talent that is called for switches increasingly from entrepreneurial to managerial. While this process leaves some creative people behind, others make the transition but become more "enterprise managers" than enterprisers themselves (see Gilad, 1984; Whiting, 1988), and have to adjust or even suppress aspects of their personalities and thinking styles. Not necessarily negative in itself, this suppression will call for further decision making on the investor's part as to where the future will lead.

Evaluating Investments

Like judgment of market demands before investing, evaluation of an investment is heavily dependent on the environment or marketplace. In a fundamental sense, therefore, evaluation of financial and creative worth are parallel, because in both cases evaluation is based largely on social consensus. A product is deemed creative when appropriate judges collectively agree that it is (Amabile, 1982). A stock is valuable when other investors collectively desire to possess it. As we noted in chapter 2, people's conceptions of creativity suggest that novelty, high quality, and appropriateness are the main criteria for judging creative performance (Amabile, 1982; Jackson & Messick, 1965; MacKinnon, 1962a; Sternberg, 1985b, 1988b).

Evaluation of an investment furthermore depends on the judges' characteristics, which in turn somewhat depend on trends and mores in the cultural and economic environments. Sometimes the value of either a company or a creative product is not initially obvious in a particular context. Long ago some people considered the advent of books to be calamity. Writing down ideas and stories encouraged laziness in memory and thinking in a way that would undermine intellectual civilization! The original thinker must be prepared for the fact that it can take years before creative value is fully recognized by society at large— witness also the many artists, writers, and composers who gain fame only posthumously.

There is also a potential paradox in judging the value of a creative product, just as there is in valuing many kinds of financial investments.

How much is a rare coin worth? Is it a good long-term investment? The silver or gold in the coin may be worth just a few dollars. Yet discriminating buyers with knowledge of the numismatics market may pay hundreds of thousands of dollars for that coin. A novice might not be willing to buy it at any price because she does not recognize its value. The same can happen in the evaluation of a fine new idea or a rare antique chair. So who is really making the correct judgment as to worth?

In an attempt to gain some evaluation standards, we use consensus techniques. These techniques are not perfect, however. Although one might think that the collective good sense of a group would be better than that of any one individual—after all, why else have committees?—ample evidence suggests that sometimes the reverse is true. Irving Janis (1972) described a phenomenon he referred to as "groupthink," or "instances of mindless conformity and collective misjudgment of serious risks" (p. 3).

Any number of investment crazes have exemplified groupthink. Probably the most often cited is the seventeenth-century tulip mania. In the early 1600s tulips were fashionable in Europe, and in Holland—the chief source of bulbs—Dutch horticulturists had developed many rare varieties. In 1633 the public in general began investing in tulip bulbs, and prices began to rise. The Semper Augustus variety reached a value of somewhere between $6,000 and $8,000 (converted from Dutch florins) per pound. One pound of the variety Gheele Croohen sold for $30 one month and $1,575 the next. Rumors of foreign orders fanned the flames, and a futures market developed. But in 1637 dealers began to have difficulty finding buyers. In short order the market collapsed, and the "valuable" bulbs were suddenly next to worthless (Dreman, 1977).

In fact any investment collectible is susceptible to such trends, as one can see in the sometimes wild gyrations of the markets in art, precious gems, rare coins, and rare stamps. The same is true in real estate and stocks and bonds. There is no supreme judge of a financial investment, any more than there is an ultimate judge who can state the true value of a new idea. But despite its relativism, it is the working tradition to use consensus techniques for judging both financial and creative worth. We must hope that those who are involved in the evaluation of original works will strive to see beyond their own time and place and to develop knowledge and appreciation of creativity in themselves, so that they can better judge it in others.

Costs

Many of the costs and benefits of economic investments apply equally to investments in creative work. Take one of the most lamented costs: taxes. As people earn more from investments, they pay more in taxes. (In graduated tax structures, their proportional contribution increases as well.) One not infrequently hears complaints that it simply isn't worth the work to earn more because one ends up paying it back in taxes. Thus one will need the knowledge and intelligence to predict costs before the bills come due, to know later on how to minimize them, and the motivation to find ways of cutting costs.

In creative work other kinds of taxes may effectively rob an individual of his or her drive for originality. For example, people may be called on to pay back awards and public or professional recognition by serving on panels that evaluate the award nominations of others. Such committees almost invariably require great amounts of time without proportionate— or perhaps any—recompense. Similarly someone whose writing is frequently published may be asked to review the work of others, and ultimately, to edit journals and books—all of which will take time from her own writing. Successful individuals in business and education find themselves more and more in demand as mentors, spokespeople, and committee members. Furthermore, as one's reputation grows, the demand increases for speeches or articles that reiterate one's unique contributions for different audiences—and the repetition of content is not conducive to groundbreaking thinking! As a result of all of these time thieves, it is not uncommon for the creative individual eventually to find him- or herself with almost no time left for creative endeavors. One must learn how to say no to the pileup of demands in order to leave time to continue one's creative work.

Paradoxically, among the potential costs of creative endeavor, especially in the early stages of a career, are rejection and even ostracism for attempting to buy low. It was noted that fledgling innovators have less investment in the established order. If they then try to overturn that order, those with vested interests rarely express thanks for being shown that they have been wrong for many years, or that they have been passing their time on work that will soon be passé. Rather there may be attempts—not always subtle—to punish the creative individual for upsetting the apple cart. Thus the creative individual may find him- or herself at odds with the community of investors, having to convince them of the value of the innovation, when these others have a stake in the status quo. The most creative discoveries and inventions may even go unheeded because colleagues simply aren't ready for or don't want to hear them. For example, there is now strong evidence that antacid medications are relatively ineffective against stomach ulcers because such ulcers are caused by bacteria rather than stomach acid. According to *Science* (Apr. 9, 1993), however, pharmaceutical companies have been reluctant to embrace new antibacterial drugs against ulcers because of the companies' vested interest in antacids. Again, the contrarian spirit and willingness to believe in oneself are invaluable at such times.

Last, as an individual acquires a more and more valuable portfolio of creative accomplishments, he or she faces the same danger as does a mature company—that he or she may not be able to muster the resources to deal with a rapidly changing world and thus will be a bad investment in terms of potential for future human-capital gains. Indeed, there is even the possibility that the person will enter creative bankruptcy. Such deadwood may make few creative commitments and have trouble meeting the few they *have* made. This kind of creative bankruptcy can happen at any time in a career.

Individuals can nonetheless recover from such bankruptcies, just as they can from financial ones. Modes of recovery are variable; they may involve changing fields, reeducating oneself, or simply deciding on a fresh angle from which to approach one's work. Creative bankruptcy, like the personal kind, need not be permanent, as long as the motivation to adapt and succeed remains strong. B. F. Skinner, the greatest behaviorally oriented psychologist of the twentieth century, wanted to be a novelist but eventually found his greatest talent elsewhere. (In fact, as a psychologist, he did write one novel, which has never been held up as a paragon of literary virtuosity.)

Benefits

All these cautions about the risks and costs of creativity, while they must realistically be acknowledged, are perhaps unduly discouraging. The world is full of people, from the famous to the ordinary, who have developed and capitalized on the confluence of the six facets of creativity in their own lives. These creative individuals receive valuable dividends from their work, just as do financial investors.

Personal satisfaction and a sense of fulfillment from having championed one's own ideas against naysayers are among the profits reaped by the creative investor. Just as financial dividends can be reinvested in one's capital and to generate more interest, so too do creative accomplishments build on themselves. Good work snowballs into more and perhaps greater work as one gains confidence in oneself, as others' expectations increase, and as new challenges—contracts, commissions, assignments—are offered. Those whose standards for themselves are high are usually those who achieve the most, and innovative success starts a self-perpetuating cycle of creativity.

The sheer fun of working on a project that is important, challenging, *and* potentially beneficial to others cannot be overlooked either. We test ourselves most when we take stock of our abilities and set our sights on doing the best we can as innovatively as we can. Perhaps it should be reiterated that there is a continuum of creativity, and that it can occur in almost any context. One's best, most creative contribution may possibly be in designing a new technique for brain surgery, but for most of us it is more likely to be in landscape design, or counseling, or accounting, or sales, or coaching—anywhere we find ourselves in the course of our days. Living and working more imaginatively is a joy in itself.

The history of human endeavor attests to the fact that the benefits of creativity to the individual and potentially to society almost certainly outweigh the costs. Those who take risks are those who make major, lasting contributions for which they are long remembered and even handsomely rewarded in material terms. But not everyone will be an Einstein or a Carnegie, and making it into the history books or striking it rich, while desirable, should not be one's source of motivation. Instead the impetus for creativity and change must come from within, for that is also where the rewards will be enjoyed most intensely. Each person must find his or her own place in the spectrum of creative expression in order to reap the highest returns on the investment. Everyone differs on the six facets of intelligence, knowledge, motivation, thinking style, personality, and environment. Hence the returns will vary with the person, but all will know the pleasure of having changed the world in some definable way.

The Investment Metaphor: Limitations and Comments

Since metaphors are imprecise by nature, we recognize that creativity and investment are not strictly analogous. In using metaphors, therefore, it is important to recognize points of dissimilarity as well as similarity—in fact, examining where the metaphor is imprecise often yields more understanding of the concept. The investment metaphor is no exception.

One example of a difference between the investment and creative realms is the starting point for each endeavor. Financial investors generally buy into existing stocks or other instruments. For creative work, people may join an existing field or genre but must generate the specific project or starting ideas.

Another example of a difference between financial investment and creativity is the source of the "value added" after buying into a stock or an idea. The financial investor usually monitors a stock, which may gain in value because the business or economy as a whole succeeds; he or she does not usually go to work for the company to help it succeed. For creativity, however, the individual must roll up his or her sleeves, apply the cognitive, personality, motivational, and environmental resources to the problem, push the project toward a final product, and sometimes promote the product to win acceptance. Creators, therefore, must work personally (and hard!) to bring their ideas to fruition. Such work may be done by employees or assistants, but only after the creator has done the thinking and laid the intellectual or technical groundwork. Thus, for creative work, an individual's resources are actively applied throughout a project whereas, in the financial world, an investor uses his or her resources primarily to make just the "buy" and "sell" decisions.

One other caution is necessary regarding our investment metaphor: In our experience some people find an economic parallel distasteful. Others see financial considerations of any kind as antithetical to creativity. But such concerns, although understandable, are superficial. We want to show that there are major conceptual points of comparison between financial and creative investments; we are not equating creativity and money. Perhaps this point will be clearer when one considers that the concept of investment is by no means limited to the financial domain. In a broad sense people constantly invest time, effort, and intellectual and emotional energy in careers and relationships. Our theory makes only structural parallels, not those of content. Again our goal in saying that creativity is like investing in financial instruments is not to link creativity with money but to show similarities between the psychological components involved in monetary investments and those involved in creative performance.

Metaphors are helpful frameworks for comparison, and nothing more. They should guide rather than control thinking. Although we find the investment metaphor useful for discussing effective creative performance, we also know that theorists run into trouble when they start taking their own metaphors too seriously. The tail starts wagging the dog, to use yet another familiar metaphor!

We believe that "buying low and selling high"—with the accompanying considerations of market and specific risk, investment strategies, investment vehicles, capital, market demands, skills, costs, and benefits—accurately parallels the process of effective creative involvement in a field.

Some Implications of the Investment View

Before discussing each facet of the investment theory, we want to point out some general implications of the theory.

Anyone Can Do It

When it comes to abilities our cultural background leads us to think in terms of some people having more of them and others having less. People's levels of ability are often viewed as fixed.

When you think of creativity in terms of buying low and selling high, however, these conventional notions just don't apply. Buying low and selling high is something anyone can do. Perhaps not everyone will do it equally well, but to some extent creativity is a state of mind—one that a person can choose to adopt. Here are some illustrations from the business world.

Mark McCormack, for example, is the founder and director of International Management Group, an organization that represents athletes, dancers, musicians, models, and others in various kinds of negotiations and also helps them manage their money. With athletes this management is particularly important, because athletes often have only a few years of serious play before they are essentially forced to retire.

Recognizing certain facts about athletes, McCormack was the first to come up with the concept of representing them in this way. One fact is that athletes' contract negotiations can involve a lot of money. Another is that they are not necessarily trained in negotiating contracts. And another is that if they mismanage their money, as many have (Bjorn Borg is a famous case), they may actually spend much of their lives poor.

Then McCormack had another idea: People think so highly of athletes—well, at least they used to—so why not have athletes endorse products? Today, of course, such endorsements are taken for granted, but the concept is actually relatively new. McCormack has made a fortune out of these ideas and others. In addition to running the largest talent management firm in the world, he has found time to write several books, among them best-sellers such as *What They Don't Teach You at Harvard Business School* (McCormack, 1984).

We're not going to argue over whether McCormack had some kind of inherited talent or not. What we will argue is that he is a man who has constantly been looking for new angles—for the service that he can provide that others haven't thought of. Another example of someone who saw a new angle is Ted Nierenberg, who began Dansk International (Ray & Myers, 1986). He attended an industrial fair in Hannover, Germany, and noted a display of stainless steel flatware. In the United States at that time this product was not used in homes. Yet, stainless steel utensils are cheap, durable, and potentially stylish. Nierenberg saw a need and a market. After consulting Scandinavian designers, he introduced stainless in the 1950s when the timing was right—suburbs were growing and women were returning to work. Nierenberg attributes his vision to "an ability to see the exceptions," a part of buying low that we will call "selective encoding" and discuss in greater detail later.

Peter Kasoff also had a creative entrepreneurial vision that led to the beginning of his nonprofit company, the Philanthropic Initiative. Kasoff's innovation was to combine the various aspects of philanthropy under one roof. His company helps potential donors find their area of interest and motivation for giving, locates relevant organizations that match the donor's interests, invests donor money to maximize philanthropic potential, facilitates the connection between donor and recipient, and provides follow-up to keep the donor informed of the recipient's progress.

For one more example at the individual level, there's Tom Monaghan, founder of Domino's Pizza, who had an idea of providing take-out-only hot pizza to the customer with rapid delivery (Landrum, 1993). Monaghan knew he had a good idea and a potential market. He was buying low because there was no strong competition in the take-out food market at that time. Eventually, after overcoming financial difficulties and a dispute over the "Domino's" name, the novel idea led to a highly successful organization that delivers fresh pizza dough and related ready-to-assemble pizza products from a central location to franchised stores.

The same principle of buying low and selling high also applies at an organizational level. Let's look at IBM's initial efforts in the mainframe computer business. When it started selling mainframes, IBM was indeed buying low. There wasn't much competition, and IBM made some of the best equipment money could buy. But as smaller computers became more and more powerful, IBM was slow to react. Apparently, instead of staying a step ahead of the crowd, it fell behind. When everyone else seemed to see that IBM would have to redefine itself—and find some other niche that others had not yet discovered—IBM didn't seem to see it, or if it did, it didn't act on the knowledge. Today, however, IBM is turning itself around.

In contrast, Apple, a company that was on the decline, was taken over and turned around by a concentration on products that were always one step ahead of the market, rather than on products that everyone else had, which people would soon tire of or view as passé.

And then there's the automobile industry. Back in 1974 Japanese manufacturers started exporting small cars to the United States at a time when Detroit was thinking in terms of bigger and bigger cars. The idea that people would actually prefer small cars was a novelty at the time. The U.S. companies had always charged more for the larger, luxury models, and Detroit assumed that everyone would want the largest car he or she could possibly afford. The Japanese didn't have any innate abilities that the Americans lacked. Rather, they took the attitude of seeking the edge that Detroit, in its complacency, was not seeking. Today, with the dollar falling against the yen and Detroit more savvy as to what people want, American cars are staging a comeback.

Perhaps the best example of a company that has taken a creative attitude toward its product is Nike, which—together with a few other sneaker companies—has changed the American conception of what a sneaker is. As a child one of the authors had a choice between two or three types of sneakers. There were Keds, there were PF Flyers, and there were some store brands. There were two principal types of sneaker within each brand: basketball and tennis. But basically sneakers were used for sports. There was no glamour in them; they were simply utilitarian.

Today's youth has a very different image of sneakers, which have become products with panache. One could not even count the number of brands of sneakers, much less the number of different models. What was a commodity has become, in the upper ranges, a luxury item that can cost in excess of two hundred dollars. We won't attempt to judge whether any sneaker is worth even half that. What we can judge is that Nike saw a market that many others did not, and literally created a desire among the nation's young that did not exist before.

Although these examples may sound like ones that don't apply to the ordinary person, the principle is exactly the same. Certainly you have noticed how two people can go into a job that is defined in exactly the same way, and one of them seems always to have an edge that the other lacks. Part of this edge is the edge of buying low. One author's father grew up during the depression. He noticed something that anyone else could have noticed—and that most people probably did: Many people lacked the money to buy clothes. He opened a sewing supplies store. People could buy in one place everything they needed to make clothes. Soon he was sending sewing supplies by mail order around the country, especially to towns too small to have a store that sold similar merchandise. He never owned eight houses (as does McCormack), just one, and he was far from being a millionaire. But he looked for what people needed that they didn't have, and he provided it. And that point of view is available to anyone. It doesn't take any super inborn talent, but a fresh way of looking at the world that can be developed with practice.

We end this section with yet another true story—in some ways, the most impressive of all. The story was told to one of the authors by his wife. A man from her hometown of León, Mexico, the richest man in the city, was asked by a reporter how he had acquired his fortune in the shoe business. He explained that when he had taken his first job as a night watchman in a shoemaking plant, he had been illiterate. When his boss discovered this fact, he immediately fired him. He was forced to find a new way in the world, which he did, starting his own shoe business and eventually buying his boss's plant as well as many others. After all these years he is still illiterate. The reporter then commented: "But if you had known how to read and write, just imagine where you might be now!" And the wealthiest man in León replied, "I know exactly where I would be. I would still be the night watchman in the shoe plant where I started."

BOX 4.1

The Art of Buying Low

Hugh McMahon carved out a creative niche for himself when he realized more than a decade ago that Halloween was becoming more and more geared to adults. He combined his artistic background with a common craft that millions enjoy every October—carving pumpkins. But a pumpkin can become much more than just a scary face with cut-out eyes, nose, and mouth. McMahon carves the pumpkin to varying depths and pops out parts of the pumpkin to achieve interesting effects when the pumpkin is illuminated. He describes the process as "sculpting light" (Lubart, personal communication, 1990).

McMahon bought low and pursued his novel approach just as the market was becoming ripe. He began to market his idea by showing one of his carved pumpkins to restaurants in New York City. After being turned down at about twenty establishments, he began to think that perhaps he was out of his gourd. Then he got a break, when a restaurant called Ichabod gave him his first sale. The fit was right: Ichabod Crane is a Washington Irving character who is chased by a headless horseman. The image he selected boasted a glowing pumpkin head in the horseman's arms.

McMahon has gone on to turn pumpkin carving into a lucrative seasonal business. He carves pumpkins into cats, owls, elephants, tigers, turkeys, and other animals. He also carves nature motifs, such as designs with leaves that play on the fall season. And he has carved pumpkin portraits of Ronald Reagan, Prince Charles, Lady Diana, Elvis Presley, Willie Nelson, Sylvester Stallone, American Indians, and others. His pumpkins have been featured in the *New York Times* and in *Life* and *People* magazines. His work has been displayed at the White House and at numerous restaurants and nightclubs. McMahon has come to be known as the Michelangelo of pumpkin carvers; he is a good example of how buying low and selling high can pay off in the long term, even when it doesn't seem to in the short term.

Creativity is a frame of mind, and even people who can't read or write can have it.

Buying Low and Selling High Is a Way of Life

Our second point follows closely from the first. Buying low and selling high can be a way of life—it's an attitude toward living. Some people choose to live creatively, others don't. But it is a choice.

You can choose to follow the crowd, or you can choose to go your own way. Architectural design has been Jordan Mozer's means of expressing his unique ideas and imagination (Lawson, 1994). He calls his approach "surreal" and contrasts it with the "linear, rational" approach to architecture. Since 1990 he has focused on designing the interiors of restaurants such as the Cyprus Club in San Francisco and, most recently, Iridium in New York City. In designing Iridium Mozer tried to answer the question, "What would music look like if you could see it?" (p. 8). He described his design for the restaurant as "animated" and "liquid." For example, "Chair legs evoke the look of ballerinas en pointe . . . and the back of every chair . . . 'dances'" (p. 8). But according to New York designer Sam Lopata, "Most restaurateurs want much more subdued design" (p. 1). Yet Mozer continues to pursue his style. Mozer says, "I'm a gambler, and I'm aggressive and obstinate, and I'm not afraid to put in 80-hour weeks" (p. 8).

A similar choice is available, of course, in the stock market. Instead of doing their own thinking, many people seek the advice of experts, some of whom have dubious credentials. They wait with bated breath for their investment newsletter to come with its latest recommendation: "Buy Twiddlekins." How exciting—a chance to make money! But there's just one problem. The same investment newsletter is advising thousands, perhaps tens of thousands, of people to buy Twiddlekins, and unless someone has the speediest mail service in the country, by the time he or she puts in an order, the price will already have been bid up by the thousands of others buying Twiddlekins. It's too late to buy low. Even worse, what often happens is that savvy investors realize that—since the price has been bid up for no particular reason—there is no particular reason to buy Twiddlekins or to hold it if they already own it. So they sell Twiddlekins, and the price goes back down. Those who recently bought may then start to panic, and very soon the price is even lower than it was before. Following the crowd in investing is a good model for following the crowd in any endeavor—you usually end up behind.

Moving beyond business examples, we believe that the same principles apply in one's personal life. One of us has studied intimate relationships for a number of years (see Sternberg, 1988d, 1991), revealing, among things, that in one respect personal relationships are like any other institution: When they stagnate, they die. Couples who keep doing the same things day in and day out, thinking the same thoughts day in and day out, and fighting the same battles day in and day out usually end up either unhappy or just plain bored with their relationships. These couples are not necessarily "uncreative" people. Either or both partners, for example, may be very creative in the workplace. But they seem to believe that, whereas businesses need to grow and change, relationships don't. And then they wonder why slowly, month after month, year after year, they see their intimate relationships becoming less intimate and less satisfying. To thrive, relationships—just like anything else—need to be creative. The most successful relationships are those in which couples continually have new experiences and share new ideas. We're not saying that there have to be changes each day, or even each week or month. The point is not how often there is change but to keep the relationship dynamic: The creative couple is likely to be much happier than the couple who believes that a relationship will just take care of itself. The lesson is, you constantly have to help a relationship grow, the way you would a plant or a child.

What's Low and High Changes with Time and Place

If you're over thirty, you've almost certainly heard someone say, "If only I'd bought Xerox when . . ." (or Berkshire-Hathaway or Disney or any of a number of other companies). These are good examples of the old saying that everyone has twenty–twenty hindsight. The creative person needs to be ahead of the crowd, not with it.

We should add, "A *bit* ahead of the crowd." One of the saddest aspects of life is that someone can be too far ahead of the times and not live to see his or her work appreciated (or worse, to see someone else come up with the same idea later, and receive the credit). In fact, the very well-regarded graphics of the Apple Macintosh were antedated by the Xerox Star System. The case even went to court, and Xerox lost. Xerox was a bit too ahead of its time. It also made some mistakes: It didn't market the product well, and it priced the system so high that few could afford it. For another example, we know that Vincent van Gogh, whose paintings now bring record-breaking sums at auction, died penniless. He was not alone.

The phenomenon of being too far ahead is not limited to the historical greats. It happened to one of us, who submitted a grant proposal to study "concept naturalness." The idea was that some concepts, like "tall and dark," seem natural, whereas others, like "short and light," do not. The proposal came back with reviews ridiculing the very idea the author was proposing—that some concepts are somehow more natural than are others. About seven years later, the same foundation that had rejected the idea was busily funding research on concept naturalness.

As we mentioned before, what is considered creative differs not only with time but with place. For example, John James Audubon initially met with rejection in the Philadelphia of the early 1820s. His illustrations of wildlife represented not only experimentation with watercolors but also the portrayal of animals in more naturalistic poses and settings. Audubon couldn't find financial support because his work differed radically from traditional drawings, based on rigidly posed, stuffed wildlife. Also, he had spent years in the territories doing illustrations and his back-country manners were looked down upon. Shortly after his experience in Philadelphia, Audubon sailed to England with his work. His art was well received and his woodsman style appealed to the English. Audubon wrote, "I am fêted, feasted, elected honorary member of societies, making money by my exhibition and by my painting" (Staff, 1994, p. 99). His famous book of engravings, *The Birds of America*, was first published in London.

Furthermore, regarding differences due to place, anyone who gives lectures for a living, as we do, knows that you can give exactly the same talk to two different audiences, with raves flowing from one audience and total disgust oozing from the other. Similarly, anyone who teaches knows that exactly the same course can work terrifically with one group of students and fail totally with another. Businesses recognize that what is appreciated in one place is often not appreciated in another. For example, if you visit the Coca-Cola public exhibit in Atlanta, you will enter a room that has soft drinks bottled by Coca-Cola around the world. Some of the flavors are sold widely, and others are sold in just one country or in a small number of countries. Businesses recognize that tastes vary, country by country.

The same principle applies to us all. When we choose a job, we need to base our choice not only on the money it may pay or the prestige it may offer, but on whether it is in an institution that values the kind of creative ideas we have to offer. If it is not, we are not likely to be appreciated and may well end up not staying there long.

Good interpersonal relationships are founded on the same principle. Often we find our self-esteem undermined when we are in a relationship with someone who does not appreciate what we have to offer. If we are lucky we find someone else who does appreciate our creative gifts—what is distinctive about us—and who can live with our faults. In studying relationships the senior author has lost count of the number of people with whom he has talked who are in dead-end relationships with others who don't appreciate their strengths but instead focus on their weaknesses. Obviously no one is perfect. Everyone has strengths and weaknesses: What you need is someone who can value the former and tolerate the latter!

Seeing What's Low and What's High

By now you may be saying that it's obvious that one should buy low and sell high. The trick is knowing when things are really low and when they are really high.

For example, interest rates on mortgages recently reached lows that had not been seen for several decades. As we write, rates are on their way back up. But very few people were able to predict the exact low point, and the large majority who refinanced their houses did so either before rates reached the bottom or after they had started climbing. Similarly, the Japanese stock market recently reached a low beyond which it had not fallen in many years, but who was buying? And, on the very day these words are being written, the Dow-Jones industrial average has reached yet another all-time high—and people are buying stocks like hotcakes. Perhaps the market will keep going up. As for one of us, he sold stock a month ago, certain the market was ready to decline. He's still waiting.

Obviously we don't know any magic trick to tell you just when any market—whether of stocks or ideas—will hit top or bottom. If we did, would we be writing this book, or would we tell anyone else? Indeed, we have to laugh when we think of people who pay fortunes to supposed experts who claim to know. If the experts knew, believe us, they wouldn't have to sell the advice to even one person. Using the secret, they could become as rich as they liked for as long as they liked.

Yet there *are* strategies, and there *are* clues. In the last chapter we discussed the use of technical analysis to follow market trends when examining the value and investment potential of a field of work or an idea for a project. Now we would like to extend these general concepts with some commonsense rules of thumb for buying low.

One clue is that if everyone is doing it—no matter what it is—and you do it too, you are buying high. Back in the 1980s people were buying so-called "junk bonds" as if there were no tomorrow. These are bonds with low ratings that bear extraordinarily high rates of interest precisely because they are risky. Even insurance companies, which normally invest only in relatively safe debt instruments, were putting more and more money into the junk bonds, as were savings and loan institutions. The rest is history. The market crashed, and the crash was followed by a string of all kinds of bankruptcies—not only of the companies that floated the junk bonds but of the companies that bought them. When everyone is doing something, we sometimes let common sense go to the wind. If bonds or anything else are paying an extraordinary rate of interest, there has to be a reason, and the reason is that they are inherently extremely risky. The old saying that if something appears to be too good to be true it probably is, applies quite well here.

When everyone is doing something, it is tempting to follow the crowd (and it's a hell of a lot easier than going against what everyone else is doing). Yet, if you offer a product that everyone else is offering, you will be able to make sales only if you find some edge that others don't have—in other words, if you are creative. If you write books that have the same plots and characters as everyone else's, you need some way of distinguishing your own product, or else you will have trouble getting your readership to pay attention to you rather than to others. Recently, one of us went to Paris. In Montmartre there were hundreds of artists selling—their pictures of Montmartre. The pictures looked practically identical, and while the art may have been technically competent, it sure wasn't very creative. And they were having trouble selling their work, too, because everyone's work looked like everyone else's. Do you get the point? Buying low and selling high is not just an academic theory—it makes good sense in practice. Those who succeed, in whatever field, succeed because they somehow distinguish themselves from the rest.

A second clue to whether you are buying low or selling high is that if people think you're slightly nuts in whatever you decide to do, you are probably on a buy-low path because you are deviating from the norm. Also, if you yourself feel at least slightly uncomfortable with what you are doing, you may well be on the right track.

A man who made a fortune in the work of expressionist painters was asked how he had known to buy the paintings when everyone else seemed to hate the paintings. (Indeed, for example, the first show in Germany of Edvard Munch, the great Norwegian painter, closed the day it opened, a total failure.) The investor's answer is worth noting. He said that he, too, had been turned off by the work, and that, to him, was a sign he was making the right decision to buy. The fact that the paintings made him uncomfortable suggested to him that they were ahead of their time. And the paintings of the expressionists are no special case: Who would ever have thought that Andy Warhol's paintings, many of which were ridiculed when they first came out, would later bring small fortunes?

A third clue is that you are honestly facing up to a situation involving yourself and others when most people aren't or wouldn't. Instead of just seeing things a certain way because everyone sees them that way, you ask yourself whether perhaps the normal and shared way of perceiving a situation is wrong.

We tend to believe that there is safety in numbers. If everyone sees (or is likely to see) a situation in a certain way, it is natural to assume that this way of seeing things is correct. Yet history is riddled with examples of such errors. The junk-bonds case mentioned above is one example. In the foreign policy arena Vietnam is another. At the beginning of the Johnson administration, a majority of the public supported the intervention; by the end of it practically no one did. Yet the basic flaws in the Saigon government, and the basic U.S. reasons for supporting that government, hadn't changed.

The history of this country and every other is littered with such foreign policy fiascoes. These are often cases of groupthink (Janis, 1972). When everyone starts to see things in a certain way, we start to believe that things must *be* that way. After all, how could everyone be wrong? The group acquires an illusion of invulnerability and starts to see its decisions as unassailable. Often people in the group will implicitly appoint themselves as "mindguards," whose job it is to make sure everyone sees things the same way. Those who don't are at first chided, then perhaps strongly rebuked, then isolated, and possibly finally expelled if they do not conform. All the while the group members' illusion that anyone who does not agree with them must be nuts is being reinforced.

Possibly, a recent political example is the House of Representatives post office scandal. Politicians ripped off money from their accounts at the post office. The people involved probably thought there was safety in numbers. However, the representatives involved did not judge the anticorruption sentiment of the country correctly, and a tremendous backlash ensued with several of the culprits losing reelection campaigns.

The Bay of Pigs fiasco during the Kennedy administration is one of the examples used by Janis. How could a group of highly intelligent, well-educated men (most of them with Harvard degrees), men who were well versed in government, have thought that a ragtag band of refugees landing at the Bay of Pigs could somehow take over the island? Wasn't there anyone in the group who was willing to "buy low"? Someone needed to go against the group and say: "Hey, let's look at this from a fresh perspective. The plan we're coming up with is crazy—it just doesn't make any damn sense." In fact, there were such people. But as happens in so many political groups, such people were isolated and made to feel that *they* were the ones who were out of step.

The tendency of people to adopt the views of a group rather than think for themselves and see things differently is not limited to foreign policy. During the Nixon administration, a horrendous decision was made to burgle the Democratic National Headquarters at the Watergate apartment complex in Washington in search of documents. The burglars were caught. Bad luck for the planners. But the planners made their bad luck worse. Working as a team, they developed a conspiracy to try to contain the damage and dissociate themselves from the burglary. The subsequent coverup was one of the biggest public relations disasters for any presidential administration in history.

It is ironic that people referred to the members of the Nixon administration as Machiavellian, when, in fact, the administration did exactly the opposite of what Machiavelli advised politicians to do. Machiavelli said that if politicians had good news, they should dribble it out slowly, but if they had bad news, they should dump it out all at once. The Nixonians had bad news, and they could hardly have dribbled it out more slowly. Each day seemed to bring another revelation. Again, in retrospect, it is not clear how they thought they would be able completely to cover their trail, but at the time that decisions are being made, people in a group often selectively exclude information that does not fit their agenda and their emerging consensus.

The tendency of groups to engineer coverups is not limited to political administrations. The attempt to cover up the damage done to women by a defective intrauterine device resulted in the manufacturer going into Chapter 11. Instead of immediately halting production when problems started to emerge, the manufacturer continued to produce and distribute the product. Countless examples of such coverups can be found.

Generally the creative solution is to fight the natural tendency to do what is expected. Some years back the Johnson & Johnson Company was hit by a major public health and public relations disaster. Poison had been inserted into Extra-Strength Tylenol, causing some people who took the product to achieve the permanent cure to headache. In this case it wasn't even the fault of the company but of a madman. But the company decided as a group not to cover up. At first they pulled all Extra-Strength Tylenol from the market, and later they pulled all the other types of Tylenol as well. People in the marketing world were aghast. Here was the maker of the number one analgesic in the country pulling all its medicine off the shelves and admitting that there was a problem. Marketing experts said that Tylenol would never recover. In fact, fairly soon thereafter Tylenol was again the best-selling analgesic in the country.

No one ever knows for sure just what the "buy-low" solution is. But people with a creative frame of mind do not join the crowd in its beliefs simply because there is safety in numbers, or because if everyone believes something it must be true. They think for themselves and resist tendencies toward groupthink and blind conformity. The people at Johnson & Johnson didn't have any inborn ability that people at other companies lack. Rather, they went for the surprising option and faced a situation for what it really was, rather than for what they would have liked it to be. In the end they won.

You Can't Just Buy Everything That's Selling Low

By now it's probably occurred to you that in the domain of creativity, as in the stock market, you can't just buy everything that is selling low. In fact, the majority of stocks that have low price-earnings ratios just aren't very good investments. And in almost any domain the majority of ideas that are unpopular are so because they are bad ideas. For example, probably no one believes that the world is shaped like a football, coming to a point at each end. The fact that the idea is unpopular obviously doesn't make it good. Similarly, people today are worried about who will control nuclear missiles in various republics of the former Soviet Union, such as the Ukraine. An agreement that they would go to Russia seems to be going to the winds. To our knowledge no one has suggested that the United States go in and try physically to prevent the Russians or other republics from controlling the missiles. The mere fact that the idea is not being actively bandied about certainly doesn't make it a good one. In short, how do you know which of the ideas that are "selling low" are good ideas?

In fact, you *don't* know for sure. Moreover you are likely to make mistakes. A point to which we will return again and again throughout the book is that creative people have to be willing to make mistakes. They are people who learn from their mistakes and who don't keep making the same ones again and again. But people can ask themselves a few questions to help them decide whether a particular idea that is selling low is also a good idea, albeit an unpopular one. These questions serve as a form of fundamental analysis for making the decision to invest one's personal resources in an idea or endeavor. In other words there are methods for assessing the intrinsic value of an idea, just as financial investors can assess a company based on its earnings, management structure, and proportion of income spent on research-and-development activities.

The first question is whether there is any good evidence to support the soundness or, in cases of factual issues, the truth of your idea. Galileo had good evidence to suppose that two objects dropped from a height would fall to the earth roughly at the same time, even though they were of different weights. People could argue all they wanted that the heavier one should fall first. All they had to do, as he did, was actually to try the experiment.

The evidence in favor of your proposed idea need not be direct. Niels

Bohr and others proposed the atomic model of matter despite the fact that none of them had actually seen an atom. Similarly, no one has directly seen a black hole; because light can't escape from it, one cannot actually see it. But the evidence in favor of the existence of black holes is strong and persuasive. If people only accepted as true what they could see, they would be limited indeed. For example, chances are that you accept the existence of Tibet, despite never having seen it.

The second question to ask yourself is whether there is any good evidence opposed to what you or other people currently believe. There was good evidence against the theory that the world is flat before there was any really good evidence in favor of the view that it is roughly spherical. In the same vein, people began to see errors in Newtonian physics before they had modern physics to update it. Recognizing a problem in existing ways of seeing things almost always precedes the finding of some new way of seeing things. But people can evaluate the worth of a current idea or approach to a task only if they are open to recognizing that problems may exist.

While people may be slow to recognize problems in the way others see things, they are usually slower in recognizing the flaws in their own beliefs. Over a period of several years, one of us was teaching a class on "teaching for thinking" to a group of teachers from around the country. Each year the author did the same experiment. He asked teachers in the class to write down on a piece of paper some belief that was important to them and to which they held strongly. After all had done so, they were given time to prepare an argument—defending the position opposite to their own. They all did so. Then they were asked to prepare an argument supporting their own position. To the surprise of almost everyone in the room, people were more effective in defending the position opposite to the one they believed in than they were in defending their own. Why? Is everyone a born lawyer? No. People often accept their own position on grounds of emotions, values, or religious beliefs. But the positions of the opposition, which they don't accept, are positions against which they may be used to arguing rationally. The result is that when they reverse their own arguments, they can argue rationally in favor of other positions, but they often don't have rational arguments pertaining to their own. People accept much of what they accept not because they have thought about it, but because— well—it is what they believe.

A third question you can ask yourself is what a particular thing looks like from someone else's point of view. Ideally, you should look at the thing from as many different points of view as possible. Sometimes people's beliefs fly in the face of what would seem to others to be the most basic common sense, yet they don't see it. They are locked into a belief system that won't allow for creative and innovative thinking. Earlier in the book we talked about the tyranny of testing. Let us offer an example here of the kind of silly belief that has not only stopped people from developing and using more creative tests but has hurt the prospects for countless children in our schools. The inability of school personnel to see things from outside their own internal point of view hurt a child and, ultimately, the school itself.

Seth, the son of the senior author, was in third grade when he changed from one public school to another. Both schools were roughly comparable in terms of quality of education, socioeconomic groups of students, and the like. But whereas Seth had been placed in the top reading group in the first school, he was placed in the bottom reading group in the second. What happened?

The first day Seth was in the new school, he was given a test to determine his reading level. First, it does not require incredible perspicacity to realize that the first day a student is in a new school is not an ideal day for testing. Of course, the administrators of this school were not alone. When immigrants used to arrive in the United States, earlier in this century, the first thing they would see was the Statue of Liberty and the second was an intelligence test. For some reason, the immigrants—almost none of them English speaking—did not do so well on the tests, and people came to the conclusion that people from other countries were stupid. That's the impression Seth gave; his mind just wasn't on the test.

After a while the reading teacher noticed that Seth was reading at a level beyond that of the bottom reading group. So what did the school do? Move him to the middle group? No. Incredibly, they decided to give him the reading test again to decide where to place him. In other words the assumption was that the test—which is, after all, only a predictor of reading skill—was a more valid index of Seth's skill than was his actual in-class performance. To those outside the system, the assumption might seem ridiculous. To those inside, however, the assumption somehow made perfect sense.

Fortunately Seth did well on the reading test and was moved up to the middle section. But soon his teacher noticed that he was reading better than the children in *that* section. So what did they do? Gave him the test again, of course. This time Seth scored at the level of the first group. Did the school put him in the first group, following the backward logic of their earlier decision? Strangely, no.

Seth's mother and father went to talk to the reading teacher, the principal, the classroom teacher, and the school psychologist. They explained that Seth was now one full book behind the children in the top reading group, and they were leaving him where he was so that he would not miss all the skills in that book. Seth's parents offered to take the reading book home and work with him at home to help him catch up. It made sense. Seth's mother, the associate commissioner for education in charge of curriculum for the state of Connecticut, presumably knows something about reading. And Seth's father has done research on reading. But no way. The school has a policy—reading books can't leave the school—and policy is policy.

We have yet to find anyone on the outside who did not find the school's logic absurd. But no one inside the school seemed to. The point is that things that seem completely obvious when you are inside a system often seem ridiculous from the outside. People inside the system essentially pass up the opportunity to do creative things because they can't imagine things being any other way.

The same principle applies in interpersonal relationships. Many relationships get stuck in ruts because one or both persons in the relationship are unable or unwilling to see things from another point of view. One of the best ways of evaluating the worth and creative potential of an idea is to try to see it from another's point of view.

The fourth question you can ask yourself is whether an idea—your own or someone else's—has a certain kind of class. Class, of course, is a matter of taste, of aesthetics.

As editor of a scientific journal, the *Psychological Bulletin*, one of the authors needs to select reviewers to evaluate articles. He has found that reviewers come in different varieties, of which two kinds are of particular interest here. One kind evaluates articles more or less in accord with how much the reviewers agree with what the article says. If the article is consistent with their own approach or point of view, and especially if it mentions their work, they will go to great lengths to recommend that the article be accepted, even if it isn't very good. The other kind evaluates quality pretty much without regard to the point of view taken. Rather, these reviewers ask whether it is good, given its own approach and its own point of view. In the author's experience, the latter kind of reviewer tends to be the more creative, not only in reviewing, but in his or her own work.

The advantage of the latter reviewers over the former is that they look for quality, even if the product is not done in the way they would like to see it done. These people have good taste and appreciate it in others. The former reviewers don't look for aesthetic value, just for whether others agree with them. An idea that is not very popular may be creative, or it may just be stupid. Good taste in ideas is part of the knack for separating the two.

Where does good taste come from? Can it be taught? We believe that it *can* be—not directly but rather through role modeling. Sometimes a person's parents serve as role models. For example, take the case of Matt Groening, creator of *The Simpsons* show. Groening's father, Homer Groening, was a cartoonist, filmmaker, and advertising artist. When Matt was growing up, his father subscribed to many magazines. "I'd see cartoons from *The New Yorker* and *Punch* and was always being guided by my dad in what was good and bad animation" (Morgenstern, 1990, p. 12). People can also acquire good taste and a creative sensitivity by observing it in their teachers and then acting in kind. To us, a really good teacher is a role model—not only in what he or she knows but in how he or she approaches problems.

An example of a teacher who conveys aesthetics and a creative approach to problems is Jim Wheeler of Westport, Connecticut. He often begins his high school class by reading aloud from a children's book to help his students rekindle their intuitive, imaginative tendencies; Wheeler believes that drawing is partly a process of reaching within to discover lost childhood feelings. Wheeler explains that he tries to teach more than art, however. For example, he encouraged a student who feared erasing part of her drawing, saying that change was really part of building the drawing (and the artist) rather than subtracting from it. He also criticizes analytically focused education. "I teach [my students] that the world around them must be thought of in its context. The positive shape of the object and the negative space around it create a complementary relationship" (Newman, 1993, p. 19).

Another example of conveying much more than the course content comes from a New York City school teacher of autistic children. Dan Bailey was a role model for students, parents, and other teachers in the way he could look past external behaviors to the real person inside. He developed innovative lessons to teach a range of topics, from academics to travel training, job coaching, and sex education. His curriculum ideas came partly from his daily experiences. For example, "On a city bus he noticed a retarded man touching himself inappropriately. From this grew Mr. Bailey's famous sex education course on public versus private behavior" (Winerip, 1994, p. 20).

As these examples suggest, the advantage of having excellent teachers is often not so much in the explicit content of the courses they teach, but rather in the implicit content—in the way they think about the content, act on it, and react to it. If you think back to your really excellent teachers, you are likely to find yourself agreeing. The best teachers are not necessarily those who gave the most entertaining or even fact-filled lectures, but rather those whom you have taken after in your own ways of thinking about problems.

Expect to Be Ignored or Even Actively Opposed

In 1769 Sir Richard Arkwright patented the spinning jenny, a machine to make thread from cotton. This invention was received with hostility from hand spinners and weavers, who burned Arkwright's mills and boycotted his thread. Around the same time Edmund Cartwright invented a mechanical loom, and his textile mills met a similar fate. In the nineteenth century, Ignaz Semmelweis, a Hungarian obstetrician, suggested that hospital medical staff might be infecting patients by not washing their hands properly before operations. The not-yet-accepted germ model of disease made good sense and fitted the evidence. When Semmelweis introduced a chlorine disinfectant, the rate of puerperal fever in the wards dropped substantially. However, Semmelweis was ridiculed by his medical colleagues and eventually he went crazy.

One would like to believe that when people have creative ideas, others will come running after them, demanding to sign on board. Or at least, one would hope, others will appreciate the newly proposed creative ideas. However, as Charles ("Boss") Kettering, an innovator at General Motors, maintained, "The hardest substance in the world [is] . . . the human skull, [given] the force needed to drive any new idea through it" (Kingston, 1990, p. 42). If you buy low and sell high, you are going to confront vested interests both when you buy and when you sell. In other words you will be going against what everyone else thinks they know you should do. And when you go against the crowd, it doesn't make others happy. On the contrary, it often makes them feel insecure about themselves and as though you need to be put in your place.

When one of us first left graduate school, he had developed a new theory of intelligence that he hoped would break what he saw as a gridlock in a field that seemed unable to get beyond IQ-based conceptions of the construct of intelligence. One of his first invitations to speak was from the Educational Testing Service, a company that produces many standardized tests, such as the SAT, the GRE, the LSAT (law boards), and so on. Naively he expected that people would be delighted to hear his new point of view on intelligence. Instead their reaction was more one of "How can this twenty-five-year-old presume to tell us what intelligence is? We've been studying it for as long as he has been alive, and he's telling *us*?" In short, the reaction was not what anyone would call warm and friendly. However, the point isn't whether the theory was right or wrong. The point is that when people have a vested interest in a given set of ideas, and especially when they have millions of dollars invested in those ideas, they may not be eager to hear others. And they weren't.

Of course, you may say, that's the price paid by the very young in a field. Thank goodness things change when you become more advanced. At least that's what *we* used to think. Unfortunately, it's not true: Things don't change a whole lot, and when you have ideas that shake up the establishment, it's almost always an uphill battle, no matter where you are in your career.

Take as an example the very investment theory of creativity on which this book is based. Our articles on the theory have been selected for the honored position of lead article in three different prestigious journals in the field of psychology. The journals have in common that they are of high quality but somewhat offbeat. We hasten to add that we also submitted to a fourth prestigious, but very conventional, journal. Well, no lead article—in fact, no article at all. Total turndown. Although it may sound bizarre, we are at least a little bit proud of the turndown. We won't lie: We'd have rather been accepted. But if you believe, as we do, that new and creative ideas always encounter at least some resistance, you should not be too upset when you do in fact encounter it, especially from the entrenched establishment of the field.

Several weeks ago one of us attended a conference that was also attended by Ken Clark, among founders of the Center for Creative Leadership, a leading training center for managers in Greensboro, North Carolina. Its programs have attracted thousands of middle to upper-middle managers over the years. Clark is a highly regarded psychologist, so it should come as no surprise that the center he helped to found is so successful.

What we didn't know before is how much opposition Clark had to face when he was trying to get the center going. Academics were suspicious of it, and when some mistakes were made early on, as happens with any program, there were those outside who were just waiting to pounce. It took more than five years, Clark said, for the center really to get on a solid footing. We are in no position to judge the quality of this or that program. What we can say, though, is that Clark's experience is the rule, not the exception. When you have a creative new idea or program, don't expect people to come running to you. If they do, beware of the poison darts!

Some years ago one of us went to a conference at which there was a presentation by a young psychologist from Boston University who was doing highly technical work in mathematical psychology. Although the meeting was for elite young people in the field, they were overwhelmed by the complexity of the talk. There was enormous sniping behind the professor's back. The general consensus was that the guy was just a bit crazy and that maybe his equations didn't really mean anything.

Recently that same one of us was at a conference in Washington, D.C., where a representative of one of the primary agencies that provides funding for psychological research mentioned that we should all be proud of a certain psychologist. His work has proved so useful that a whole industry is literally being built up around the applications of what had once seemed about as pure and unapplied as psychology could be. Of course it was the same psychologist. The ideas of the guy who had been derided as crazy were leading to a new industry, something that could not be said of anyone else who attended that conference years ago.

The investment theory suggests that ideas that are fresh and creative will meet resistance. When you buck vested interests, don't expect a ride on Easy Street. Be prepared to work hard to defend your ideas, and to encounter resistance. And be prepared to have to fight hard after you buy low before you ever get the chance to sell high.

You Need the Courage to Fight for What You Believe

Mark Twain once said, "The man with a new idea is a crank until the idea succeeds." When the chips are down, you need the courage to fight for what you believe in, because you may find that you are the only support you have!

A theme we have tried to emphasize throughout this chapter is that people who are creative cannot expect their ideas immediately to be believed or accepted. They very often have to fight for what they believe in, sometimes against strong odds. It often seems easier just to forget the whole thing.

Marcian Hoff, inventor of the microprocessor, which revolutionized the computer industry by drastically reducing the size of computer components, speaks of the need for courage in creative work: "You must not only have the idea, but also must believe in it so strongly that you're not going to take 'no' for an answer. You have to push for it and argue for it. That may mean that you will have to go out and start up your own company . . . but if the idea is as great as you think it is, then you should be more than willing to take those risks and put that effort into it" (Brown, 1988).

We are sometimes surprised when we read about models of creativity that focus exclusively on the mental processes involved in creativity. There is no doubt that intellectual skills and knowledge are crucial to creativity. However, we believe that creativity is not wholly a cognitive phenomenon, or even just inside the head. To be creative you need more than good ideas: You need guts. And that's something that's hard to model in a computer program, and hard to put into a set of mathematical equations. If you want to do creative work, you've got to have the courage to try, and then try again, even when others would like to see you disappear, or even be punished, for going against the established way of doing things. You can either choose creativity, or choose conformity and the safety of the crowd. It's up to you—no one else.

The Role of Intelligence in Creativity

Intelligence is a wide-ranging and complex construct. Our discussion of the relevance of intelligence to creativity will be guided by the triarchic theory (Sternberg, 1985a, 1988e). According to this theory intelligence has three basic parts—a synthetic, an analytic, and a practical part—each of which is involved in creativity. Readers interested in learning more about this or other theories of intelligence might consult any of several sources, such as *Metaphors of Mind* (Sternberg, 1990a), *The Triarchic Mind* (Sternberg, 1988e), *Frames of Mind* (Gardner, 1983), or *The Handbook of Human Intelligence* (Sternberg, 1982a).

The Synthetic Part of Intelligence: Generating Ideas

Redefining Problems

A high-level executive in one of the Big Three automobile firms in the United States was faced with a dilemma. On the one hand he loved his job and the money he made doing it. After all, high-level executives in Detroit are well paid, whether or not their cars are selling. On the other hand he absolutely detested his boss. He had put up with this would-be ogre for a number of years and now found that he just couldn't stand it anymore. After carefully considering his options, he decided to visit a headhunter— a specialist in finding high-level executives new jobs. So the executive made an appointment, not knowing exactly what to expect. Fortunately the headhunter indicated that there would be no problem in placing him somewhere else.

The executive told his wife how the appointment had gone and that he was confident he would find another job. After he described his day, his wife described hers. At the time she happened to be teaching *Intelligence Applied* (Sternberg, 1986b), a program for teaching thinking skills to high school and college students. She described the particular technique she had gone over that day—redefining a problem. The basic idea is that you take a problem you are facing and turn it on its head. In other words you look at the problem in a totally new way—one that is different not only from how you have seen it in the past, but that is also different from how other people would be likely to see it. As she described her lesson, the executive felt an idea sprouting within him. He saw how he could use the technique his wife was teaching in her class to his own personal advantage.

The next day he returned to the headhunter and gave him his boss's name. He asked the headhunter to look for another job—not for himself this time but for his boss. The headhunter agreed and, before long, found something. The boss received a phone call offering him another job, not realizing, of course, that the offer was the result of the teamwork of his subordinate and the headhunter. As it happened, the boss was tiring of his current job and in short order accepted the new position.

The icing on the cake was that, as a result of the boss's accepting the new job, his old job became vacant. Our high-level executive applied for it and ended up with his boss's job.

This true story—told to one of us by the wife of the executive—illustrates the importance for creativity of redefining problems.* Other examples of the importance of redefining problems are shown in box 5.1, along with comments by various theorists of creativity on the importance of this skill. In the foregoing example the executive had originally defined the problem as one of finding himself a new job. But after talking with his wife, he realized that the technique she was teaching in the classroom was relevant outside the classroom as well. He solved his problem by turning the problem on its head—that is, by finding his boss rather than himself a new job!

---

*This story, whose source is Sternberg, is incorrectly referred to as "mythical" in another book on creativity, where it is used without attribution.

BOX 5.1

Problem Redefinition

"A problem well put is half solved."
—John Dewey

A group working on automobile safety at Tennessee Technological University realized that the problem of protecting people from injury during a crash had always been taken as the need to keep people in their seats—to stop the passengers from moving around and hitting the car. The Tennessee group was able to generate a creative approach to automobile safety by redefining the problem. They shifted the focus from the person to the car and worked on making the interior of the car less likely to hurt a person if a crash occurred (Stein, 1989).

"To regard old questions from a new angle requires creative imagination and marks a real advance in science."
—Einstein and Infeld (1938, p. 92)

"We had discovered . . . that a complex of sugar with iron is very important for iron to get into human beings. I tried to work on this problem and got nowhere. . . . In brooding about this, I said we ought to look at the data not as if it were an inorganic problem but as if it were a protein chemical problem. And we just developed a whole new approach. It was a matter of three or four weeks, and we had sort of broken a whole new field of chemistry wide open."
—Robert Saltman, molecular chemist (quoted in Rosner & Abt, 1970, pp. 117–18)

Some of the most creative solutions have come about as a result of people redefining problems and, in certain cases, doing exactly the opposite of what they are expected or supposed to do. Such instances provide particularly good examples of how important it is to "buy low" if one wishes to be creative. One needs to look for ideas exactly where no one else is looking or even dares look. If you stay with a problem definition that everyone else has bought into, then you have already limited the range of possible solutions you might consider.

One of us came across an example of problem redefinition that helped a halfway house to open its doors and serve the community. A home for mentally ill adults was being set up by a community group. A building had been acquired and renovations completed. Unfortunately almost all the funds for the project had been spent on renovations, and there wasn't enough left to furnish the place. At a committee meeting, however, someone suggested a creative solution. Instead of trying to buy furniture with insufficient money, the committee could use the money to publicize a contest and provide prizes.

The halfway house ran a "painted furniture" contest. People from the community were invited to take old furniture and decorate or paint it in some way. All entries became the property of the halfway house and quickly solved the furniture problem. In fact, instead of acquiring drab, institutional furniture, the house now boasted a unique, vibrant set of tables, chairs, lamps, beds, and dressers.

A jury selected the contest winners—submissions that were the most fun, most contemporary, or most unusual, for example. And, to top it all off, since the entries not only fulfilled but exceeded the house's needs, the excess furniture was auctioned to raise even more funds.

Redefining problems is something anyone can do, even in the most mundane situations that one confronts in everyday life. In fact, as one of us was literally writing these words, another example of problem redefinition emerged.

This chapter was written in a small hotel room in Paris on a small rectangular metal table that was never meant to serve as a desk. The problem was that the table had shelves at two levels: The higher shelf easily accommodated a portable computer, but the lower shelf effectively left the author nowhere to put his legs. In other words it was damned uncomfortable to write at that table.

The author was complaining to his wife about how uncomfortable he was when using the computer. She took one look at him and turned the computer so that the front of it was flush with the narrow rather than the wide side of the table. Now there was plenty of room for the author to spread his legs along the floor space by the two longer sides of the table.

Here we have an personal example of how some people write about a thing and others do it.

You don't have to write books on creativity or anything else to confront the need to redefine a problem. Take one last example that illustrates the need for problem redefinition in everyday life.

A couple of years ago one of us faced an annoying problem—every morning he would wake up and discover garbage strewn all along his driveway. The opened, overturned garbage can provided what seemed to be the obvious clue: A raccoon had knocked the can over so as to eat the remains of the author's dinner. The problem was to trap and remove the raccoon.

The solution seemed obvious. The author went to the local Ace Hardware Store and bought a trap designed not to hurt the raccoon. The idea of the trap is that you put the bait (such as the contents of a can of sardines) in the center, open the side doors, place the trap near the garbage cans, and then wait for the raccoon to enter.

As soon as the raccoon enters, the doors slam shut and cannot be opened from the inside. The raccoon is trapped. You then place the trap, with the raccoon securely in it, inside your car. Next you drive to the house of a neighbor you don't particularly like, open the doors of the trap, and dump the raccoon in the neighbor's yard. Evening drives are generally recommended, when it's dark and not obvious that you're dumping the raccoon on your neighbor's property. Note that the problem is now the neighbor's and not yours.

The author followed the prescribed steps and assumed he had washed his hands of his raccoon problem. However, his garbage cans continued to be overturned each day. The good news was that the doors to the trap had closed and the bait had been eaten. The bad news was that there was no raccoon in the trap. The question arose: How could the animal eat the bait and not get caught in the trap, given that the spring mechanism ensured that the doors would close as soon as the animal stepped on the release mechanism on entering the trap? At this point it appeared that the darn raccoon was cleverer than the person who designed the trap!

The author decided to redefine the problem. He asked himself why he had ever thought that it was his role in life to trap a troublesome raccoon. His problem was really quite simple: to find a professional animal trapper to do the job. He called one, who came to the house with a bunch of traps

that looked curiously like those the author had used; but what the hell—
now it was the animal trapper's problem! The trapper placed the traps,
with bait inside them, all along the area occupied by the garbage cans.
And sure enough they trapped animals—several squirrels, a cat, and other
assorted backyard fauna. The one thing they didn't trap was a single raccoon. It was $210 later, and the author had yet to see a trapped raccoon.

Further information about the problem became evident one morning
around 3 A.M., when the author was awakened by a loud clanging noise em-
anating from the area of the garbage cans. There was an enormous dog
reaching inside the trap. The doors had closed, all right, but not completely—the dog was so large that it did not even fit inside the trap. Thus the
dog was able to pull out the bait, with the doors sealing shut only after the
dog had departed. Basically the raccoon had not been caught because there
never *was* a raccoon—only an enormous dog that didn't fit inside the trap.

The author called the trapper, who assured him that he had traps to
catch dogs as well as raccoons, but that sometimes the neighbors were
not so happy when their dogs were trapped. Wishing neither to offend his
neighbors nor to invite their retaliation, the author decided to redefine
the problem once more.

This time he went to the hardware store and bought $10 garbage cans
with handles that ensured seal-tight lids. Instead of defining the problem
as one of trapping the animal, he now defined it as one of keeping the animal out of the garbage. Indeed, the dog was unable to get through the
handles, and the problem was solved—for a while.

But several months later the new garbage cans were attacked by the
real thing—hungry, clever raccoons. The raccoons, unlike the dog, had
no trouble prying open the seal-tight lids of the garbage cans and thereby
extracting the choice morsels of garbage.

The author—not one to be beaten in a test of wits by raccoons—
bought himself a few bungee cords and connected them to the handles
of the garbage cans by crossing them over the top of each can. After several days, however, the raccoons had figured out how to get through the
cords. Eventually the author solved the problem by redefining it one last
time. He built an enclosure with locking doors that completely sur-
rounded the garbage cans—this the raccoons could not enter. And from
that day to this, no one but he and the trash collector has gotten to the
garbage cans.

This example illustrates not only how mundane can be the uses of problem redefinition, but also another important point about real-life creative problem solving. We have a notion—false, as it turns out—that problem solving is a linear process. There is a problem, we solve it, and the problem is over. Problems thus have a clear beginning, middle, and end. In life this image of an arrow pointing from one direction to another is almost never correct. Rather, the solutions to today's problems soon become tomorrow's problems. In other words the seeds of the next problem are planted in the solution to the last.

If you don't like your job, your solution may ultimately be to find another. But the next job won't be free of problems either. Thus your solution to the last problem plants the seeds for the next set of problems. Let's take another example. You and your spouse no longer get along. Finally you decide in despair to seek a divorce. Your divorce now brings you the problems of living alone. Perhaps you eventually remarry. You quickly discover that the new marriage has its problems too. Our point is not that no problem in life is ever solved. Rather, it is that the solution eventually becomes the next problem. The next problem may be better, or it may be worse. We tend to think that life should be problem-free, and that problems are a disequilibrium we need to correct in order to bring us back to the normal, problem-free state of living. In fact nothing could be further from the truth. The normal state of life is to have one problem, which leads to another, which leads to another. Thus problem solving is not like a straight line pointing from one direction to another, but more like a spiral, with new problems emerging from old ones. The need for creative problem solving—for redefining problems—never ends. We need constantly to be on the lookout for new ways of defining problems in order to keep up with the demands life keeps placing on us. People who buy low and sell high don't just do it once. It's a habit with them—a way of living. They are always on the lookout for creative solutions, even to mundane problems.

Measuring People's Ability to Redefine Problems

With all the anecdotes above, we may seem more like storytellers than scientists. In fact, were we to be so labeled we would not be ashamed, because we believe that much of creative science lies in telling stories. The trick is to know the right story to tell. For any given scientific phenomenon there are many stories, some of which help elucidate the phenomenon, while others serve to obfuscate it. Good stories help make concrete the various phenomena we are studying.

But as scientists we are also interested in measuring the phenomena we illustrate through our stories. So the question arises, Can we measure the ability to redefine problems? In other words, Can we predict who will be adept at redefining problems and who will not be?

We mention here two of the types of measures we have used to assess the ability to cope with novelty by defining problems in unconventional ways. Both of them use a multiple-choice format, and both are timed, meaning that we record both speed and accuracy as people solve the problems.

The first kind of problem is called a conceptual-projection problem (Sternberg, 1982b; Tetewsky & Sternberg, 1986). Here's how it works. If you look at an emerald or at fresh spring grass, you will notice that they are both green. Probably no one would question their color. Yet we cannot be sure that the grass is actually green rather than "grue," meaning green until the year 3000 and blue thereafter. Similarly, although a sapphire or the sky on a cloudless spring morning both certainly appear to be blue, we can't be sure that they are not actually "bleen," meaning blue until the year 3000 and green thereafter. (Both of these concepts are borrowed from Nelson Goodman [1955], formulator of the so-called "new riddle of induction," which raises the question of why we describe certain concepts in one way, such as green, rather than in another, such as grue, when there is no strong reason to favor one description over another.)

Now, you might say that such concepts as grue and bleen are ridiculous, because if something has been, say, green every year up to now, there is no reason to expect that it won't continue to be green into the indefinite future. Similarly, if something has always been blue, it can be expected to stay that way. Suppose, though, that you had been brought up believing that emeralds truly are grue, and sapphires bleen. Then you would believe that up to now emeralds have always been grue and sapphires have always been bleen, and moreover, that they can be expected to stay that way.

"Nonsense," you may say. Grue and bleen are complicated concepts, both of them involving changes (in the first case, from green to blue; in the second, from blue to green). One thing we learn when we are very young is that it is always better to go for the simpler rather than the more complex explanation of something. Therefore, we ought to say that emeralds are green and sapphires blue.

It turns out not be so simple, however. Suppose you were brought up on a planet, say Kyron, where people learn that emeralds are grue and that sapphires are bleen. Then a Kyronian comes to Earth for the first time and is introduced to the concepts of green and blue. These concepts seem strange at first, but finally the Kyronian understands. In his conceptual system an object that is green is one that is grue until the year 3000 and bleen thereafter; in contrast, an object that is blue is one that is bleen until the year 3000 and grue thereafter. Note that whether our or the Kyronians' set of concepts is more complicated depends on the conceptual system with which one starts. For us the Kyronians' system is more complicated, but for the Kyronians ours is! Think about it: A Kyronian would argue in favor of the simplicity of his or her concepts, just as we would argue in favor of the simplicity of ours.

In other versions of the same type of problem, subjects learned some other interesting facts about Kyron, such as that it has four kinds of people: twes, who are born young and die young; nels, who are born old and die old; bits, who are born young and die old; and deks, who are born old and die young.

In both kinds of problems people are given incomplete information and have to infer whether a given object is blue, green, grue, or bleen, in the case of the first; or a twe, nel, bit, or dek, in the case of the second. If you wish, you can try a few problems, as illustrated in figure 5.1.

FIGURE 5.1

Conceptual-Projection Problems

In these problems you must predict states of the future from limited information.

On the planet Kyron, in a faraway galaxy, there are four kinds of unisex humanoids:

A twe is a Kyronian who is born a child and remains a child throughout its lifetime.

A nel is a Kyronian who is born an adult and remains an adult
throughout its lifetime.

A bit is a Kyronian who is born a child and becomes an adult.

A dek is a Kyronian who is born an adult and becomes a child.

Your task will be to analyze two pieces of information about a particular Kyronian and decide whether these two pieces of information
describe a twe, nel, bit, or dek. The two pieces of information will be
a description of the Kyronian in the year of its birth, 1979, and a description of the Kyronian twenty-one years later, in the year 2000.
The description of the Kyronian in the year 1979 will appear on the
left, and a picture of the same Kyronian in the year 2000 will appear
on the right. Your task will be to judge which of three labels correctly identifies the kind of Kyronian depicted in the verbal description
and the picture.

There is one important thing for you to realize in this problem.
Since it is not possible to tell at birth whether the individual is a twe
or a bit on the one hand (since both appear as children), or a nel or a
dek on the other (since both appear as adults), the verbal description for 1979 can be counted on to identify correctly only the physical appearance of the Kyronian; it may or may not correctly predict
the appearance of the Kyronian twenty-one years later. Consider the
following example:

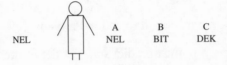

The correct answer is nel, since the Kyronian appears to be an adult
in 1979 and appears to be an adult in 2000 as well. Nel therefore
correctly predicted the Kyronian's physical appearance in 2000.

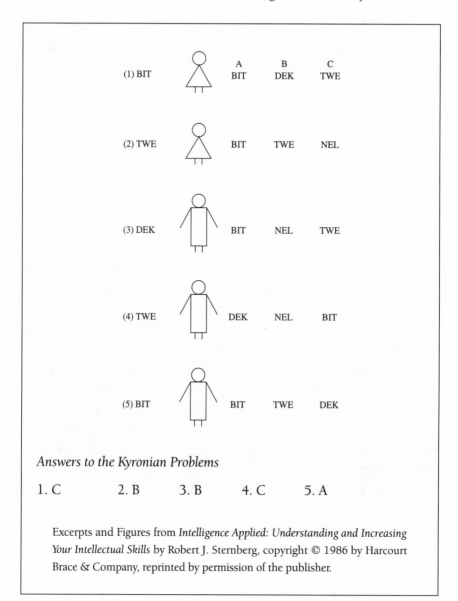

Answers to the Kyronian Problems

1. C   2. B   3. B   4. C   5. A

We have formulated information-processing models for the problems that specify the mental processes people use to solve them from beginning to end. We have also formulated mathematical models that enable us to predict and evaluate each person's performance. In scoring performance on these kinds of problems, of course, we can look at overall speed of response and number of correct responses. But more interesting are scores for individual information-processing components. A component of this kind is an estimate of the time it takes the person to complete a single mental process. For example, one process can be defined as the time it takes a person to encode (store in memory) a single word, such as "blue" or "green"; another process would be the time it takes the person to hit a response key, and so on.

The crucial finding in this research is the information-processing component that best distinguishes more creative from less creative people. This component is the amount of time it takes a person to switch from "green-blue" thinking on the one hand, to "grue-bleen" thinking on the other, or back again. In other words creative people are well able to transit between conventional and unconventional thinking. They find the transition relatively comfortable and make it with ease. Less creative people, by contrast, even though they may have the facility to use with ease (and even speed) an array of more routine mental processes, find it difficult to transit between conventional and unconventional thinking. Many people who are "smart" in the sense of doing well in school or on conventional tests are in their element as long as they are reading the words of a problem or making simple comparisons; it is when they must think in terms of concepts that are truly novel to them that they have difficulty. In other words they are fine with conventional problems based on conventional assumptions, but have more trouble with problems requiring unconventional assumptions and inferences.

A second type of problem that we use to assess people's abilities to think in unconventional ways is illustrated in table 5.1. We call these problems novel analogies. As you may imagine, conventional analogy problems do not provide a particularly good measure of people's ability to think in unconventional ways. Standard analogies appear on a variety of intelligence and scholastic aptitude tests and generally measure conventional intellectual abilities. Standard verbal analogies, moreover, measure vocabulary and general information at least as much as they measure reasoning skill. Thus someone who is a good reasoner may find verbal analogies relatively difficult if he or she does not recognize the meanings of the words in the analogies.

Although the analogies we use contain only fairly simple, common words, they come with a twist. Notice that each analogy is preceded by a presupposition. The presupposition is counterfactual, meaning that it

TABLE 5.1

Novel Analogies

In solving the analogies below, assume that the statement given before the analogy is true. Then solve the analogy, taking this assumption into account.

1. GOATS are robots.

    CHICKEN is to HATCHED as GOAT is to:

    BORN   FARM   BUILT   FACTORY

2. NEEDLES are dull.

    THIMBLE is to BLUNT as NEEDLE is to:

    SHARP   SMOOTH   STAB   BRUISE

3. PIGS climb fences.

    GOLDFISH is to BOWL as PIG is to:

    PEN   CAGE   DIRTY   GRACEFUL

4. DIAMONDS are fruits.

    PEARL is to OYSTER as DIAMOND is to:

    MINE   TREE   RING   PIE

5. TOASTERS write cookbooks.

    SPATULA is to UTENSIL as TOASTER is to:

    WRITER   APPLIANCE   BREAD   BOOK

6. GHOSTS are athletes.

    WEREWOLF is to MONSTER as GHOST is to:

    DRAMA   SPIRIT   HAUNT   ACT

Answers to Novel Analogies

1. BUILT	4. TREE
2. SMOOTH	5. WRITER
3. CAGE	6. SPIRIT

states as true something that is not. Subjects are instructed to solve the analogies as though the presuppositions *were* true. Thus if the presupposition is "Canaries play hopscotch," subjects have to solve the analogy as though this were indeed correct.

Again, we have constructed fairly detailed information-processing models of how people solve these problems. We have also constructed mathematical models that enable us to analyze an individual person's score in terms of how long the person takes on each processing component, and how accurate the person is on that processing component.

What we find is that many of the best solvers of ordinary analogies find these novel analogies extremely difficult to solve. In other words they just find it really hard to think in unconventional terms. So long as the analogy is based on the problem solver's ordinary knowledge of the world, solving it is a piece of cake. But the uncreative problem solver has a devil of a time imagining any state of the world except the one to which he or she is accustomed. We are reminded of a well-known politician in Washington, who, after the demise of the Soviet empire, commented to the press that, as far as he was concerned, nothing had changed. The sad thing was that, for him, it was true. He just couldn't quite deal with a world in which the Soviet Union was no longer the monolithic enemy it always had been and—as we were brought up to believe—always would be.

Both the above kinds of problems are verbal, but it is possible to measure the ability to think in novel ways with other kinds of problems as well, such as quantitative ones. Figures 5.2 and 5.3 show two of the kinds of quantitative problems we have used that measure the ability to think in novel ways. In the first, the novel number matrix problem, subjects are introduced to new symbols that substitute for numbers. They are then presented with numerical matrices that contain a mixture of conventional numbers and novel symbols. Subjects then have to fill in the missing entry in the number matrix.

In the second kind of problem, the novel numerical operations problem, subjects are introduced to mathematical operators they have never before encountered. For example, they may have to add two numbers if the first is less than the second, subtract the second number from the first if the second is less than the first, and multiply the two numbers if they are equal. Subjects then are given mathematical problems, such as those in figure 5.3, to solve.

FIGURE 5.2

Novel Number Matrix

In each problem below, the numbers in the boxes go together in a certain way. The information below the boxes gives you another way to show a certain number or numbers. Decide what number or symbol goes in the empty box.

MATRIX 1

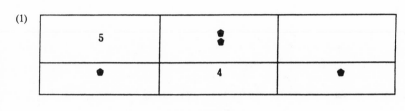

(1)

A. 9   C. 5

B. 6   D. 3

MATRIX 2

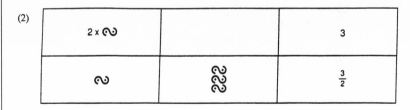

(2)

A. 4 x ∽   C. 5 x ∽

B. 2   D. $\frac{3}{2}$

Novel Number Matrix Answers

(1) C   (2) D

FIGURE 5.3

Novel Numerical Operations

In each problem below, you will employ unusual mathematical operations in order to reach the solution. There are two unusual operations: graf and flix. First read how the operation is defined. Then decide what is the correct answer to the question.

There is a new mathematical operation called *graf*. It is defined as follows:

$$x \text{ graf } y = x + y, \text{ if } x < y$$
but $$x \text{ graf } y = x - y, \text{ if otherwise.}$$

There is a new mathematical operation called *flix*. It is defined as follows:

$$a \text{ flix } b = a + b, \text{ if } a > b$$
but $$a \text{ flix } b = a \times b, \text{ if } a < b$$
and $$a \text{ flix } b = a + b, \text{ if } a = b$$

1. How much is 4 graf 7?

A. -3   B. 3   C. 11   D. -11

2. How much is 4 flix 7?

A. 28   B. 11   C. 3   D. -11

3. How much is 13 graf 5?

A. 5   B. 18   C. 13   D. 8

4. How much is 3 flix 7½?

A. 10½   B. 21½   C. 22½   D. 4½

Novel Numerical Operations Answers

(1) C   (2) A   (3) D   (4) C

Once again we find that people who are good at solving conventional kinds of problems—in this case mathematical problems—are not necessarily very good at solving these. Solving these problems requires not super math skills but the ability to let go of conventional assumptions about the numbers and operations that are permissible in math.

Yet another kind of problem is figural, as shown in figure 5.4. Subjects have to complete the figure series. The trick, though, is that the problems do not contain just a single row of figures, with each figure representing a continuation of the sequence from the last. Rather, after the sequence is started, subjects are given a figure that looks different. The subject needs to continue the series from this last figure—the one that has a different appearance from the previous ones.

All the problems described above are of the multiple-choice variety, in which subjects are given a series of answer options and must choose the best one. But we believe it important to measure subjects' abilities to think in novel ways using testing formats that are not exclusively multiple choice. Thus we also use essays that require subjects to think about problems they have probably not thought about before, or at least to think about familiar problems in new ways. Table 5.2 gives some examples of some of the kinds of essays we have used with high school students.

In sum, we use a variety of different kinds of problems to measure people's ability to think in novel ways. In each case conventional definitions of problems just don't work.

Other ways to measure the ability to redefine problems have been proposed as well, some of which are shown in box 5.2 (pp. 112–13).

We use a different kind of problem, however—the insight problem—in order to measure specific information-processing abilities that we believe contribute to the redefinition of problems and to their solution in novel ways.

Insight and Its Measurement

An insight is a new way of seeing something that usually feels as though it has occurred to you suddenly, and thus evokes a feeling of surprise and, often, delight. We propose that three basic kinds of insights form the foundation of creative thinking: selective encoding, selective comparison, and selective combination insights. (For other views on insight see Stern-

FIGURE 5.4

Figural Problems

In each question the shapes in the first row of boxes go together in a certain way to form a pattern. The second row of boxes follows the same pattern. Decide what shape goes in the empty box.

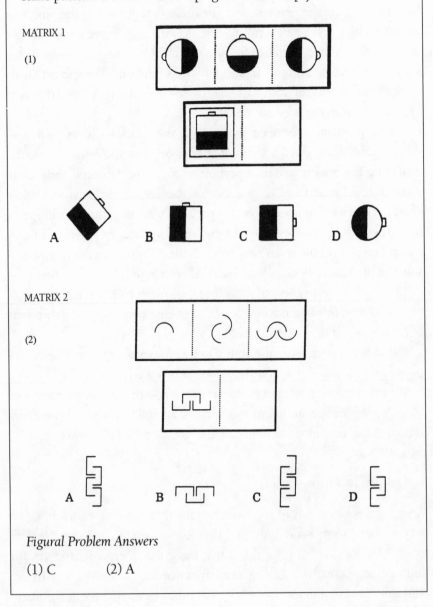

MATRIX 1

(1)

MATRIX 2

(2)

Figural Problem Answers

(1) C   (2) A

TABLE 5.2

Essays

Write an essay in response to each of the following three questions.

1. Many high schools now have police or guards present in the building for security purposes. Analyze this issue: What are the advantages and disadvantages of having extra security people in the schools? How would you solve the school security problem?

2. Suppose you are the student representative on a committee that has the power and the money to reform your school. Describe the ideal school that you would create. Include in your description any aspects of schools that you feel are important.

3. Think of a problem that you are currently experiencing in real life. Briefly describe the problem, including how long it has been present and who else is involved (if anyone). Then describe three different creative things you could do to try to solve the problem.

berg & Davidson, 1995). These selective information processes can lead to problem redefinition and to novel ideas for problem solution. In other words, these skills are an important part of the way that people "buy low" in the realm of ideas.

The first kind of insight, to which we refer as a selective encoding insight, occurs when someone who is trying to solve a problem recognizes the relevance of information that may not be immediately obvious. In other words the person zeroes in on one or more critical pieces of information for the solution of a problem at hand.

A famous scientific example of a selective encoding insight is Alexander Fleming's discovery of penicillin. Fleming was doing a laboratory experiment in which he was growing bacteria in a petri dish. The experiment went bad when bacteria infiltrated the petri dish, resulting in the growth of a mold. Most scientists, when their experiments go bad, curse their bad luck and label their experiment a "pilot experiment." They then keep doing pilot experiments until they get the thing to work, at

BOX 5.2

The following are some insight problems and their solutions:

1. *Two-String Problem*

Problem: Consider the room below. How may the two strings be tied together? You may use any of the objects in the room.

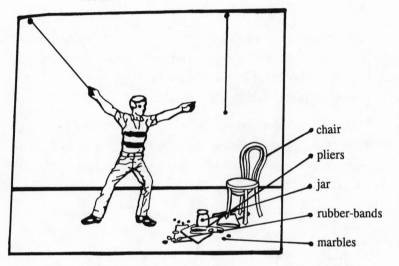

Solution: Attach the pliers (in front of the jar on the floor) to one of the strings to tie the strings together.

2. *Nine-Dot Problem*

Problem: Draw four straight lines without lifting your pencil from the paper so that each of the nine dots in (A) is crossed by a line.

Solution: Shown in (B)

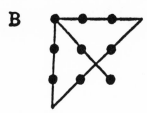

B

3. Hat-Rack Problem

Problem: Using two long sticks and a C-clamp, build a structure sufficiently stable to support an overcoat and hat. The opening of the clamp is wide enough so that both sticks can be inserted and held together securely when the clamp is tightened.

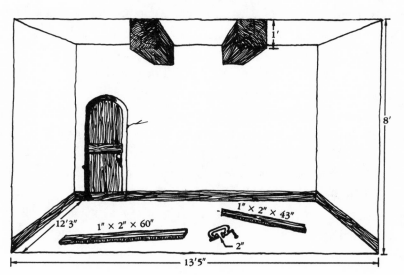

Solution: Clamp the two sticks together and wedge them between the floor and ceiling. The clamp handle serves as the hook for the coat and hat.

which point they label it the "real experiment." But Fleming was more observant than many scientists might have been. He noticed that the mold had killed the bacteria in the petri dish. And everyone knew that bacteria are very hard to kill. In noticing the bactericidal power of the mold, Fleming experienced a selective encoding insight. His observation later led to the isolation of the critical antibiotic penicillin from the *Penicillium* mold.

A selective encoding insight was also at the heart of the discovery of Super Glue. Chemical researchers at a division of Eastman Kodak were searching for a heat-resistant material to cover aircraft cockpits. When one of the compounds was applied between two lenses to test the effect on light, the lenses would not come apart. The researcher who applied the compound was upset at the loss of expensive lenses, but the supervisor, Dr. Harry Coover, saw things a different way: They had just discovered a powerful new adhesive (Feder, 1992).

Selective encoding insights are not limited to scientific discoveries. Lawyers need selective encoding insights in order to figure out which facts of a case are critical. Then, too, clients are frustrated that the facts that seem important to them do not seem important to their lawyers. That's because lawyers know that cases often turn on minute points of law of whose existence clients might well be unaware. Doctors use selective encoding insights when they are able to isolate the critical symptoms they will need in order to make a diagnosis. Business executives use selective encoding when, confronted with a bewildering array of information, they realize that certain facts are the keys that will enable them to make a decision that may have enormous financial implications for their company. Indeed, practically everyone needs selective encoding insights at various points in life. A spouse may use a selective encoding insight in realizing that certain pieces of his or her partner's behavior don't seem quite right in the context of how the partner has always behaved before. Some other examples of selective encoding insights are described in box 5.3.

The second kind of insight, to which we refer as a selective comparison insight, is used to figure out how information from the past can be brought to bear on the problems of the present. Such an insight usually involves what we call "analogical thinking," in the sense that the person sees how something from the past is somehow analogous to something in the present. A famous selective comparison insight was reported by the nineteenth-century German chemist Friedrich Kekulé von Stradonitz in describing his discovery of the structure of benzene, which he had been trying to make for some time without success. One night Kekulé had a

---

BOX 5.3

Selective Encoding: Keeping Your Eyes Open

Hans Paetzold, a creative pastry chef at the Culinary Institute of America, discusses his sources for new "ornaments," which are motifs for decorating cakes and pastries: "Ornaments, you get from curtains . . . old buildings . . . old movies. . . . You just have to have an eye for it" (Lubart, personal communication, 1990).

Choreographer and dancer Merce Cunningham commented on one source of his new ideas: "I may see something out of the corner of my eye—the slight way a person climbs a curb, the special attack of a dancer to a familiar step in class, an unfamiliar stride in a sportsman, something I don't know about, and then I try it" (quoted in Rosner & Abt, 1970, pp. 178–79).

---

dream in which he imagined a snake curling around and biting its tail. When Kekulé awoke he realized that the snake curling around on itself was a visual metaphor for the structure of benzene—namely a ring.

Selective comparison insights, like the other kinds of insights, are useful in everyday life. The lawyer who recognizes the relevance of a past precedent, or the relevance of prior information about the parties in a case, is having a selective comparison insight. A business executive facing a tough decision who remembers a similar decision in the past and an outcome that led to disastrous consequences is experiencing a selective comparison insight. In all these cases the past is brought to bear on the present in a nontrivial, nonobvious way. Some other examples of selective comparison insights, and some comments about their importance, are in box 5.4.

We call the third kind of insight a selective combination insight. A person has a selective combination insight when he or she sees how to fit together pieces of information whose connection is not obvious. For example, Charles Darwin's formulation of the theory of evolution was based at least in part on a selective combination insight. The information available to Darwin was available to many other scientists as well. They could equally well have come up with the theory, and one of them, Alfred

BOX 5.4

Selective Comparison: Finding Connections for Creativity

"Metaphor, the perception of likeness in dissimilars, is the sign of genius."

—Aristotle

Johannes Kepler: Planets and Clockwork

Kepler, a seventeenth-century astronomer wrote, "And I cherish more than anything else the analogies, my most trustworthy masters. They know all the secrets of nature." Regarding the movement of planets: "The celestial machine is to be likened not to a divine organism but rather to a clockwork . . . insofar as nearly all the manifold movements are carried out by means of a single, quite simple magnetic force, as in the case of a clockwork, all motions are caused by a simple weight" (quoted in Polya, 1973, p. 12; Rutherford, Holton & Watson, 1975, p. 68).

Alexander Graham Bell: The Telephone and the Ear

On his inventive process Bell wrote: "It struck me that the bones of the human ear were very massive, indeed, as compared with the delicate thin membranes that operated them, and the thought occurred that if a membrane so delicate could move bone relatively so massive, why should not a thicker and stouter piece of membrane move my piece of steel . . . and the telephone was conceived" (quoted in Barron, 1969, p. 134).

Russell Wallace, eventually did. What Darwin saw was how to fit the disparate pieces of the puzzle together.

Louis Comfort Tiffany revolutionized the art of stained glass in the late nineteenth century, when he selectively combined elements from English Stourbridge glass, the work of the French artist-craftsman Emile Gallé, and his own traditional knowledge of glass production. He used the natural color gradations and texture variations of the glass to make his windows, lamps, and other products, and he combined the cames (grooved strips that held the glass segments together) with the stained glass itself in a new way. For example, he would vary the width or texture of the cames and use them to depict tree branches or other integral parts of his stained-glass-window compositions.

Selective combination insights, like selective encoding insights, are critical in everyday life. A concrete example is the formulation of a creative recipe. With guests coming, the cook has to figure out how to make a good-tasting dish out of the available ingredients. A teacher can make a creative curriculum through a selective combination of students' interests, materials, and assignments. For example, the mother of one of the authors taught remedial English to twelfth-grade students who had previously failed. In a typical class she might have students read a newspaper article on an issue of interest (such as gun control), learn vocabulary based on the article, and write a letter to the editor about the issue. The effectiveness of this strategy—combining diverse materials with the students' own interests—was such that her lesson plans easily held the students' attention. In business, entrepreneurs essentially engage in selective combinations. They bring together disparate parties who fit each other's needs and create new ventures. More examples of selective combination, and comments as to their importance, are shown in box 5.5.

Insight abilities, like the ability to define problems in novel ways, can

---

BOX 5.5

Selective Combination: Putting the Pieces Together

"Combinatory play seems to be the essential feature in productive thought."

—Einstein

The music of the Talking Heads involves selectively "scrambling and rearranging" elements from diverse sources. The well-known song "Once in a Lifetime" began as simple guitar riffs that were combined in different permutations in a sound studio. David Byrne, lead singer, then added the idea of a preacher who questions the rewards of bourgeois life. The basics of the song were complete with the addition of a tribal-sounding chorus. In a 1985 interview, band member Tina Weymouth described the creativity of Talking Heads music in terms of a *New Yorker* cartoon: "A man on a sofa says to the woman beside him, 'Yes, I know I'm just one long line of clichés, but I put them together in a really interesting way, don't you think?'" (Emerson, 1985, p. 54).

"My mind works by having all of these little things that people would believe are totally unrelated all around me and being able to pull them together as meaningful parts of one whole." Michael Sullivan Smith, an inventor of a new printing technique, earned a Gold Medal for Excellence in Creativity and Utility at the 1990 Inventors' New Product Exposition. In his graphic design work Smith saw a 60 percent rejection rate for the silk-screen printing method that was being used; more than half the products were unusable due to printing mistakes. Earlier Smith had discovered that a printing screen could contact the receiving surface all at once, rather than a portion at a time. Combining these observations, Smith came up with the starting idea for a new printing technology. His invention combines air pressure, suction cups, and ink consistency to produce high-quality, reliable, carefully controlled prints on standard and non-standard surfaces (Lubart, personal communication, 1990).

Anne Hamburger, founder of the En Garde Art Company in New York City, brings a new concept to theater by selectively combining the site of the play, such as a particular theater, with the playwright and content of the play. For example, in her 1990 production of *Crowbar*, Hamburger combined the talents of a contemporary playwright with the historical Victory Theater, built in 1899 by Oscar Hammerstein I. *Crowbar* portrays what happened in the Victory Theater during the intermission of the first play performed in the theater in 1900, *Sag Harbor*. The actors perform *Crowbar* all throughout the theater. Tom Wellman, the playwright, describes the purpose of the play: "The various characters, all of whom are dead, hopefully reveal something about that period and the contradictions of that time, as well as the contradictions of our own time. It ends up being about the way our country's evolved in the last ninety years" (Lubart, personal communication, 1990; Rothstein, 1990).

be measured. Table 5.3 shows some examples of insight problems we have used (for example, Sternberg and Davidson, 1982) to measure these abilities. You may want to try the problems yourself to challenge your own insight abilities.

Our study of insight problems has reminded us at times of just how

---

TABLE 5.3

Arithmetical and Logical Insight Problems

1. You are at a party of truth tellers and liars. The truth tellers always tell the truth, and the liars always lie. You meet a new friend. He tells you that he just heard a conversation in which a girl said she was a liar. Is your new friend a liar or a truth teller?

2. A recipe calls for four cups of water. You have only a three-cup container and a five-cup container. How can you measure out exactly four cups of water using only these containers?

3. In the Thompson family there are five brothers, and each brother has one sister. If you count Mrs. Thompson, how many females are in the Thompson family?

4. Susan gets into her car in Boston and drives toward New York City, averaging 50 miles per hour. Twenty minutes later Ellen gets into her car in New York City and starts driving toward Boston, averaging 60 miles per hour. Both women take the same route, which extends a total of 220 miles between the two cities. Which car is nearer to Boston when they meet?

5. A bottle of wine cost ten dollars. The wine was worth nine dollars more than the bottle. How much was the bottle worth?

Answers to Arithmetical and Logical Insight Problems

1. Your new friend is clearly a liar. If the girl about whom the friend was talking was a truth teller, she would have said that she was a truth teller. If she was a liar, she also would have said that she was a truth teller. Thus, regardless of whether the girl was a truth

teller or a liar, she would have said that she was a truth teller. Since your friend said that she said she was a liar, your friend must be lying, and hence must be a liar.

2. Fill the five-cup container with water. Pour as much of the contents as you can into the three-cup container. Now spill out the contents that you just poured into the three-cup container. You now have two cups in the five-cup container. Pour the contents of the five-cup container into the three-cup container. Now fill the five-cup container again. Pour as much of the contents of the five-cup container as you can into the three-cup container. This container will take only one cup. You now have four cups left in the five-cup container.

3. Two. The only females in the family are the mother and her one daughter, who is the sister to each of her brothers.

4. Each car is the same distance from Boston when they meet, as the cars are immediately next to each other.

5. Fifty cents.

modest we, as investigators, need to be about our own insight abilities. For one thing, we have had many subjects solve problems that we ourselves could not solve. For another, we sometimes encounter surprises even when we can solve the problems.

Consider the example of a good problem for measuring intelligence that one of the authors gave in an article he published in the *American Scientist* (Sternberg, 1986a). This well-known insight problem is the so-called "water lilies" problem: "At the beginning of the summer, there is one water lily on a lake. The water lilies double in area every twenty-four hours. At the end of sixty days, the lake is completely covered by water lilies. On what day is the lake half-covered?"

The "correct" answer is "Day 59," because if the water lilies double in area every twenty-four hours, and if the lake is completely covered with water lilies after sixty days, then one day before, on Day 59, the lake will be half covered. About a month after the article was published, the author received a page-and-a-half, singled-spaced typewritten letter from a famous aerodynamic designer. In the letter the designer proved that if life-size water lilies really doubled in area every twenty-four hours, at the end of sixty days the world would be almost completely covered with water lilies. Oh, well: It's certainly an alternative perspective on the problem! The author found, as have so many testers before, that sometimes the people tested are more insightful than those doing the testing.

Many different kinds of problems, above and beyond those we happen to have used in our research, have been used to measure insight. Some examples are shown in table 5.4.

TABLE 5.4

Additional Insight Problems

Scientific Insight Problem

Dr. Eureka and his fellow scientists suspected that germs cause diseases and that they could live and travel on the air or in living creatures. But they had a problem: They thought that each kind of germ caused a different kind of disease; however, they could never grow one kind of germ by itself without a lot of other kinds of disease germs appearing.

Still, Dr. Eureka wanted to try the experiment again. He took a test tube and cleaned it carefully. Then he prepared a soup that the germs liked to eat and put it in the test tube. Finally, he took a germ and put it in the liquid. He placed the test tube in a warm place so the germ could grow.

A week later he came back and discovered that some other germs had somehow gotten in, and now all the germs were swimming together, completely mixed. Oh, well, he thought sadly, I guess my samples will always be contaminated.

Then, while he was walking around his lab, he found a baked

potato he'd left lying on his desk after lunch the previous week. On it were little dots, each a different color. Looking at the potato closely, he realized that the little dots were germs—but they hadn't gotten mixed together: Each kind sat on its own part of the solid potato surface. He had perfect samples of individual kinds of germs.

Suddenly, he slapped his forehead and said, "How stupid can we be? It's easy to keep germs from mixing together: This potato tells us what's wrong with our soups!" What's the difference between the potato and the soup?

Information-Evaluation Problems

In each of the following problems, you are presented with a question and a number of facts. Mark each fact as either relevant (R) or irrelevant (I) for answering the questions. In some cases pieces of information may be relevant only when considered in conjunction with each other. In such cases both pieces of information should be marked as relevant.

1. How much work is performed in pulling on a stuck drawer?
   a. Many people think studying involves hard work.
   b. To the scientist work is a measurable physical quantity in the same sense that length and height are measurable.
   c. Work can be accomplished in pushing a car up a hill.
   d. To qualify as a form of work, a force must push an object for a distance.

2. Why is it necessary to add detergent to water in order to wash clothes?
   a. The combination of detergent and water allows the detergent to penetrate between the clothes and the dirt.
   b. One hundred pounds of domestic washing is soiled with between two and four pounds of dirt.
   c. Most dirt cannot be dissolved by water alone.
   d. One hundred pounds of domestic washing usually has 0.9 pounds of protein-free organic matter (waxes, alcohol), 0.3

pounds of protein (hair, skin), 0.15 pounds of grease and sweat, as well as sand and dust.

Mystery Problem

Trying to fight his seasickness, Detective Ramirez went through the long corridor that led to the cabin of the late Mr. Saunders. Once he got to the cabin, Detective Ramirez saw Saunders's body slumped over the dresser. A small gun lay in one of his hands. Approaching the dresser Ramirez could see some loose papers on it. Among them was a suicide note. In the suicide note Saunders explained why he had suddenly decided to end his life. A pen without its cap was also on the dresser.

While reading the suicide note, Ramirez thought he would never understand how a famous writer such as Saunders could have committed suicide. Saunders was Detective Ramirez's favorite mystery writer, so Saunders's death upset him deeply.

Ramirez shifted his eyes from the note to Saunders's body, which was lying on its left side. Saunders had been a tall man in his forties with a fair complexion and blond hair that masked a long scar on his upper right cheek. The body was dressed in a well-cut dark suit that showed the writer's taste for the good things in life. "What a loss," Ramirez thought.

A noise in the background reminded Ramirez that there was another person in the cabin besides him: Mr. Saunders's nephew, Mr. Prince, who had discovered the body. Detective Ramirez asked Prince to tell him everything he had heard or seen regarding the incident.

"We came back to Mr. Saunders's cabin shortly after the captain's reception was over," said Mr. Prince. "Mr. Saunders—my uncle—told me he wanted to be alone. He wanted to take some notes for his new book. So I left the cabin and went directly to my own cabin, which is next door."

"What happened after that?" asked Detective Ramirez.

"Shortly after I left, I heard a shot," Mr. Prince continued, "and when I came in, I saw my uncle's body slumped on the dresser. I called his name and then I noticed the bullet through his left temple."

"Did you touch anything?" asked Detective Ramirez.

"No, I did not. I left everything the way it was."

Ramirez was certain that the apparent suicide was in fact a murder. He said to Mr. Prince, "You'd better tell me the whole truth." How did Detective Ramirez know that Mr. Saunders's death was murder, not suicide?

Answers to Additional Insight Problems

SCIENTIFIC PROBLEM

The potato is solid. Therefore, when germs land on it, they remain in the same place. The soup is liquid, and when germs land in it they can move around without difficulty.

INFORMATION-EVALUATION PROBLEMS

1. (a) I   (b) I   (c) I   (d) R

2. (a) R   (b) I   (c) R   (d) I

MYSTERY PROBLEM

Mr. Prince could not have known his uncle had a bullet through his left temple unless he had moved the body. Mr. Saunders had fallen on his left side and Ramirez noticed Saunders's right cheek, which had the scar on it.

Excerpts and Figures from *Intelligence Applied: Understanding and Increasing Your Intellectual Skills* by Robert J. Sternberg, copyright © 1986 by Harcourt Brace & Company, reprinted by permission of the publisher.

Educational and Practical Implications

The failure of testers to recognize the superior insight abilities of some of their subjects suggests one important implication of creativity for education. Teachers and other evaluators need to be sensitive to the fact that sometimes their students will see things that they themselves don't. One of the worst things a teacher can do is to close off all possible solutions to a problem other than his or her own, and assume that if a student disagrees the student must be wrong. In our experience this kind of closed-mindedness occurs much more often than any of us would like.

And this phenomenon is not limited to the schools. In business as well, management often tends to see a certain problem in a certain way, or to define itself in a certain way. For example, in the 1970s you could go to a department store and find a dazzling selection of brands of typewriters. But if you go to a department store now and look at the typewriter section, chances are that—if you are able to find typewriters at all—there will be at most two brands. The companies that defined themselves as making typewriters, and especially manual typewriters, have for the most part folded. Companies that defined themselves more broadly—as making word-processing devices of one kind or another, for example—stayed around longer as the manual typewriter market declined. But one company, known for its word processors, also eventually hit the financial straits. Those companies that defined themselves even more broadly—as making computers and other computational devices that include machines that process words—have had more success. To stay successful in a rapidly changing world, a company has to keep redefining itself.

In their everyday lives, too, people need to keep redefining themselves. There was a time when people would start in one job at the beginning of their work life and change jobs perhaps once or twice for the rest of their career. These days people change more frequently, in part because companies come and go so quickly. But even people who stay in the same nominal job often change what they actually do in the job in just a few years. For example, if you look at what a secretary does today versus what a secretary did fifteen or twenty years ago, you will find that the job has changed enormously. Many secretaries now use computers for various on-the-job functions. Computer skills have become a must for the more highly skilled among them. Twenty years ago only a very small fraction of secretaries would have known even the first thing about a computer. Moreover, there was no reason why they should have known more—computers were not yet being used in their jobs. The same, of course, can be said for the executives for whom they work, many of whom have themselves had to learn how to use personal computers.

We believe that it is important in the schools, as well as on the job, to be on the lookout for people with unusual creative intelligence. In our own work we have put this principle into practice. Recently Sternberg and Pamela Clinkenbeard ran a summer program at Yale for sixty gifted high school students. Usually "gifted" means "high IQ," or "high grade point average." But we identified our gifted students in a different way.

We gave applicants to our program problems based on the triarchic conception of intelligence. One-third of the problems required creative-intellectual abilities, measured by the kinds of problems described above. One-third required analytic abilities, and another third practical abilities, which will be discussed below. In order to ensure that the test was as fair as possible to all the students who took it, we also used different kinds of test items. In particular, for each of the analytic, creative, and practical abilities, one-fourth were multiple-choice verbal items, one-fourth were multiple-choice quantitative items, one-fourth were multiple-choice figural items, and one-fourth were essay items. Thus students with different kinds of talents (for example, more verbally oriented or more mathematically oriented) would be equally favored by the test. Figures 5.2, 5.3, and 5.4 and table 5.2 provide examples of the kinds of items used to measure creative-intellectual abilities.

As a result of the testing we had three categories of students: high-analytics, high-creatives, and high-practicals. Basically, people were identified as "high" in an ability if their standardized score (which ranks them relative to other people) in a given ability was statistically substantially higher than their scores in the other abilities. In the 1992 summer program, comprising sixty students, these were the only categories selected for inclusion in the program. In the 1993 summer program, comprising more than two hundred students, we had two additional identified groups: a balanced-gifted group (roughly equally high in all three ability areas) and an above-average "control" group (students high in the various abilities but not scoring high enough to be identified as "gifted" in any of them).

Students were then streamed into one of several sections of a college-level, advanced-placement introductory psychology course. Because all the students were entering high school juniors and seniors, this course presented a challenge of high magnitude. As noted above, the 1992 summer program had three sections: analytic, creative, and practical. The 1993 summer program, however, had an additional section: traditional. Because students were assigned to sections at random (with the constraint that each section have the same number of students), they were somewhat more likely to be in a section that did not correspond to their own strength than to be in one that did. For example, in the 1992 summer program the high-creative student had only a one-in-three chance of being placed in the creatively oriented course (and a one-in-three chance of being in the analytic course, and one-in-three for the practical one).

The analytic section of the course emphasized the development of such skills as analyzing theories, comparing theories, critiquing experiments, and the like. The creative section emphasized coming up with original ideas for theories, experiments, and the like. The practical section emphasized the use of psychology and psychological principles in everyday life. The traditional section emphasized learning the basic facts of the discipline.

All students were also assessed in four different ways: for basic recall of the course material (the traditional emphasis in educational testing), for analysis of course material, for creative use of course material, and for practical use of course material. Examples of the kinds of questions we used are shown in table 5.5. Although your own field may well not be psychology, you should realize that the same kinds of questioning strate-

---

TABLE 5.5

Summer Program Assessment Questions

Basic Recall and Underastanding

You have recently accepted a job selling raffle tickets. You will be paid five dollars for every ten tickets you sell regardless of whether it takes you ten minutes or ten days to sell them. What kind of reinforcement schedule are you being paid on?

a. variable interval

b. fixed interval

c. variable ratio

d. fixed ratio

Vygotsky's idea of the zone of proximal development (ZPD) implies that we should change the way that we test children. Which of the following changes in testing would Vygotsky recommend?

a. more items on every test

b. giving hints to students

c. taking points off for guessing

d. giving more essay questions than multiple choice items

Analytic

Compare the theory of constructive perception with the theory of direct perception. Briefly describe each theory, and then evaluate each theory for strengths and weaknesses. Compare and contrast the theories. Last, make an argument for why you think one is a "better" account of perception than the other.

Creative

Based on everything you have learned in this course, come up with your own theory of intelligence. You should address at least the following questions, but feel free to go beyond them as well: What is intelligence? How is it acquired? Is it fluid or fixed? What are the factors that influence someone's intellectual capabilities? You can draw on theories from the readings, but be sure that your theory adds something new to the existing literature. Also be sure to state what is distinctive about your theory, and to explain its advantages over other theories.

Practical

You are a clinical psychologist who follows the behaviorist school and utilizes the principles of learning theory in doing therapy with clients. A man comes to you and asks you to help him give up smoking. What processes might you use to aid him in this endeavor? How successful do you think your treatment would be and why?

gies can be applied in any field: You can ask students to remember material, analyze material, creatively use the material and go beyond it, or think about the practical implications of the material.

Most important from the standpoint of this book, students who were identified as creatively gifted, who were placed in a section of the introductory psychology course that emphasized creative thinking, and who were then assessed in ways that allowed them to use creative thinking, excelled on these measures beyond the performance of the other groups. High-practical students also did particularly well on the practical assessments when they had been placed in a section that emphasized practical thinking.

These results show the benefit of matching instruction and assessment of students with their triarchic ability pattern. Obviously we're not saying that students should learn and be tested only in a way that matches their ability pattern. But we are saying that we believe that there are a lot of creative students out there who are withering on the vine because the way they are taught and assessed does not give them a chance to express their gifts. Creative students are not going to show their extraordinary strengths in a course that requires them basically to memorize a textbook.

The results for the high-analytic students were a surprise, although not necessarily a disappointment. We expected, of course, that the high-analytic students would do best when placed in a section that emphasized analytic teaching and learning, and then when assessed with tests that measured analytic thinking. Instead the high-analytic students were the worst of the lot, no matter how they were taught and no matter how they were assessed. In other words it didn't matter how you taught them—they still didn't do well!

At first we were baffled by these results, but their meaning quickly became clear when we identified who the high-analytic students were and talked to their instructors about them. The high-analytic students were basically the ones who had been identified as gifted throughout their schooling. They were the traditional "high-IQ" students, the ones who were fully aware of their own abilities and whose schools were fully aware as well. These were students who had, throughout most if not all of their studies, learned that they could get away with relatively little effort. For the most part they had never been really seriously challenged; they could get top marks doing a minimum of work. They came to our summer program, therefore, expecting that once again they could breeze by without working very hard. They discovered, probably for the first time in their lives, that they were wrong.

They were the lucky ones. Many such students do not discover that the days of being top performers without working end after high school. We have taught any number of freshmen who come to college expecting that they will get by without working and then discovering, often too late, that they are wrong. The summer psychology students had the advantage that they were given the opportunity to learn the lesson sooner rather than later.

In another program for upper-elementary school students, Janet Davidson and the senior author attempted to show that creative-insightful thinking could be directly taught, even to very young children (Davidson & Sternberg, 1984). We devised a five-week program that taught students how to solve insight problems of the kinds described earlier (for example, the water lilies problem). More examples of problems we used are given in table 5.6.

Students were instructed in the processes of selective encoding, selective combination, and selective comparison in a variety of domains, including the mathematical, as shown above. Instruction was in the context of science problems, verbal problems, and other types of problems. Students in this program included both those who had been identified as "gifted" by their schools and those who had not been so identified.

We found that after five weeks, students identified as gifted and those not so identified both improved significantly in their ability to solve various kinds of insight problems. The rate of improvement for the two groups was roughly the same, so that although students in both groups benefited, there was still a mean difference between groups at the end of the program. Neither this program nor any other simply wipes out individual differences. But the results clearly showed that insightful thinking can be taught, at least to some degree.

One other result was worthy of mention, however. When we initially gave the insightful thinking tests, we found them to be modest predictors of who had been classified as "gifted." Quite a few children identified as gifted were not particularly adept at solving the insight problems, whereas

TABLE 5.6

Insight Problems

1. If you have black socks and brown socks in your drawer, mixed in the ratio of 4 to 5, how many socks will you have to take out to make sure of having a pair of the same color?

2. A farmer has seventeen sheep. All but nine broke through a hole in the fence and wandered away. How many were left?

3. A farmer buys a hundred animals for a hundred dollars. Cows are ten dollars each, sheep are three dollars each, and pigs are fifty cents each. How much did he pay for five cows?

4. Suppose you have two pencils, a good one and a cheap one. The good one cost $1.00 more than the cheap one. You spent $1.10 for both pencils. How much did the cheap one cost?

5. If there are twelve one-cent stamps in a dozen, how many two-cent stamps are there in a dozen?

Answers to Insight Problems

1. Three

2. Nine

3. Fifty dollars

4. Five cents

5. Twelve

many other children not identified as gifted were quite adept at solving these problems. In other words whatever criteria the school was using to identify children as "gifted," insightful thinking did not seem to be among them. We believe that the same could be said for many, and probably most, other schools as well. Once again the creatively gifted are often those most at risk for having talents that are neither appreciated nor often recognized in the context of the school.

As this book is being written, we, together with Wendy Williams,

Melanie Grimes, and a team from Harvard University, are in the process of developing a program for upper-elementary and middle-school students called "Creative Intelligence for Schools." The goal is to help children develop the creative skills that often start to languish as they advance through the school system. The program we are developing is based on our investment theory of creativity, and will serve to put into practice the ideas you are reading about.

Our own practical interests are not limited to the context of the school. We also currently have a research program for developing creative leadership skills. We give our students case studies, such as that in box 5.6, as a basis for learning how to handle leadership challenges creatively. Through these case studies leaders learn the skills needed to supervise in new and productive ways. For a number of years Richard

---

BOX 5.6

Creative Leadership Skills

Your goal is to make sure your guidance is communicated accurately to all levels of the organization. In the past, information has been lost or distorted as it has filtered down the organizational chart, resulting in misunderstandings and hard feelings on the part of some employees. You have reason to believe that someone down the line is intentionally holding back and distorting information for his or her own ends, but you are not sure who it is. What might you do to find out, and then what should you do if you are able to identify the individual? Use the space below for your responses.

Wagner, Wendy Williams, and Robert Sternberg studied the practical intelligence of managers. The research was in many respects quite successful, producing a theory and a resulting test that could predict success in management about twice as well as a conventional intelligence test (see Williams & Sternberg, in press). But something in this work bothered us: We were assessing the ability of people to adapt to their environments, but not the ability of people to shape these environments—to turn the environments into what they wanted them to be. More and more we began to see that the people who really made the difference in corporate America were not necessarily just the highly competent managers, but the real leaders who shaped the way their companies operated. So we have recently become interested in the creative side of management—the leadership side—believing that in the world of business as in our schools, we cannot afford to squander what we believe to be our most precious human resource: creativity.

The Analytic Part of Intelligence: The Basics of Problem Solving

When one of us was in graduate school, a fellow student provoked the envy of all his classmates. This guy seemed to have a new idea every day. Most of us were happy to have a new idea once every few months, and so it was demoralizing to be with someone who was a nonstop fountain of them. Moreover, when the rest of us thought about what this one creep was going to do to our chances of ever finding a job, we were depressed to say the least. How would we ever be able to compete, especially if there were more out there like this fellow?

The student got a job, but it wasn't anything special. Moreover, he hasn't been particularly successful in his career. What happened? By the end of his time in graduate school, his problem had become obvious: He was high in synthetic ability but lacked analytic ability; he had the ability to come up with good ideas but not to decide which ones were good. He was just as likely to follow up on one of his less exciting ideas as on one of his real winners.

There is a natural tendency—one we sometimes fall into ourselves—to pit synthetic ability against analytic ability, or right-hemisphere thinking against left-hemisphere thinking. But, like most dichotomies, this one is overstated. With respect to synthetic and analytic abilities, people are not really one thing or another but some combination of both.

Creativity requires not only coming up with ideas but knowing when a problem exists to start with, how to define the problem, how to allocate resources to solve the problem, and how to evaluate the value of potential solutions—knowing which ideas are your good ones. Renzulli (1986) and many others as well have proposed that to be creative, you need some minimum threshold of analytic ability. But most scholars, including Renzulli, believe that the threshold is not terribly high. You don't have to be an IQ star to be creative.

The relationship between intelligence and creativity is often reported in terms of IQ (intelligence quotient) scores. These scores represent a standardized metric for comparing people. The population average IQ is defined as 100 with scores typically ranging between 70 (low intelligence) and 130 (high intelligence). IQ can be measured by several different intelligence tests, which focus on analytic ability.

There are three basic findings concerning IQ and creativity (Barron & Harrington, 1981; Lubart, 1994). First, creative people tend to show above-average scores, often above 120. Second, the correlation between IQ and creativity varies across studies from weak and slightly negative to moderately strong and positive. Third, the typical correlations tend to be approximately $r = .20$ (weak, positive). Thus creativity is weakly related to, but by no means the same as, intelligence. For those with IQs of 120 and above, intelligence does not seem to matter much to further increases in creativity.

We turn our attention now to the analytic skills that are basic to solving any problem. Even if you are going to solve a problem in a mundane way, you still need these skills. However, each ability can also be used to facilitate a buy-low approach to a problem.

PROBLEM RECOGNITION AND DEFINITION
The first basic analytic skill is recognizing that you have a problem to solve. To detect a problem situation you have to acknowledge that one may exist. Many a close relationship founders on people's unwillingness even to acknowledge that anything possibly could be wrong. Many businesses fail for the same reason.

How did a country like the United States, which was once financially solvent and the powerhouse of world economies, end up with such an outrageous national debt? By having a problem and failing to recognize it until it was too late. One might say the same of the Communist system and its collapse. The problems that led to the demise of the Soviet empire had been there for a long time, but the government was not acknowledging them. Many problems could be easily solved if they were recognized early on. But people often play ostrich, sticking their heads in the sand, and by the time they take them out, the problem is beyond their control.

The second half of realizing that you have a problem is figuring out exactly what it is. Earlier we talked about redefining problems. Problem definition is what occurs beforehand: You can't redefine a problem until you have an initial definition.

In an interesting study with thirty-one art students, Getzels and Csikszentmihalyi (1976) provided a set of objects and asked the artists-in-training to use some or all of them to make a drawing. The general task was defined, but the artistic problem that could be the basis of a composition was completely open. The researchers observed the students' behavior as they worked. The students who ended up producing original drawings—as judged by art critics—spent more time formulating their compositions. This differential attention of the highly original students to problem formulation was also seen in the large number of objects that they explored and manipulated before settling on a still-life arrangement. Further, the highly original students were more prone to redefine the nature of their compositions as they worked—in other words they didn't feel locked into one view, a concept we discussed earlier in this chapter in the section on problem redefinition.

DECIDING ON HOW MENTALLY TO REPRESENT INFORMATION ABOUT A PROBLEM

How you mentally represent information about a problem can have a major effect on how you solve it, and even on whether you solve it. A famous problem about a monk seeking study and contemplation illustrates what we mean (see also Sternberg, 1986b).

A monk wishes to pursue study and contemplation in a mountain retreat (see figure 5.5). The monk starts climbing the mountain at 7:00 A.M. and arrives at the top at 5:00 P.M. the same day. During the course of his ascent, he travels at varying speeds and takes a break for lunch.

FIGURE 5.5
The Monk Problem

He spends the evening in study and contemplation. The next day the monk starts his descent at 7:00 A.M. along the same route. Normally his descent would be faster than his ascent, but because he is tired and afraid of falling and hurting himself, he descends the mountain slowly, not arriving at the bottom until 5:00 P.M. the day after he started his ascent. Must there be a point on the mountain that the monk passes at exactly the same time on the two successive days of his ascent and descent? Why?

Tough problem. But it is much easier if represented in a way that is somewhat different from the usual. The answer, by the way, is yes, the monk must necessarily pass through exactly the same point (or altitude) on the mountain at corresponding times on the days of his ascent and descent. The problem becomes much easier to conceptualize if, rather than imagining the same monk climbing the mountain one day and going down the next, you imagine two monks, one ascending and the other descending the mountain on the same day. You may assume that the monks start and finish at the same time, although this assumption is not necessary for solution of the problem. Note that this rerepresentation, shown in figure 5.6, does not change the nature of the problem or its solution, but simply makes the problem easier to solve.

Related to strategy selection is resource allocation. One of the resources that each person has to allocate is time. How much time should be devoted to competing projects or parts of each project? Sternberg (1981) found that more intelligent people tend to spend relatively more time on global, up-front planning for how they are going to solve a problem, but relatively less time on local, along-the-way planning, whereas less intelligent people do just the opposite. The less intelligent just plunge into the problem without thinking about it much, whereas the more intelligent give it a lot of thought before acting on it. Creative thinking requires time, and people who are always putting out fires often don't

FIGURE 5.6
The Solution to the Monk Problem

have the time to think about anything in a very creative fashion. To be creative you most likely will need to permit yourself extra time on a task in order to search for more novel solutions.

We believe that the allocation of resources is an issue of paramount importance not only at the individual level but at the corporate and national levels as well. Many people agree that industry in the United States is losing the strong scientific and technological edge it once had. There may be many reasons why this is so, but one is almost certainly the relatively small amount of money that is being allocated to research and development, particularly when there is a long time until the anticipated payoff.

Whereas Japanese companies think in time frames of ten, twenty, thirty years, and more, American companies often seem to think only in terms of immediate payoffs. Basic research usually does not have an immediate payoff. Neither do many of the fundamental changes that can be made in the restructuring of a company. But the long-term payoffs may be much greater than those born out of short-term investments. If, as a society, we want to retain our edge, we will need to think in terms of a much longer time frame than the one with which we now seem to be comfortable.

FORMULATING A STRATEGY AND ALLOCATING RESOURCES FOR SOLVING A PROBLEM
Having figured out and represented what the problem is, you have to decide how to solve it. You need to analyze the alternatives available to you and choose the path that will best get you to your goal. Buying low can involve strategy selection, if you decide to choose a strategy that is novel and that isn't what everyone else is doing or would do.

Formulating an optimal strategy is sometimes a matter of knowing what questions to ask. Take what is one of the most routine of chores: refinancing a home mortgage in times of low interest rates. How you formulate your strategy for doing this may greatly affect the ultimate outcome.

One simple strategy is to go to your bank and see if the mortgage rate is lower than what you are paying. If the rate is lower, you refinance; otherwise you don't. This strategy, however, is far from optimal.

A second, better strategy is to ask yourself what the difference is between the current rate and what you are paying. If the difference is small, and if you expect to be paying off the mortgage soon, the optimal choice might be to stay with what you have rather than pay the closing costs of refinancing.

A third, even better strategy would be to do all the above, but also to consider that other banks might offer a better rate. By not limiting your strategy to checking just your current bank, you might be able to get a substantially better rate elsewhere.

A fourth strategy, better yet, would be to consider not only different banks but different terms of payment—fixed versus variable rate, and especially thirty- versus fifteen- or even ten-year mortgages. You can often cut the interest rate substantially by going for a shorter term, with only a relatively small increase in payment.

Of course, there are other possible strategies. We are merely trying to show that how much thought you give to setting up a strategy for solving a problem can have a major effect on its outcome. With regard to creative work, the use of divergent versus convergent thinking may be an especially important part of strategy selection. Divergent thinking refers to the generation of ideas from given information with an emphasis on the variety of new ideas (Brown, 1989). For example, if you are writing a poem, listing all your ideas for possible topics would be a case of divergent thinking. Numerous studies, including longitudinal ones following people's lives over many years, show a positive relationship (often $r = .20$ to $r = .30$) between divergent thinking and creative performance (Barron & Harrington, 1981; Torrance, 1979, 1988). People who engage in divergent thinking as part of their problem-solving strategy have an advantage. Divergent thinking provides a range of alternatives to work with and helps a person to move beyond the first acceptable idea that comes to mind. Generally these initial ideas are readily available to many people—to pursue them would be to buy high. A convergent-thinking strategy—trying to find "the" one answer—is typically emphasized in schoolhouse problems. When alternated with a divergent one, this strategy may actually be optimal because people will be providing lots of ideas *and* continually refocusing on their goal. Our observations of Yale undergraduates in experiments on creativity suggest that the less creative students tend to have a purely convergent strategy—which leads them to generate only one idea that "solves" the problem, but, as noted above, tends to be a mundane solution.

Notice how correct analysis of a problem, followed by creative rerepresentation of that problem, can greatly facilitate problem solution. Other researchers (Kotovsky, Hayes & Simon, 1985) have used a "Tower of

Hanoi" problem, which requires the problem solver to move a set of discs from one peg to another following specified rules. Research with various representations of this problem shows that the average time needed to solve the problem can vary by a factor of eight, depending on the specific way the problem is represented. Certain representations make the problem rules easier to learn and use.

The importance of problem representations is not limited to what might seem to be academic problems. People who use spreadsheet programs use them not because they provide unique information that could be obtained in no other way but because they represent information in a way that makes it relatively easy to see the consequences of various decisions. Similarly different word-processing programs for personal computers all finally accomplish about the same thing—what differs is how they represent information to the user and how much they facilitate the task of writing via their form of representation. The enormous success of the Apple Macintosh computer has been in large part because of its representing information in a user-friendly way that people can understand. There is probably little that can be done with a Macintosh that cannot be done with another processing system: The difference is in ease of representation.

The importance of representation applies in the world of the school as well. For example, we teach statistical courses to our students. Math is difficult for students in large part because of the difficulty they have in knowing how to represent mathematical information. Many mathematical techniques can be represented either algebraically or geometrically. That is, they can be represented as a series of equations or as a set of geometric forms in a two- or more-dimensional space. When we teach math ourselves we try to use both representations, realizing that some students respond better to one representation and others to the other.

For a discussion of how visual representations may be particularly useful in creative work, see box 5.7.

MONITORING AND EVALUATING PROBLEM SOLVING

When many of us were children, our teachers used to give us timed tests of arithmetic computation problems. The idea became that the best student was the first one done. There is a problem with this mentality: It encourages people to rush through what they are doing, often without

---

BOX 5.7

Representing Problems: Focus on Visual Imagery

A notable collection of scientifically creative people claim that visually representing problems through mental imagery helps them achieve novel insights. Perhaps imagery is a useful representation because images can be formed rapidly, are particularly well suited to representing physical phenomena, and do not have the trappings and extra meanings of verbal concepts (John-Steiner, 1985). Or perhaps imagery is useful because multiple aspects of a problem can be represented simultaneously, and the image can be easily altered, showing how the rest of the problem will also change (Kim, 1990). Consider these examples:

Einstein wrote: "Words or the language, as they are written or spoken, do not seem to play any role in my mechanism of thought. The physical entities which seem to serve as elements in thought are certain signs and more or less clear images which can be 'voluntarily' reproduced and combined" (quoted in Hadamard, 1945, p. 142).

When developing the special theory of relativity, Einstein visualized himself traveling along beside a beam of light. As part of this image, he mentally "saw" stationary spatial oscillations and realized that these could not be described as either light or an electromagnetic wave, causing problems for the then-current views in physics (Shepard, 1978, pp. 134–135).

James Watson, discoverer (with Francis Crick) of the structure of DNA, speaks of his use of imagery: "For over two hours, I happily lay awake with pairs of adenine residues whirling in front of my closed eyes . . . flipping the cardboard base pairs about an imaginary line" and then realizing that "each adenine residue would form two hydrogen bonds to an adenine residue related to it by a 180-degree rotation" (quoted in Shepard, 1978, p. 146).

---

thinking about what they're doing, and then to rush to turn in the work when they're done, without even checking it first.

A teacher once gave one of us and his classmates a somewhat difficult problem involving the computation of change for five dollars. Some of the students came up with answers expressed in negative terms. The fact that the answers made no sense (what is "negative change"?) escaped them; they turned in their papers anyway. Ellen Markman (1979) has done research on children's attempts at detection of blatant contradictions in texts they read and, similarly, has discovered that for the most part children don't even notice such contradictions.

Creative work is almost always fraught with errors along the way. Ben Shahn, a twentieth-century American artist, described the need for an "inner critic," saying that even "when a painting is merely in the visionary stage, the inner critic has already begun stamping upon it. . . . 'Your idea is underdeveloped' says the inner critic. 'You must find an image in which the feeling is embedded.' . . . Now find that image" (1964, p. 20). The great French mathematician Jules Henri Poincaré wrote that the mind acts like a sieve, separating good from bad ideas (Poincaré, 1921). Unless the creators analyze and correct their errors as they are en route to finishing their work, they are sure to produce something that is less than the best of which they are capable.

Indeed, if you look at the original drafts of writers and poets, you see extensive editing. The rough draft of Walt Whitman's poem "Come, Said My Soul" indicates that the first line originally read, "Go, said his soul to a poet, write me such songs." However, Whitman disliked the second part of the line and tried "such verse write." He crossed out this second attempt and tried "go write such songs." In the end the poem opened: "Come, said my Soul, Such verses for my Body let us write, (for we are one)" (Mitgang, 1984, p. C-11). For other comments on the importance of solution monitoring and evaluation in creativity, see box 5.8.

In sum we have argued that although the synthetic aspect of intelligence is certainly the most important to creative work, the analytic aspect is important too. To do your most creative work, you have to analyze problems well and, often, to analyze your own problem-solving efforts too.

The Practical Part of Intelligence: Making Good Ideas Work

Some time ago we had a graduate student in the psychology department who was considered superb by almost all the faculty. He was impressive not only in his analytic ability but in his synthetic ability as well. What more

---

BOX 5.8

Solution Monitoring and Evaluation

Tchaikovsky wrote that when working out a sketch of a musical composition, the evaluative phrase was of "primary importance." "What has been set down in a moment of ardor must now be critically examined, improved, extended, or condensed" (quoted in Vernon, 1970, p. 59).

Gordon Gould, inventor of the laser, states: "You have to be able to look critically at what you've thought up and refine it to only those things that work. . . . You have to be able to reject the ninety-nine percent of your ideas that aren't any good—and do it before you even become conscious of them—without suppressing any of the creative activity going on in your mind. At least that's how I see myself when I compare myself to people who haven't been successful inventors" (quoted in Brown, 1988, p. 328).

According to T. S. Eliot, "Probably, indeed, the larger part of the labour of an author in composing his work is critical labour—the labour of sifting, combining, constructing, expunging, correcting, testing" (1932, p. 18).

---

could anyone ask? Most of the faculty expected this chap to be an enormous success. One of the authors, on the other hand, expected him to be a flop. In fact, that's just what he became. After just a few years he left the field and had to find another line of work for himself. What went wrong, and why was it that almost nobody in the department predicted it?

Although this student had impressive levels of analytic and creative intelligence, he was a basket case as far as the practical aspect of intelligence was concerned. For one thing, the guy was unbelievably arrogant. Although he was near the bottom of the totem pole in terms of status, he acted as though he ran the place. It's one thing to be arrogant; it's another to have the practical intelligence to hide it when you must! The guy didn't show this kind of practical intelligence even when he went for his job interviews. He got a lot of interviews, but only one job offer—and that was from the worst job that he sought. No one wanted him in his or her organization, no matter how "smart" he might be.

In thinking about creativity we often fail to deal with the practical part. The practical part, however, is important, even in academic situations! Where does the practical part enter?

First, it is one thing to find a problem or an idea interesting. It is another to have a sense of whether anyone else will find it so. For example, no matter how creative an experiment someone designs to show that people remember two-syllable words better than they remember four-syllable words, few people are likely to be interested. A good choice of problems requires taking into account not only your own interests but those of others. Is it a problem that anyone in the world besides yourself is likely to find of interest? If not your work is not likely to be recognized as creative.

We say "not likely" because if there is no interest, you still have one other option available: to try to interest others. A point made above with regard to Alexander Fleming, and one that we see repeatedly in the history of creative thought, is that sometimes creative people recognize the importance of a problem whereas others don't or just aren't ready to see it. The creative person may thereby find him- or herself spending a lot of time convincing others that the problem is worth studying, or that his or her approach to the problem is one that people should listen to. This is the problem that one of us faced when he gave his first colloquium at the Educational Testing Service (as mentioned earlier): how to convince a basically hostile audience that it should pay attention and listen to what is about to be said.

It might seem slightly "below the belt" to raise issues such as these. After all, what do they have to do with creativity? Actually, a lot. Because creativity is socially constructed—creative work is creative by virtue of people designating it as such—we can't speak of creativity outside a social context. What is creative to one group of people may not be to another. Small wonder that people spend so much time speaking to and writing for the already converted. Politicians talk to their supporters; physicists spend most of their time talking to physicists. It's much harder, though, to persuade a crowd that does not share your presuppositions of the value of what you do. Yet the greatest payoff, ultimately, is often in reaching out to the unconvinced, not just to those who are already likely to believe anything you say.

What we are suggesting, which may seem offensive to some, is that there is a "sales" aspect to creativity. If you look at how people get from "buying low" to "selling high," you will almost always see a middle period in which people are not just coming up with good ideas but actively trying to convince other people of the worth of those ideas. (We would all like to believe that good ideas just sell themselves, but they rarely do.)

No one knows how hard it is to sell good ideas or products better than perfume manufacturers. That's why they spend millions of dollars hiring creative marketing talent, and also why the lion's share of the cost of perfume is for marketing, not for the product itself. Although most perfumes smell pretty good, the creativity that went into creating the fragrances is only the first step in selling them. Perfumes sell at least as much on image, including the design of the bottle, as they do on the actual scents. A delightful scent is likely to have only limited success or even to fail outright unless it is creatively—and aggressively—marketed.

Of course, the case is even tougher with such products as gasoline. Basically it probably makes little difference what brand you buy, or even if you buy a generic brand, which is often purchased from the major oil companies anyway. Thus the quality of the marketing campaign may dwarf the quality of the gasoline itself.

Most people would like to think that great ideas in science, literature, art, or music are different from perfume, and certainly from gasoline. To an extent, of course, they are. We are in no position to argue whether the creativity that goes into making a spectacular scent is any less than that which goes into making a spectacular sculpture. It's hard to compare apples and oranges, but much harder to compare perfumes and sculptures. What they have in common, however, is the need to appeal to people. Even in such rarefied fields of science as physics, it is not enough just to have ideas—you have to know how to convince others of their worth. We have talked to people in many fields, and without exception they agree that there are some whose ideas have won much more acceptance than they deserve because of the quality of the sales job, whereas there are others whose ideas have won less acceptance than they deserve because they are not well packaged.

BOX 5.9

Selling Creative Ideas

Dr. Julian Henley, a surgeon, holds several patents for medical inventions ranging from an artificial voice box to an electromolecular drug delivery system to a cancer treatment using microwaves. The story of one of his inventions, an artificial gill, illustrates the importance of practical intelligence when bringing an idea to fruition.

The artificial gill uses a special porous membrane rapidly to exchange gases between air and water, allowing a person literally to breathe under water. After approaching some entrepreneurs and building a prototype, Henley was invited to present the invention to potential buyers of the technology. When Henley went to the buyers he quickly found that they were not interested in hearing how the invention worked at a molecular level but wanted a demonstration. After sitting at the bottom of a pool for about thirty minutes, breathing with his device, Henley resurfaced and received a round of applause. Then they asked what the artificial gill could be used for. Henley said that it might be used for an underwater life-support system or a suit that could conserve heat and exchange gases. The investors replied, "Yeah, but we need something commercially more immediate. . . . Can we build breathing underwear from this that will sell?" One of the lessons of this incident is a practical one. As Dr. Henley says: "Sometimes the economy will pay for panty hose more than it will pay for life-support systems. If you want to be effective and creative, you really have to recognize the parameters of the real world" (Lubart, personal communication, 1991). Sometimes these real-world constraints will require the creative person to adapt the final product or sales pitch to fit the audience. In other cases the best solution is to find a better audience, as Henley did. His artificial gill may become part of a life-support system for outer space.

Businessman Kazuhiko Nishi, a Japanese technologist, exemplifies people who successfully sell their creative ideas. Nishi is credited with starting a computer magazine publishing house, designing the first mass-produced portable computer (Radio Shack TRS 80 Model 100), and coming up with other innovations—all while he was still in his twenties. When working with people who are instrumental in bringing a new product to commercial success, Nishi says, "What you need to do is maintain compatibility with existing society. In your own company you can be as creative as you want. But when you have to talk to the bank you have to behave like an ordinary Japanese" (Watanabe, 1990a, p. D-1). For example, although Nishi owns a Bentley, he arrives at sales meetings in a black company car and displays a soft-spoken, conservative image when pitching his new ideas.

While there is no easy formula for successfully selling an idea, several factors should be considered (LeBoeuf, 1980; McCormack, 1984). Some things that can help to sell a new idea are: (a) giving a high-quality presentation of the idea; (b) networking to find key people who may be interested in the idea or helpful in some way; (c) knowing your market—where your idea could fit in and whether the timing is right; (d) creating a need for your idea (emphasizing problems with the status quo and pointing out the benefits of your idea); and (e) looking at your idea from the "buyer's" point of view—understanding the image that you are projecting and what your idea means to the potential buyer.

The need for practical intelligence in creativity goes beyond just selling your work. It is also involved in knowing how to interpret and act on the reactions your work receives. For example, people in many fields apply for funding in order to do creative work. There are grants in all the sciences, in the humanities, in the arts, and so on. When scientists, artists, and others apply for grants, their proposals are usually critiqued and the critiques returned to the proposers. Part of the practical intelligence of creativity is knowing how to react to these critiques. It's knowing that if you are buying low, you are bound to encounter criticism, and so you have to be sure to separate the profound and useful criticism from the empty and useless. It is knowing how to take the comments of others and use them in a way that makes your ideas or product better, and not just a rehash of what other people have done before and may well want to see again.

In conclusion, to be creative involves three aspects of intelligence: the synthetic part of coming up with ideas; the analytic part of recognizing them, structuring them, allocating resources, and evaluating the quality of ideas; and the practical part of knowing how to promote and refine your ideas, based on critiques you get from others.

Related to these intellectual abilities, creativity requires a knowledge base (discussed in the next chapter) and an attitude that makes one want to use one's intellectual skills and knowledge to solve problems in a novel way. For example, a person may have the ability selectively to encode, compare, and combine information or to analyze and critique ideas when solving a problem, but not choose to put these skills into action. We will discuss the attitude for creativity in chapter 7 (thinking style) and in chapter 8 (personality).

The Role of Knowledge in Creativity

A brilliant, highly creative scientist arrived in a big city to give a talk on his work in theoretical physics. A recent Ph.D. from Harvard, he was personally unfamiliar to the faculty at the city university where he was to speak, although already well known by reputation. He had flown on a six-seater special propeller plane, the kind you practically have to use pedals to move. The plane had flown through a storm, and the trip made a roller coaster ride look tame. The professor was doing his best not to regurgitate his last meal. His talk was in an hour, and he had no idea how he was going to get through it. He hailed a cab, which started driving him toward the university.

As he was riding in the cab, he had a brilliant insight worthy of his outstanding creativity. He offered the cab driver half of his five-hundred-dollar honorarium to give the talk for him. "Look," he said. "I have all my notes neatly laid out. All you have to do is read from the notes and sound like you know what you're doing. And just in case you get into any trouble, I'll be in the back row." The taxi driver, who had only a high school education and had never studied physics in his life, assented because he needed the two hundred fifty big ones.

They arrived at the university, and sure enough the cab driver gave the talk. Because no one knew what the physicist looked like, no one recognized the substitution. The talk went fabulously and drew long and loud applause. At the end a graduate student in the audience asked a simple question. In fact, the question was so basic and even trivial that the professors practically hid their faces in shame. The only problem was that the speaker hadn't the foggiest idea what the student was talking about. Although he'd read the talk, he had no idea what he'd really said. He thought for a moment and, seeing the professors reacting in shame, responded: "Well, that question is so easy, even my taxi driver could answer it. And he's here, in the back row."

This obviously apocryphal story illustrates what we believe to be a key point about creativity. To be creative you need to know something, but sometimes not an awful lot. And what you need to know depends on just how you're being creative. The taxi driver may not have known anything about theoretical physics, and so he was in no position to be creative in theoretical physics. But he could still be quite creative in his everyday life. Creativity is not limited to the university elite or to any other.

Knowledge can be divided into two kinds: formal and informal. Although both are important for creativity, they are quite different.

Formal knowledge is the knowledge of a discipline or job that you learn in books, lectures, and other direct means of instruction. This knowledge may consist of facts, principles, aesthetic values, opinions on an issue, or knowledge of techniques and general paradigms. For example, Newton's laws would constitute part of the formal knowledge of physics, the law of supply and demand would constitute part of the formal knowledge of economics, and the plot of *Paradise Lost* would constitute part of the formal knowledge of English literature. In the stock market, knowledge would be the information available about a specific company or industry. Knowledge (both formal and informal) differs from intelligence, discussed in the last chapter, because knowledge is the raw material that intellectual processes use.

Informal knowledge is the knowledge you pick up about a discipline or a job from time spent in that arena. Informal knowledge is rarely explicitly taught and often isn't even verbalized. Moreover, its informal nature sometimes renders it difficult to sum up. For the stock market, knowing how the market works and who are the major financial players is one example of informal knowledge. In general knowing how to get a job, how to present a new idea to a superior, how to garner resources to get one's work done, and how a field is organized in terms of the power structure, would all be examples of the informal knowledge of a discipline important for creativity. Whereas formal knowledge can be viewed as "true" or "false" in a universal sense (for example, the laws of thermodynamics), informal knowledge cannot be. How the knowledge is judged depends on its context. The informal knowledge that works in a large, bureaucratic, well-entrenched company, for example, might be very different from the informal knowledge needed for success in a small, informal, start-up company. To succeed in almost any endeavor, you have to have both the formal and the informal knowledge that are necessary for adapting to the environment.

Formal Knowledge

The Role of Domain Knowledge in Creativity

Clearly, to be creative in a formal discipline, whether theoretical physics or any other, you need to know something about that discipline. Some of the research illustrating the importance of knowledge to creativity is described in box 6.1.

BOX 6.1

Knowledge and Creative Masterworks

"If I have seen further it is by standing on the shoulders of giants."
—Isaac Newton

Hayes (1989) has conducted studies of musical composers, painters, and poets. He finds that a period of knowledge acquisition lasting approximately ten years is needed before creative masterworks are produced. This finding was evidenced across creators with diverse artistic orientations, from the seventeenth to the twentieth century.

For example, seventy-six composers from Harold Schonberg's *The Lives of the Great Composers* were studied. The date at which each composer began studying music, and the dates of notable creative works (pieces recorded five or more times), were obtained. "Out of more than 500 works, only 3 were composed before year 10 of the composers' careers, and these three works were composed in years 8 and 9. Averaged over the group, the pattern of career productivity involved an initial 10-year period of silence" (p. 139).

How does knowledge foster creativity? First, knowledge helps a person to produce work that is novel for a particular domain: the ignorant risk reinventing the wheel. For example, when it comes to the opportunity to think creatively, a college professor has a big advantage over the typical student just starting the professor's course. Because the professor knows the content of the course, he or she is less likely to come up with ideas that just repeat what other people have already thought and said. For example, in the authors' undergraduate courses, it is very rare that a student will come up with a truly good new idea on a topic—one that has not been proposed before. An idea may be creative with respect to the student, who has not read every available source on the topic of his or her paper, but the idea may not be creative with respect to the world of the discipline, where the idea has been proposed previously. Graduate and professional students, knowing something more about the discipline than the typical undergraduate, are more likely to come up with creative ideas, but even many of their good ideas are not really new.

Second, knowledge fosters creativity, helping a person to be contrarian. Successful investors in the financial markets often do this; if you know where the current thinking is, you are in a better position to move against the tide and introduce the novelty that is fundamental to creative performance.

Third, knowledge helps in the production of high-quality work, which is taken into account in judgments of creativity. Knowledge helps a person transform an initial idea into a fully developed product.

Fourth, knowledge, in the form of practice, can let a person concentrate mental resources on the new ideas rather than on the basics. For example, a scientist who knows the basics of experimental design has the luxury of thinking about larger issues, whereas students may have to grapple with the basics of how to get the variables of an experiment into a suitable design. The same principle applies in any field. An expert in marketing knows the basic principles of ad design and so can think of the creative aspects of designing a particular advertisement, while a novice needs to grapple with the basics of design. Similarly, a good doctor knows how to recognize and interpret basic symptoms, so that he or she can think about what the combination of symptoms means rather than having first to figure out just what the symptoms are.

And finally, knowledge can help a person to notice and use chance occurrences as a source of creative ideas. In this vein Joseph Henry, the first director (in 1846) of the Smithsonian Institution, said: "The seeds of great discoveries are constantly floating around us but they only take root in minds well-prepared to receive them" (Rosenman, 1988, p. 135). Earlier we mentioned Fleming's discovery of penicillin. Fleming's prior experience with bacteria and destructive enzymes had primed him to notice that the bacteria were dead and see the potential of penicillin. At least twenty-eight scientists before Fleming had reported mold-killing bacterial colonies, but this result had always been viewed as an unfortunate accident rather than as a discovery.

As a foundation for thinking well in a discipline, there is no substitute for knowledge. Many educators learned this lesson in the 1960s, the hard way. Back then there was a craze in education to get kids to think—a goal no one could argue with. There was a "new math" curriculum, as well as a "new physics," a "new chemistry," and a "new biology." But the curricula were notoriously unsuccessful. What they tried to do was to teach kids to think at the expense of teaching content knowledge. It didn't work because you can't think well if you have nothing to think about. A good curriculum balances learning the content of the discipline with learning how to think well with that content.

The value of content knowledge for higher-order thinking was first observed experimentally with chess players by Allen Newell and Herbert Simon (1972). Chess masters and chess novices were shown patterns of pieces on a chessboard and asked to recall the patterns. Obviously almost no one would remember all the pieces the first time they saw them, and so it was necessary to give the participants multiple trials. The basic finding was clear-cut and striking. If the experts and the novices were given patterns to remember that were configurations of pieces from actual games, the experts were far superior to the novices in learning the positions. However, if the two groups were given pieces randomly arranged on the board—pieces that made no sense in terms of any game of chess that had ever been or would ever be played—the experts were no better than the novices in learning the configurations.

This classic experiment suggests that one of the main things that distinguish the experts from the novices is the knowledge they can bring to bear on their thinking. After all, the processes used in remembering the positions of the chess pieces would be the same for both the real and the random configurations. The experts' advantage was that they had stored in memory thousands of board positions from actual games, so that when they saw a sensible configuration of pieces, they could use their knowledge of games to aid their recall.

Newell and Simon's findings have been conceptually replicated in several domains of work. The main point of this line of research is that a storehouse of knowledge is beneficial for high-level performance, including creative performance. It is important to point out, however, that more matters than purely the quantity of knowledge; the knowledge must be stored in a usable form. There are stories of people trying to learn a foreign language by memorizing small dictionaries translating words in their native language into words in the foreign language. These people are then unable to speak even one sentence in the new language. It's one thing to know facts and another to be able to use them.

Facts can be stored as isolated units of knowledge or as part of a rich associational network. Some theorists have proposed that creativity depends on the structure and type of associations that are maintained between the items in memory. Mednick (1962), for example, suggests that knowledge can be stored in a variety of arrangements, with the two extremes called "steep" and "flat" hierarchies. People with a steep hierarchy of associations in a domain have strong links between highly related facts but find it difficult to move beyond these normal associations. For example, "dog" is strongly associated with "cat." "Cat" may be one of only a few associations that would come to mind for a steep-hierarchy person. In contrast, people with flat associative arrangements have relatively weak relationships between knowledge elements. The flat structure makes it easier to access diverse information and should be more conducive to creativity. "Dog," for example, will still be associated with "cat," but the link will be weaker and other terms will also have links, such as "days" (from the "dog days of summer").

Simonton (1988b) adds that the type of associational information between knowledge elements is important. For the "analytical" type of knowledge base, the associations between elements are based primarily on habitual use of the items together or on formal properties shared by memory items. For example, "cat" and "mouse" may have a strong link because they often occur together and are related semantically; one chases the other. For the "intuitive" type of knowledge base, there are additional behavioral and emotional types of associations that are as important as habitual or cognitive links. This broader spectrum of associations between knowledge elements is believed to facilitate creativity.

The Potential Costs of Formal Knowledge

Although knowledge may buy you a lot in your thinking, it may also cost you.

Some years back one of the authors was visiting a world-famous psychologist abroad. This psychologist is internationally renowned for his theory of intelligence and critical thinking. The psychologist wished to show the author his city, and so took him on a tour, which included a visit to the zoo. As it happened, just as they passed the cages of the primates, the animals were engaged in what could euphemistically be called "strange and unnatural sexual behaviors." The author, having been brought up in a refined household, naturally turned his head away. The psychologist from abroad, however, obviously was not so well reared, because he stared fixedly at the primates as they did their thing. Obviously his staring was in bad taste, but what can you say to your host?

After a minute or two the host psychologist started to analyze the behavior of the primates in terms of his theory of intelligence. Now, there are very few things in the world that the author believes he knows for certain, but one of them is that, whatever was behind the sexual behavior of the primates, it had nothing to do with the famous psychologist's theory of intelligence (or with anyone else's, for that matter).

This incident started the author thinking about what had happened. How could a brilliant scientist think that his theory of intelligence had anything at all to do with primate sexual behavior? But then the author realized something else: What the psychologist had done was by no means unique. B. F. Skinner had done the same thing. He had proposed a model that accounted well for very simple learning phenomena. The basic idea was that if you are rewarded for doing something, you will tend to do it more. For example, if certain aspects of your spouse's behavior particularly please you, and you reward your spouse when he or she acts in these ways, then the spouse will tend to do what pleases you more often. On the other hand, if you are not rewarded for doing something, you will tend to do it less. Thus if your child acts in ways that annoy you, often the best thing to do is to ignore the behavior. If the behavior is rewarded neither by you nor by anyone else, eventually it is likely to be "extinguished," meaning that it will probably disappear. Skinner's theory worked well for simple behavior. If people are rewarded for good behavior, they are likely to repeat it. If people are ignored when they behave badly, they are likely to stop behaving badly. But Skinner then tried to apply his theory to very complex forms of behavior, such as language learning. Although the theory didn't work for complex forms of behavior, to his dying day, Skinner was one of the few who believed that it did.

Cases such as those of our psychologist from abroad and of Skinner are common. As shown in box 6.2, many experts have come to realize that expertise can have its costs. Sometimes, when we are very knowledgeable about something, that very knowledge interferes with our seeing things in a new way. Knowledge thereby can interfere with, rather than facilitate, creativity.

BOX 6.2

Fixation Effects: When Your Mind Gets Stuck in a Rut

"Learned conventions can be windowless fortresses which exclude viewing the world in new ways."
—Gordon, 1961

A number of studies have shown fixation effects during problem solving (Finke, Ward, & Smith, 1992). For example, Luchins and Luchins (1959) conducted research with "water-jug" problems, in which water must be poured from jug to to jug to achieve a desired end result. When people solve a number of these problems using one specific formula, they tend to persist with the same formula on a new set of water-jug problems, even though these new problems could be solved with an easier formula.

Birch and Rabinowitz (1951) offered a more concrete demonstration of the effect of past experience on novel problem solving. In their study there were two experimental groups and one control group. One experimental group used an electrical relay to solve a circuit design problem. The other group used an electrical switch to solve its circuit design problem. A control group, familiar with both relays and switches for engineering problems, was given no pretest experience. The critical test consisted of the two-string problem (described in chapter 5). Two strings hanging in a room need to be tied together, which is possible only if one string is set in motion so it can reach the other. A switch and a relay were provided in the testing room; either could be used as a weight to set one string in motion.

The control group used each object equally often. The experimental groups, however, almost always (about 90 percent) used the object with which they did not have prior experience. For example, the experimental group that had used the relay for an electrical problem used the switch as a weight to solve the two-string problem. When questioned why they chose either the switch or relay, people pointed to the extra weight or special shape of the object they had used. Many remarked that anyone could see that one object (either the switch or relay, depending on the experimental group) was obviously a better weight for the pendulum motion. This effect is called functional fixedness because people cannot break away from the original function of an object. In general, previous experience and knowledge of standard ways for conceptualizing and solving a task can block creative solutions.

Such cases are not limited to psychology or to any other one area of endeavor. In the April 9, 1993, issue of the prestigious journal *Science* there appeared an article entitled "Ulcers as an Infectious Disease." The point of the article was that there is now overwhelming evidence to suggest that although antacids are used to treat 90 percent of all ulcers, and are among the top-selling drugs in the United States, these antacids have been notoriously ineffective. In fact, according to the article, the relapse rate for ulcers treated with antacids is 50 percent over six months and up to 90 percent over two years, scarcely an impressive record for a widely used treatment. Would you use aspirin for headaches if it worked only 10 percent of the time? Would you want to have an operation if you were told that the chances of your surviving it were only 10 percent?

In contrast, according to the article, recent studies show that the use of antibiotics to fight the bacteria associated with ulcers results in success rates of more than 80 percent. Yet many physicians and especially drug companies are not rushing to change either their theories of the causation of ulcers or their views of how ulcers should be treated. They have too much of an investment in the treatments they now use. When people are accustomed to think about a problem in one way, they often are reluctant to think about it in any other way.

The same principle applies to many of the inventions that are still in use. Why are we still using essentially the same tests for measuring abilities that we were using at the turn of the century? Why is the computer language FORTRAN, one of the first such languages, still in use when there are so many newer languages with many more desirable properties? Why has it taken many businesses years to computerize their files, when doing so years earlier would have saved them uncounted dollars? Once people get used to doing things a certain way, they often have trouble imagining doing them any other.

If you are thinking right now that you know people like those we are describing—people who can't seem to let go of old ways of thinking and doing things—you are not quite getting our point. The point is not that some people become entrenched in their ways of thinking and acting, but that everyone does. The question isn't whether it will happen to you but what you will do about it.

In order to emphasize that we are no more exempt from this problem than anyone else, consider the following. About a year after one of the authors formulated the "triarchic," or three-part, theory of intelligence (Sternberg, 1985a), he formulated a "triangular" theory of love (Sternberg, 1986c), which also had three parts. This theory was soon followed by the author's first published article on creativity, called "A Three-Facet Model of Creativity" (Sternberg, 1988c). At this point some people began asking the author why all his theories had three parts. He explained there were at least three good reasons for it. You get the idea: We can talk about the dangers of entrenchment, but we can't prevent it from happening to us. What we can do is to take steps to fight it.

How do you fight it?

The first thing is consciously to try to vary your routine. If you always order the same thing at the same restaurant, try a new restaurant, or at least a new dish. If you always go to the same locale for a vacation, try a new one. If you always wear the same kind of clothes, try a new kind. In the case of one of the authors, he realized that for a while he was stuck in a really bad routine. When an employee would do something well, he might offer a small compliment. But when the employee did something wrong, he offered a detailed critique—not the greatest way to improve employee morale. Realizing what he was doing, the author changed his routine and started to be as detailed in his compliments as in his critiques. And everyone was happier. Our point is that even in the most ordinary things we do in everyday life, we often find ourselves locked into a routine that we can break only if we first realize that we are stuck in a routine and then decide that we want to alter it.

The second thing you can do is actively to invite feedback from others. Don't wait for others to tell you how you could change; ask them. Seek constructive feedback, and you may be surprised to learn just how many things you could do differently—and better. When the senior author teaches a course, he tells students on the very first day that if they have suggestions as to how he could improve the course, they shouldn't wait until the end of the term when they are filling out a university course evaluation to let him know. By then it's too late to change the course, at least for them. By getting feedback early, it is possible to change things before it is too late.

A third thing you can do is to seek actively to learn. When the senior author was in college, courses on developmental psychology—the psychology of how people change as they grow older—basically ended with the study of young adults of age eighteen or so. The implication was that people develop until they are about eighteen, and then live happily, or if they are not so lucky, unhappily ever after. One would think that nothing—or no one—changes after the age of eighteen. Today courses on developmental psychology often extend to the study of people seventy, eighty, and older. We can always be learning. It is *never* too late. One of us started learning Spanish at about age thirty, and now speaks it fluently. His mother, who is seventy-three, is now taking Spanish lessons. Reading, attending lectures, visiting new and interesting places, meeting new people—all these experiences afford us an opportunity to learn. Creative people are those who are never satisfied that they know it all—they are always seeking to learn more.

The senior author does a lot of public speaking, in the course of which he has learned a valuable lesson. Whenever you go to speak somewhere, some people take the time out from whatever else they are doing because they want to, and others come to hear you only if they have to. The lesson he learned, which other public speakers learn as well, is that the best people (in whatever occupation) are always those who come to lectures, seminars, and workshops because they want to, not because they have to. Unfailingly the teachers, business executives, and others who believe that they know everything that's worth knowing and therefore don't need to waste their time on lectures are the ones who are evaluated lowest by their supervisors. They may well know much of their discipline—as it existed thirty years ago. Some of them aren't even aware of how much it has changed, much less what the changes are.

The authors try to practice what they preach. For example, often a student will come to one of the authors with an idea for a project. Sometimes the author likes the idea; other times he doesn't. And he will tell the student what he thinks and why. But if he doesn't like the idea, he will encourage the student to try the idea out on him again in a few weeks. Often an idea whose merits are not apparent on one day may seem quite meritorious on another day. Occasionally an idea just doesn't make contact with what you know the first time it is presented, whereas it does later on. It happens that the student will come back after a couple of weeks, and, sure enough, the author will see value in an idea that just two weeks earlier seemed pretty worthless. Other times the idea still won't seem so hot. In such cases the author suggests that the student try out the idea with members of the author's work group, who meet once a week explicitly to discuss ideas that they're thinking about. And as often as not, someone in the group will see value in an idea that the author didn't.

We all need to realize that no matter how much we may know about a given area of endeavor, our judgments about new ideas in that area are never perfect. Some of the best ideas go unrecognized because people can't see their value, even when it stares them in the face.

An example of this came when the two of us were at a meeting in the south of France, held at an enormous estate of the Schlumberger family, one of the wealthiest families in the world. Naturally it occurred to us to wonder how the family had acquired its wealth. Apparently, years ago, two Schlumberger brothers came up with a novel idea for more effective oil exploration. They took the idea to several oil companies in the United States, none of which was interested. Finally, in disgust, they took the idea to the newly formed Soviet Union, where the government was very interested. Eventually they put their ideas into practice throughout the world, even in the United States, and their idea brought them their fortune. But the United States lost an opportunity to be ahead of the international competition because the oil companies failed to recognize the value of a new way of doing things.

An implication of our point of view is that it is not always the world-renowned expert who has the best ideas. Sometimes it is a person who is relatively new to an area of endeavor, and who is able to think in new ways precisely because he or she has not yet been co-opted by the standard ways of looking at things.

For example, Ken Meyers, a founder of Smartfood popcorn, attributes Smartfood's success in marketing its product to a lack of marketing knowledge (Staff, 1991). Because Smartfood did not know the "right" way to market its popcorn, it invented its own highly successful "guerrilla" strategies. (For example, Smartfood had people dress in giant popcorn bags and ski at popular resorts.)

As another example, an article in *U.S. News & World Report* (Mar. 1, 1993), called "Triple Teaming the Deadly AIDS Virus," also showed the advantages of not being trapped by what everyone supposedly knows.

A number of different substances have been shown to have some effectiveness in combating the AIDS virus—AZT and DDI are only two of several drugs now routinely used. However, a feature of the AIDS virus that makes it especially hard to fight is the ease with which it mutates. No sooner is there a drug that is effective against one form of the virus than it mutates and produces another form against which the drug is ineffective. The problem is that none of the known drugs is in itself sufficiently effective to knock the virus out once and for all. Yung-Kang Chow, a thirty-one-year-old medical student working in Massachusetts General Hospital, had an idea one day while he was eating dinner. Instead of defining the problem as one of finding the right drug to combat AIDS, why not define it as one of finding the right combination of drugs to knock out the virus? To us as laypersons this idea might seem rather obvious. But that's precisely the point: Often the people who are least blind to new possibilities are those who know less, not more, about a given area.

Chow combined the two standard AIDS therapies, AZT and DDI, with each of two other substances, pyridinone and nevirapine. When the virus was assaulted by either combination of three drugs (AZT, DDI, plus pyridinone or nevirapine), the virus was forced to mutate so fast that it was no longer able to survive. In essence the virus's ability to mutate was turned against itself—attacked by the three drugs, the virus mutated itself out of existence.

Chow attributed his coming up with the idea to his own lack of knowledge about the ways in which we are "supposed" to fight AIDS. He is a good example of how often the people who are best able to solve a problem are those who don't know so much that they can only see the problem in a single way. Chow also attributed his success to the support of his advisers, an aspect of creativity we will discuss in chapter 10. (As it turned out later, the experiment didn't replicate. Even Chow himself could not repeat his own results. So here's another lesson: When you have a creative idea, it makes good sense to make sure it works before you call your press conference.)

We can see various examples of the costs of knowing too much in everyday life, but is the phenomenon demonstrable under the more carefully controlled conditions of a laboratory? Frensch and Sternberg (1989) tried to show in such controlled conditions that being an expert can actually hurt you under certain circumstances.

Their experiments involved having expert and novice bridge players compete against a computer in a game of bridge. Since computers can be programmed to play quite well, it is no mean challenge to try to face one in this game. In one of the experiments, both experts and novices played bridge against a computer while the computer kept score. It will come as no surprise that the experts played better against the computer than did the novices. But the point is not merely whether experts play better than novices (of course they do), but rather the effects of knowledge on how people play.

In addition to a standard-play condition, there were also two other conditions of play. One was a "surface-structural" change condition. In this condition people played bridge against the computer, but the form of the game was slightly altered. What was altered was either the rank-ordering of the suits (which is normally, from lowest to highest, clubs, diamonds, hearts, spades) or the names of the suits. The names were changed from the usual ones to made-up words, such as "gleebs," "fricks," and so on. We called these changes "surface-structural" because they altered only the most superficial aspects of the game. The new conditions of play could be mapped in a one-to-one fashion to the old conditions. Nothing fundamental about the game was really different. When the players were subjected to this surface-structural alteration, their play suffered momentarily but quickly recovered. All they had to do was to learn the new order or names of the suits.

In a "deep-structural" change condition, a more fundamental change was made in the game. The game of bridge starts with a "bidding" phase and then converts into a playing phase that occurs in a number of successive rounds. In the game the player who puts out the high card in a given round is normally the one who leads off play in the next. Our deep-structural change was to make it so that the player who put out the low card led off the next round. To total novices, the change makes little difference. It doesn't disrupt their complex strategies of play, because they don't have any! But an expert who has developed such strategies would be more likely to be disrupted because he or she could no longer use them.

The results came out exactly as predicted: Experts were more hurt by the deep-structural change than were novices. Although the experts eventually recovered, it was hard for them—so used were they to their normal rules of play. Thus their expertise actually got in the way of their adapting to the new rules.

Many of us have seen this phenomenon operate in our own lives and those of others. Often the people who have been in a field the longest find it hardest to adjust to changes in that field. Sometimes they are not even aware of the changes. But other times they are and simply don't want to adapt.

Earlier we mentioned the idea that knowledge forms part of a person's human capital. Essentially a person with a lot of knowledge in an area has invested a great deal to acquire his or her knowledge base. For the most part the person seeks to draw on and to protect the value of this knowledge base whenever possible. Accumulated knowledge, therefore, can become an impediment to further creativity; the person becomes unwilling to "buy low." We do not wish to oversimplify a complex problem. Sometimes the changes that occur in a field of endeavor are not favorable ones, and it is not clear that the right thing to do is to adapt. At the very least, though, you should examine what you are doing and why you are doing it.

Informal Knowledge

Consider a leadership problem faced by one of the authors recently. As acting chair of the Department of Psychology at Yale, he decided that one of his major goals would be to try to increase the team spirit of the members of the department. Although the people in the department worked well as individuals, they did not display the kind of cohesiveness and sense of shared mission that he believed would make them maximally effective as a group.

He tried to come up with a creative idea to instill a sense of team spirit in the department. His first effort in this direction was to organize a group picnic at a beach in a community about fifteen miles from New Haven. Everyone in the department was invited to come to the picnic. The picnic seemed to be a good way of getting people together and starting toward a new spirit of cooperation and team play. There was just one problem: Few people came to the picnic; almost none of the faculty showed up.

The author's first reaction was one of frustration. The group members were not a cohesive team, and they were displaying their lack of cohesion by not taking even a minimal step to unite them into a more unified group. After venting his anger, however, the author realized that he should have been able to predict the outcome, and if he had predicted it, he might have organized an event more likely to set things on the right course. On the surface, the decision to have a group picnic at an attractive beach would seem to be a good one. But there were a number of problems:

1. The event was organized over a weekend in late summer. Many people have alternative weekend plans, however, especially as they try to enjoy the last days of summer before the weather cools.

2. The event was some distance from Yale, and moreover, one could reach it only by car. But many students and some staff don't have cars. Thus, unless they managed to hitch a ride, they would be unable to come.

3. The event was basically a social event. Even if it served a useful social purpose, many people in the department separate their professional lives fairly clearly from their personal lives, so that fostering personal contacts might do very little to foster team spirit in the workplace.

4. Although some people love beaches, others hate them. The latter view visiting the beach as tantamount to inviting skin cancer to enter their bodies.

The picnic at the beach may have been a creative idea, but it was a bust, as are many other efforts that leaders and managers make to achieve certain goals. Not long ago President Bill Clinton proposed a BTU tax on energy as a way to help pay off the staggering U.S. national debt—a creative idea but one that quickly became apparent was DOA (dead on arrival). There was too much opposition from oil states, from people living in colder regions, from people promised a middle-class tax cut, and from many others as well. How can ideas that initially sound so creative fall flat so fast?

The answer has to do with informal knowledge. In studies of expertise and creativity, scholars investigating creativity have tended to focus on formal knowledge—what a biologist needs to know about biology to do her work, or what a business executive needs to know about finances to make a financial plan. But the world does not revolve around a classroom or the kind of knowledge that is taught there. For most decisions informal knowledge—the kind you pick up from living, from working on a job, being in a relationship, and seeing how people respond to their environments—is probably much more important than is formal knowledge.

In fact the importance of informal knowledge was highlighted in a study of scientists from university and industry R&D laboratories. Kasperson (1978) found that the more creative scientists (as judged by peers) differed from less creative scientists, in part, by their emphasis on informal sources of knowledge. The creative scientists placed more emphasis on speaking to people at conventions and on interacting with other people in scientific societies—often in fields other than their own. It is interesting to note that accessing these sources of informal knowledge—rather than reading books, journal articles, or other formal sources of knowledge—distinguished the highly creative scientists from the less creative ones.

For the past decade we have been studying informal knowledge and its uses, especially in school and business settings (see, for example, Sternberg, 1985a; Sternberg & Wagner, 1992; Wagner & Sternberg, 1986, 1991; Williams & Sternberg, in press). We believe that to make creative products that are both novel and appropriate, people need to draw on informal knowledge of the environment in which they are working.

Informal Knowledge and Creativity in Everyday Life

Informal knowledge impacts on creativity in daily life. Consider an example of how they relate: Many people lose opportunities in life because they are procrastinators. People often come up with new ideas for how to stop procrastinating, just as they come up with new ideas for losing weight and for stopping smoking. But the fact is that most of the ideas don't work: They may be novel; they aren't creative.

Indeed, consider one of the questions Wagner and Sternberg have used on a form of their tests of use of informal knowledge:

> You are concerned that you habitually put off completing disagreeable tasks and wish to improve this aspect of your work-related performance. On further examination, you think that your problem is one of procrastination—you are unable to start tasks you need to get done on a given day. You have asked for advice about dealing with this problem from several friends . . . who seem to be especially productive.

What would be the best advice they might give you? In order for them to give you good advice, or for you to give it to yourself, you would need the informal knowledge of why you couldn't get started. Informal knowledge is not the knowledge taught in school, and often it isn't taught anyplace else either. But it is hard to function effectively without it. Let's consider some of the kinds of advice you might receive, or the ideas that you might generate, and then whether they are good ideas:

1. Wait to begin a task until you really want to do it. This advice is probably not very useful, because some tasks that you need to do you may *never* really want to work on. For example, if someone procrastinating on his or her income taxes followed this advice, they'd probably never get paid.

2. Spend some time considering just what it is you dislike about a particular task, and then try to change that aspect of it. This strategy can work for many tasks: For a period of several months, one of the authors found himself reluctant to go to his office but didn't know why. He would

procrastinate about leaving the house until as late as possible in the morning and would try to pack up and leave for home early in the evening. One day a colleague pointed out that the author seemed not to be around very much; the author then asked himself what it was about going to the office that he was avoiding and realized that it was having to deal with a certain member of his staff. Once he recognized the problem, he saw the solution: She's no longer working for him. Often if you will just admit that you are not doing something you should be doing, and take the time to figure out just *why* you are not doing it, you will be a long way toward solving the problem.

3. Get rid of all distractions—not a bad suggestion for getting things done. This page is being written on a Friday afternoon. It should have been written Monday afternoon, four days ago. But every day the author went into the office, the entire day was eaten up by distractions of every conceivable kind, and even some inconceivable ones, such as the uproar created by the receipt of a letter bomb by a professor in another department. Finally, as the author saw the week disappearing before his eyes, he decided to stay at home to write, and thereby get rid of all the distractions of the office. So here's the text: The lesson is that if you have to go into the office, seal the place off! The day you must get a certain task done, just don't take the phone calls and don't answer the door. It may seem harsh, but sometimes it's the only way to get things done.

4. Force yourself to begin the day by spending just a small amount of time on the task, perhaps fifteen minutes, starting with the easiest part. Everyone has tasks that just seem too big to start, with the result that often they don't get started until much later than they should. Some years ago one of the authors contracted to write an introductory psychology text—about as big as a task can get. It took him five years to write but six years to complete, because the first year, he just couldn't get started. Every time he thought about the task of writing such a mammoth book, he froze. Finally, come January 1 of the second year, he realized that he couldn't wait any longer, and he also realized why he hadn't been able to start the book.

He had been trying to start with chapter 1—an overview of the field and also probably the most difficult chapter to write. And if he tried to start with the most difficult chapter, he might well procrastinate indefinitely. But a good piece of informal knowledge is to start a complicated, multifaceted task with a small, easy step, not a large, difficult one. So he redefined the problem: He started with chapter 11, the one (on intelligence) he thought would be easiest for him to write.

When we talk about everyday creativity, this is the kind we mean: the big and little insights in life that may or may not mean much to others but mean a lot to you. In order to start the project, the author had to redefine what he meant by starting. Not much of a creative insight, you may say. But it is that kind of creativity—the kind that lets you break through a block that is preventing you from achieving your goals—that is probably ultimately the most important kind in your life. You may or may not ever make a groundbreaking scientific, literary, or other kind of discovery. Certainly, though, you will have everyday problems that can be solved by seeing them in a new way and using the informal knowledge at your disposal to solve them in an optimal way.

Informal Knowledge and Creativity in the Workplace

We have conducted many studies of the role of informal knowledge in success in management and sales (see Sternberg, Wagner, & Okagaki, 1993, for a review of many of these). We believe that our results offer implications for creativity in a wide range of workplaces.

In our research we often give managers scenarios of problems they might actually face on the job. Sometimes they are given multiple options and are asked to choose among them; other times they would have to generate their own creative options for solving the problems. For example, problems might be about how to award a contract or how to handle a particularly sticky interpersonal situation. Here's an example of the latter:

> You have just learned that detailed weekly reports of sales-related activities will be required of employees in your department. You have not received a rationale for the new reports. The new reporting procedure appears cumbersome and will probably be resisted strongly by your group. Neither you nor your employees had input into the decision to require the reports or in decisions about its format. You are planning a meeting of your employees to introduce them to the new reporting procedure.
>
> OK—what might you do?

Well, here's an opportunity to be creative. And the range of responses we get is wide. For example, some proposals have been to (a) emphasize that you had nothing to do with the new procedure; (b) have a group discussion about the value of the new procedure and then put its adoption to a vote; (c) give your employees the name and number of the director responsible for the new procedure so that they may complain directly to that individual; (d) promise to make their concerns known to your superiors but only after the employees have made a good-faith effort by trying the new procedure for six weeks; (e) use the meeting for something else and inform the employees about the procedure in a memo, thereby avoiding the unpleasantness of a contentious meeting; and (f) postpone the meeting until you find out the rationale for the new procedure. Note that a number of these solutions might be labeled as "creative," but a number might also lead to your losing your job. For example, when you hold a vote among the employees, you are probably simultaneously voting yourself out of a job, whether you know it or not. Again, a lack of informal knowledge can lead to decisions that just aren't practical in the context in which one is working. In business as in many other domains, creative ideas meet with success only when they are also practical.

Our work on informal knowledge in business settings has yielded some interesting results.

First, although informal knowledge and the ability to use it tend to increase with the number of years of experience people have, it is not experience per se that matters but how well they take advantage of it. Some people can be in a job for ten years, yet have less informal knowledge about it than other people who have been in the job half the time.

Second, scores on tests of how well a person can use informal knowledge predict job performance about twice as well as do IQ tests. Let's face it: After you graduate from school, IQ may still make a difference, but for most jobs it doesn't make that much. Most people aren't in jobs that require loads of the kind of academic intelligence IQ tests measure. What really matters is what you learn from the job and how you exploit it creatively in the problems you face on the job. We emphasize the *creative* part of exploiting tacit knowledge. The people who get ahead are often those who don't just do what everyone else is doing but find a way of doing things differently and better.

Third, scores on our tests of how people use informal knowledge are uncorrelated with scores on IQ and similar tests. If you have noticed that it is not just the high-IQ types who succeed in life, you are right. Obviously people with a very low IQ are going to be at a disadvantage when dealing with demanding jobs. But after a certain level of IQ (theorists disagree just what this level is, and it probably varies from one job to another), other things start to matter much more—two of them being the possession of informal knowledge and its creative use.

Ironically, people who score the highest on standardized tests and do the best in school are often somewhat less successful than people who were not at the top of the class in high school or college (see Sternberg, 1988e). Why? Because those who are not at the top of the heap on the academic measures usually realize that they will need something more than their scores on tests or grades in school to succeed in life. Thus they find other talents in themselves and try to make the most of them. Many outstanding test takers and achievers, however, never learn that lesson. They try to make a go of their lives on the basis of high test scores and eventually discover that they just can't do it. By then it is often too late for them to get completely back on track.

Fourth, the ability to use informal knowledge creatively is somewhat domain-specific, just like the kinds of creative production we considered in chapter 2. When people take tests of informal knowledge across several occupations, there is a moderate but not a high correlation. In other words some of the informal knowledge you need to succeed on the job is common across occupations, but other informal knowledge is specialized. The best entrepreneur, for example, may have informal knowledge that can assist her in management but other knowledge that doesn't, or that actually gets in the way. For example, she may have found it to be advantageous for entrepreneurship to do things her own way without outside interference, whereas this strategy is not so advantageous for management.

Finally, informal knowledge can be taught. One of us has actually taught a course on how to get jobs, how to keep jobs, what to do if you get fired, how to write a résumé, and the like. All these aspects of informal knowledge are teachable. People can learn them if they set their minds to the task.

Some uses of informal knowledge are simply routine, and, though they may be important, they are not the focus of this book. Rather, we focus on situations in which people can use informal knowledge to advantage in ways that others don't see—that is, we focus on ways to use informal knowledge to buy low and sell high. That's why fruit-flavored teas are such a hit as this book is being written. The idea is creative: It is based on the informal knowledge that we live in a time when people are seeking purity in products, and in which they associate purity with clarity of the product. They may not stay a hit, though, as the novelty wears off.

Some other researchers have also drawn links between informal knowledge and creativity. Csikszentmihalyi (1988), for example, has noted the importance of a person's having informal knowledge of a field in order to move around among the gatekeepers—the people or institutions that control progress in a field. For example, in the art world the gallery owners control the flow of creativity, to some extent, by the work that they choose to show. Knowledge of various gallery owners and how to attract their interest is important for the success of creative work. Similarly, in science, informal knowledge regarding journal editors, their publication standards, and their preferences is important for bringing creative work to fruition.

Taking another angle on informal knowledge, Langley, Simon, Bradshaw, and Zytkow (1987) have proposed that heuristics, "rules of thumb," are an important part of creativity. Heuristics are guidelines for searching a set of possible solutions in a fairly rapid way. The researchers have developed a set of computer programs that uses heuristics to examine data, "execute" new experiments to gather information, and rediscover scientific laws. For example, given the original data that Johannes Kepler had available, the program can rediscover Kepler's third law of planetary motion ($D^3/P^2 = C$; D = distance, P = period of revolution, C = a constant). Some of the heuristics used by the program are: (1) if the values of two numerical terms increase together, consider their ratio; and (2) if the value of one term increases as that of another decreases, consider their product. Of course, these programs address only one limited aspect of creativity (especially because the numerical data are provided as a starting point). The programs demonstrate, however, that heuristics—informal knowledge for attacking a problem—are part of creativity. They also demonstrate that so-called "creative" programs can easily make rediscoveries but not new discoveries.

Informal Knowledge and Creativity in the School

Some years back the son of one of the authors showed the author a paper he planned to hand in to his teacher. "Seth," said the author. "You've got some really good ideas in this paper. But you're not really going to hand it in like, this, are you? It's full of typographical errors, and it's messy besides." Seth's response was definite: "Sure I'm going to hand it in," he said. "The teacher only cares about the ideas. She doesn't care whether the paper is neat or not or whether it has a few errors in it." The author tried to assure Seth that the teacher *would* care, but to no avail. Seth handed in the paper and received a bad grade.

Seth is by no means unique. Lots of children are brimming with creative ideas but don't know how to present them in a form that will win them the praise—and the grades—they seek. And for that matter, many adults are the same way. Experiences such as that with Seth convinced the author of the need for a program to teach informal knowledge in the schools—one that would balance this informal knowledge with instruction on how to be creative. But the most important element would be instruction on when to be creative and when not to be. In other words children would be given the informal knowledge of how most effectively to use their creativity so that it would benefit rather than hurt them. Thus was born the combined "Practical and Creative Intelligence for Schools" project, currently in progress. Table 6.1 shows an example of a lesson from that project.

TABLE 6.1

Lesson 1: Why Be Creative?

What

A discussion to introduce students to the concept of creativity and convince them it's worth learning more about.

Why

If we expect students to work through eight lessons on creativity, they have to know what creativity is and why they should want to be creative. This lesson begins to show children that creativity is a goal worth pursuing, a joyful and fulfilling part of being alive.

How

1. Begin the discussion by writing the word "creative" on the chalkboard. Ask the class if anyone knows what it means. Write down interesting answers. Some questions to pose to the class: Can clothes be creative? Dogs? Brick houses? Pizza? Graveyards? Jump ropes?

2. Read aloud a dictionary definition of "creative," such as, "Marked by the ability or power to create—to bring into existence, to invest with a new form, to produce through imaginative skill, to make or bring into existence something new" (*Webster's Ninth New Collegiate Dictionary*, 1983, p. 304). (Tell students not to worry if their ideas differed from this definition.)

3. Ask students to nominate some people they think are or were especially creative. List the names on the board. Discuss what is creative about each person—something he or she did well, insights or views on things, and so on.

4. Ask whether students think the people on the list took pleasure in their work—did they love doing what they did or was it drudgery? What made them want to do it? Where did they get their inspiration? What did they gain by being creative?

5. Distribute the handout containing the poem "Bantams in Pine Woods" by Wallace Stevens. Give students time to read it. Now ask what they think of it. Is it creative? Why or why not? What might be considered creative about this poem? How do you think Stevens got the idea for this poem? What does it make you think about?

6. Tell students that over the next few weeks they will be thinking more about the topic of creativity. Distribute blank notebooks and explain that each student is to begin a journal, a place to record his or her creative thoughts and ideas about how to become more creative. These journals will not be graded in the traditional sense; rather, students will be praised for coming up with unusual ideas and different ways of thinking about things.

7. As a first exercise ask each student to write four more lines that sound just like the Stevens poem. Read the first two lines of the poem aloud again as students shut their eyes. Then ask students to write whatever comes to mind as long as it sounds like it could be part of the same poem. If time permits have a few students share their contributions with the class.

Our studies of informal knowledge in the classroom have shown that this type of knowledge is as important to success in the classroom as it is to success on the job. In fact it predicts school performance as well as do academic aptitude tests (Sternberg, Wagner & Okagaki, 1993). And it predicts adjustment to the school setting better than do academic aptitude tests. As a student you need to know how to study, what teachers expect when you write a paper, what kinds of comments in class are appreciated and what kinds are not, and so on.

From some points of view all this is too bad. We see many students at our own university who have made their way here precisely because they are so good at psyching out the system. But they have put so much effort into psyching out the system that they have become afraid to do anything at all that goes against the grain. They may adapt well, but they rarely do anything creative, because they try to do exactly what is expected of them rather than to go beyond those expectations. Nothing scares them more than the idea of buying low and selling high, because it entails too much risk. They play the game safely, but in playing it that way the lesson they are learning is that creativity just isn't worth the risk.

In schools and in the workplace, we need to teach people the need to balance adaptation with shaping of the environment—to balance conformity with creativity. If we don't, our society will pay a steep price. We believe that society is already paying. People need to learn in school what the system expects, but they also need to learn how to go beyond and transcend those expectations. That is the only way to be creative.

The Role of Thinking Styles in Creativity

Suppose a French teacher wanted to teach the conjugation of regular -*er* verbs in the present tense. One thing he could do is teach traditionally the concept of action verbs, how verbs function in sentences, and the importance of knowing how to conjugate verbs as part of language study. The class could then complete exercises provided in their textbooks.

This approach to teaching exhibits an "executive" style of thinking about lessons. Thinking styles in general are preferred ways of applying one's intelligence and knowledge to a problem or task to be completed. A thinking style is not an intellectual ability but rather a way of using the intellectual abilities we have. For example, a classroom teacher's thinking style can influence how he or she teaches a class. The teacher discussed above was exhibiting an executive style because he was executing a predesigned plan for the lesson.

Another teaching approach to the French lesson exhibits a "legislative" style. A teacher might think up a whole situation or method of getting the students to use the verbs. For example, she could designate each row as a team. For each team she could put a different infinitive form of a regular -*er* verb on the board. A team relay race would show which students knew their verb forms. Another legislative idea would be to organize students to playact typical scenes and use vocabulary and idioms. Ordering a meal in a café or greeting a friend at the airport are examples.

Finally, if a teacher preferred a third style, the "judicial" one, he or she

175

might be inclined to give students sample papers that contain mistakes and have the students correct the papers to learn about verbs. In this style people make judgments and evaluations.

Styles of thought can also be seen to guide approaches to problems in a business. Workers at a computer company had been taking an "executive" approach to problems of controlling work flow between subgroups in the company; people were implementing the procedures set forth by management. Each team worked on a problem case a little and then sent it to the next group for further work. Eventually the problem would get resolved after circulating among many specialized teams.

Some workers, however, went to management with a "legislative" approach for controlling the work flow on computer problems. These workers designed a new way of dividing up the work; they proposed a new set of rules for routing problems.

Three tiers of people would be involved: the project leader, the technical team leaders, and a sampling from the rest of the technical people covering all groups in the project. The whole team (twenty to twenty-five people) would meet once a week for two to four hours and review significant problems. From interactive discussions it would quickly become apparent which team leader should take the lead on a particular problem. A subteam of people involved would be formed to pursue and resolve problems. The group could refuse to handle a problem if it felt it was beyond its scope.

A key to the success of the new method was that the problem was efficiently solved in one step rather by its circulation among groups. Problem resolution time went from three months on average to one.

The thinking styles that we have been describing in these examples—the legislative, the executive, and the judicial—come from a taxonomy of thinking styles called the "theory of mental self-government" (Sternberg, 1988a, 1988e, 1990b), which describes how people can choose to channel their thinking.

Creative Styles

The basic idea of the theory of mental self-government is that, just as governments are needed to govern various countries, states, and cities, so people need to govern themselves. The kinds of governments we see in the world, therefore, can be viewed as external mirrors of what goes on in the mind. More important for our purposes, just as some kinds of governments actively encourage or at least allow creative thinking among their citizens, whereas others actively repress such thinking, so people's styles of thought either encourage or discourage creativity.

Before we describe in detail each of the styles, some general comments are in order. These comments apply to many other conceptions of styles as well as to our own.

First, as mentioned above, styles are proclivities, not abilities. They deal with how people like to approach tasks, not with how well they handle them. Someone may love to come up with creative ideas, but the fact that she loves to create does not guarantee that her products will be creative. Similarly, other people have a lot of creative talent but don't particularly enjoy creative work. In some people abilities and styles match; in others they don't.

Second, people do not always show the same styles across all tasks and situations. Some tasks may lead to one style, other tasks to another. Thus, although people may have preferences, they can't always have it their way. For example, a person who likes to see the big picture and deal with sweeping generalities will nevertheless have to be fairly detail oriented when he or she is doing income tax forms.

Third, people differ in the strengths of their preferences. Some people just hate details, and so strong is their aversion that they find ways of avoiding virtually any task that requires them to attend to details. For example, they may have an accountant do their taxes, a bank service pay their bills, a financial service manage their savings and investments, and so on. Other people may mildly dislike details and avoid thinking about them when it is easily convenient. People also differ in their flexibility—that is, how well they can move among styles to fit situational demands.

Fourth, styles are to a large extent socialized. By this we mean that although heredity may play some role in the styles we have—we just don't know how much—to a large extent we have those styles because they are rewarded by factors in our environment. If children repeatedly have teachers who discourage creative modes of thought, there is a good chance that their creativity will start to flag. If children (or adults) are rewarded for thinking in creative ways, on the other hand, they are more likely to develop creative styles of thought. To a large extent we have the styles we have because of the people we have role modeled—parents, teachers, peers, and the like.

Fifth, styles can vary across the life span; they are not fixed for all time. Some people find that, as they become older, broader issues become more important to them and the details less interesting. Other people become more conservative in their ways of thinking as they grow older. People may think very differently when they are seventy from the way they thought when they were twenty. To take an example, when one of the authors was in college, a number of his classmates were hippies. Today many of these same classmates are suit-and-tie Wall Street lawyers. Whereas once they accepted practically nothing about the "system," today they are the last ones to want to see it change.

Sixth, styles can be taught. Because styles are socialized and because they vary over time, people are not "stuck" in any sense with the styles they have. Even children whose creativity has been driven into the darkest recesses of their minds can find it again if given the proper instruction. And it's never too late: Many older people are finding within themselves the wellsprings of creative thought that they never had thought possible.

Seventh, what is valued in one time or place may not be valued in another. We shall give many examples of this principle as we go along. But not all schools discourage creative styles of thought, and not all businesses suppress new ideas. Indeed, among mutual funds, there are actually so-called "value funds," whose goal is to find undervalued stocks and to invest in them. The managers of these funds purposely pick what others consider to be the "dogs" of the stock market in the belief that among them are the winners of tomorrow in the investment sweepstakes. These managers truly buy low.

Eighth and finally, styles are not "good" or "bad." As authors of a book on creativity, we have a bias toward favoring those styles that promote creativity. But as we shall show, people can lead happy and successful lives (defined by different goals) even if their styles do not lend themselves particularly well to creative thinking.

So, having given you the basics, we'll now proceed to tell you what the styles are that are relevant to creativity in various ways. For each style we'll start with three sample items from one of the inventories we use to measure styles of thought (Sternberg & Wagner, 1991). In this way you can very roughly assess the extent to which each style characterizes you.

For each statement rate on a scale of 1 (= low) to 9 (= high) the extent to which the statement characterizes you as an individual. Each style will have three statements associated with it. If you average the numbers you assigned to the three statements, you will get an average score ranging from 1 to 9. Generally speaking a score of 1 to 3 indicates that the style does not characterize you well at all; a score of 4 to 6 indicates that the style characterizes you to a typical degree; and a score of 7 to 9 indicates that the style characterizes you particularly well.

Functions of Mental Self-Government

Just as governments have different functions, so do people's mental self-governments. The three functions of government are the legislative, executive, and judicial, and people can be legislative, executive, or judicial as well.

THE LEGISLATIVE STYLE

1. When I work on a project, I like to plan what to do and how to do it.
2. I like tasks that allow me to do things my own way.
3. I like to pursue tasks or problems that have little structure.

Remember to rate yourself on a 1 to 9 scale for each item, average the three scores, and then evaluate the extent to which the style characterizes you. In this way you will have a more active appreciation of what each style means for you individually.

The senior author's graduate advisor once said that the worst thing he could do was to suggest a project to the author, because as soon as he suggested it, the author wouldn't want to do it. Such a reaction is rather typical of people with a legislative style. Like good legislators, they like to create their own rules, do things their own way, and generally speaking, set their own course. They prefer problems that are not prestructured or prefabricated. In school they prefer writing papers or doing projects to taking short-answer or multiple-choice exams, which they see as straitjackets to their thinking. They generally prefer discovery learning to expository learning, meaning that they would rather figure out how to do something than be told how to do it. As adults they may become entrepreneurs, creating new businesses or business systems. Or they may become writers, scientists, artists, sculptors, architects, policy makers, or deal makers. Whatever occupation they choose, they are happiest when allowed to do things their own way, free from outside interference.

The legislative style is the single style most conducive to a creative mode of thought. A person can have all the ability and knowledge in the world—without a legislative style, he or she is unlikely to exploit that ability and knowledge in a creative way. But having a legislative style does not guarantee creativity: Without the knowledge one needs to go beyond where things are, for example, one cannot use the legislative style to one's best advantage.

THE EXECUTIVE STYLE

1. I like situations in which it is clear what role I must play or which way I should participate.
2. I like to follow instructions when solving a problem.
3. I like projects that provide a series of steps to follow to get to a solution.

When one of the authors was in college, he had a classmate we'll call Alex. Alex was a brilliant student, both in terms of his grades in school and in terms of having aced the college admission tests. In fact Alex did very well in virtually all his courses, right up to his senior year. In his senior year, he had to do a completely independent project. He certainly had the ability to do a fine job on such a project, but he didn't particularly like doing it. He ended up receiving a mediocre grade on the project, probably the first such grade he had received in college.

Alex was someone who had an executive style, the kind characterizing someone who likes to be told what to do rather than figure it out for him- or herself. Executive stylists prefer expository to discovery learning, like to follow rules, and prefer problems that are prestructured to prefabricated. If given a task, they may do it fantastically well, but they would rather be given the task and the structure within which to work on it. In school, executive stylists prefer the multiple-choice or short-answer test to the essay test and are happy in courses that require essentially memorizing a book or doing problems at the backs of chapters. Executive stylists enter a wide variety of occupations. Like legislative stylists they may become writers, but if they do, they prefer writing about the ideas of others to writing about their own, and they are more likely to become, say, reporters than novelists. If they give talks, they are more likely to try to explicate clearly the ideas of other people than to use their talks as forums to push their own ideas. If they become builders, it will be of other people's designs. They do well as enlisted soldiers or as policemen, or even as proselytizers, but of other people's systems rather than their own. They may even go into mathematics, but they are more likely to become applied than pure mathematicians.

Clearly people with an executive style can succeed just as well as those with a legislative style. For example, Alex is today a well-respected contracts lawyer. He puts down on paper the deals that other people make, and enjoys doing so. His ideal of the job is to make the contracts airtight, so that if any of the parties to the contract wants to get out of it, one or both or all of them will have to pay him more legal fees. A legislative stylist would find such an occupation a deadly bore. But again, styles are not better or worse, only different.

The difference between legislative and executive stylists is the difference between someone who buys low and sells high and someone who buys high and sells low. Executive stylists may have creative abilities and the knowledge to be creative but be unlikely to exploit either toward creative ends: It's just not what they enjoy doing. Moreover, there are plenty of other uses to which they can put their abilities, because a wide range of occupations are tailor-made for people with an executive bent.

Our concern, as theorists and as unabashed promoters of creativity, is that many organizational structures tend to support only the executive and not the legislative style. Consider the school, for example. The ideal student is often seen by teachers as the one who does what he or she is told and does it well. The kinds of assessments used to measure abilities, especially multiple-choice tests, are tailor-made for executive rather than legislative stylists. And people who have the legislative style are often downgraded for having it. As mentioned earlier, even science courses— which prepare students for an occupation that is consummately legislative (that of the scientist)—are usually taught in an executive mode, with students memorizing textbooks and doing fixed problems at the ends of chapters. Even many of the labs that students take are simply canned exercises that have the students doing experiments that have been done by countless others innumerable times before.

Businesses also often reward the executive over the legislative style—at their own peril. If you ask yourself what you would most want in a lower-level manager, you will probably rightly conclude that you would want someone who is executive. Lower-level managers don't get the opportunity to set company policies: For the most part their job is to implement them. In the military Sternberg and his colleagues and collaborators, both at Yale and at the United States Military Academy at West Point, are likewise finding that at the lower levels of leadership, visionary and other legislative activities are only the most minor part of the day-to-day life of the officer. At the lower levels of management and even of leadership positions, people implement policies that come from above. People who don't wish or choose to implement these policies are often derailed early in their careers and have to find something else on which to spend their time.

The irony is that, at the upper levels of management and leadership, probably what you need more than anything else is a legislative style of thought. At the upper levels are the people who need to set the principles and policies for the lower-level people to follow. If the upper-level people are primarily executive stylists, they are likely to flounder, simply continuing with old policies even in the face of a rapidly changing world. The cost to the organization is therefore stagnation and, ultimately, the opportunity to become a dinosaur in a world no longer fit for the species.

Often, the problem is that the people promoted to the upper levels are those who have best succeeded at the lower levels, and often these are the people who have a consummately executive style. The cost is that they cannot change fast enough, and either they or their organization goes down. We believe that the so-called Peter Principle (that people rise to their level of incompetence) often reflects promotion to levels at which people fail not because of incompetence with respect to abilities but because of inappropriateness with respect to styles.

Mikhail Gorbachev is a prime example. For most of his life he was basically a party apparatchik. When he reached the top, he gave it his all and even tried to switch from being the consummate follower of directions—the executive thinker—to being a legislative thinker. But he just couldn't change fast or far enough. If you get used to thinking a certain way all your life, it is by no means trivial suddenly to change your entire way of thinking. The result of the failure to change, in his case, was problems for his country, and ultimately, for him. He went some distance toward be-

coming a legislative thinker, but he didn't go the whole distance necessary, given the crises confronting the country.

As another example, take George Bush, who was successful in many aspects of his presidency. Bush had a background of succeeding in a large variety of executive-style jobs. But even he admitted he had trouble with "the
vision thing." He didn't even seem quite sure just what it meant. The cost
was that Bush's popularity slid from record highs after the Persian Gulf War
to record lows shortly before the 1992 presidential elections. When the
country needed a new vision of economic policy, he didn't have one. The
result was that he was voted out of office, largely because of his failure to
come up with the new economic ideas people felt were needed at the time.

Strange as it may sound, you don't necessarily have to be a consummate
legislative stylist to succeed, even at the highest levels of leadership. Many
people who reach the top succeed not because they are idea persons but because they know how to surround themselves with such people. The key
here, as in so many aspects of life, is to know your own pattern of styles: If
you are primarily an executive stylist in a legislative job, find staff who will
complement you. Similarly, a legislative stylist in an executive job needs
people around him or her to do the chores that he or she may find aversive:
If you can't find the flexibility in yourself to adapt adequately, a major part
of your job may be to hire the people who can do for you those aspects of
the job that you are averse to doing yourself.

To a large extent the same principle applies in intimate relationships. Legislative and executive stylists often function well together as a couple because one person takes more of the responsibility for deciding what needs
to be done, while the other takes responsibility for seeing that the things actually *get* done. The two are less likely than some other couples to come
into conflict because they have naturally complementary roles. Where they
may run into problems, though, is if the legislative stylist becomes bored
with or resentful about always being the person with the ideas, or if the executive stylist becomes resentful when his or her ideas are ignored, or when
he or she feels like a lackey for the other partner. Thus, even in relationships
where there is a natural complementarity, it helps if people sometimes take
turns and vary their roles as different kinds of occasions arise.

Two people can nevertheless do well in an intimate relationship if they are both legislative or both executive. If they are both legislative, the relationship may be especially stimulating because both like to come up with new ideas and ways of doing things. The legislative person may feel more appreciated in a relationship with someone like him- or herself than in a relationship with someone who just doesn't seem to understand. The downside of a relationship between two legislative people can come if both always want to do things their own way, or if each one wants to be the person to come up with the ideas, and wants the other person to be the one who follows up on the ideas. If both people are executive, they will probably be happy following the lead from others—perhaps "keeping up with the Joneses."

The same principles apply in business relationships as well. For example, a manager with a legislative style will probably pair up well with another manager who has an executive style, because there will be one person paying more attention to what to do and another person paying more attention to getting it done. But if both people want to come up with the ideas, and both want the other to implement them, there's no one to get the work done! In business things can work only if there are people to do what the chiefs decide needs to get done. If everyone wants to be a chief, the organization becomes inactive.

Sometimes people's styles change over time, and there are built-in opportunities for people who start off more legislative and become more executive to capitalize on their change in preference. For example, professors may become administrators, or scientists in research-and-development laboratories may become managers of research and development. Less often people go in the opposite direction, and administrators decide to go back into basic research. By allowing a diversity of paths, organizations can allow people best to capitalize on their styles as they change over time.

THE JUDICIAL STYLE

1. I like to analyze people's behavior.
2. I like projects that allow me to evaluate the work of others.
3. I like tasks that allow me to express my opinions to others.

A person with a judicial style likes to evaluate things and people as well as rules and procedures. If you know someone who tends constantly to evaluate other people—especially to form snap judgments of them—you are probably dealing with someone who has a fairly heavy dose of the judicial style. People with this style prefer problems in which they analyze and evaluate, and in which they judge other people and their work.

In school judicial students like to write critical papers, such as ones comparing two novels or periods of history, or papers evaluating the actions of a certain historical figure, or essays judging the success of a particular political regime. They are comfortable with analytic essays but much less so with multiple-choice and fill-in-the blank tests, unless such items happen to test critical thinking rather than rote recall.

Later on in life judicial people are likely to be more satisfied if they find occupations that enable them to exercise their judicial preferences, for example, judge, critic, program evaluator, consultant, admissions officer in a private school or college, systems analyst, and the like.

A college classmate of the senior author is a good example of someone with a judicial style. As a student he was editor of the publication that evaluated all of the courses at the college. When he went out on dates, he would give the women a test of values that he created. If they passed the test, he would go out with them again; if not, that was the end of that relationship. Needless to say he is still unmarried.

However, this individual has found a career that is a good fit to his own stylistic preference. Today he is a psychotherapist who spends his time evaluating the problems of others and prescribing treatments for them. He has thus been successful in translating his judicial style into a line of work that is a good fit with what he likes to do.

Couples in which one or both people are judicial can fare well if the judicial partner directs his or her evaluative tendency outside the relationship. Two judicial people can have a ball critiquing others, but the danger is that they will turn their proclivity inward, toward the relationship, and become hypercritical within it. In such cases the relationship may have some difficulties surviving.

Although the legislative style is the key one of the three functional ones for creative work, the judicial style can serve an important function as well: When you do creative work you not only have to come up with the ideas but critique them as well. Some people just hate doing so. As a teacher and an editor of both journals and books, one of the authors has seen many such people—both younger and older ones. They turn in papers that look as if they were written in fifteen minutes, or written while the person was under the influence of something. People who are totally lacking in the judicial style just don't want to critique their own work and won't proofread it, analyze whether the arguments are sound, ask whether the work really has a contribution to make, and so on.

In business creative people who are almost purely legislative may do all right in the creative department of an advertising firm, but they're likely to run into trouble almost anywhere else. They don't see the flaws in their plans, nor do they want to look for them. They tend not to analyze problems carefully, nor to think through the consequences of courses of action. They may tend toward impulsiveness, which can lead to flashes of brilliance or unmitigated disasters. Ideally the creative person balances enough of the judicial style with his or her preference for the legislative style so that the person can recognize when his or her ideas would be better served as a Thanksgiving turkey dinner than they would be put into action.

Forms of Mental Self-Government

Just as governments must serve different functions, so can they be organized into a variety of different forms. People can also organize themselves in various ways when approaching a task. Four of the forms that are most common are the monarchic, hierarchic, oligarchic, and anarchic.

THE MONARCHIC STYLE

1. I prefer to finish one assignment before starting another.
2. I like to devote all my time and energy to one project, rather than dividing my time and attention among several projects.
3. I like to put in long hours of work on one thing without being distracted.

A person with a monarchic style is one whose thoughts and actions tend to be motivated by a single goal or need at a time. The person is single-minded, driven, and often intolerant of other priorities and points of view. The person may tend toward rigidity and toward a mind-set in which he or she always seems to want to go "full speed ahead—damn the obstacles." The monarchic person may also believe that the ends justify the means—that when something needs to get done, it should get done without regard to the cost.

Monarchic people can be difficult to live with. If you are not the object of their drive, you may find yourself all but ignored. If you are the object of their drive, you may find yourself smothered. Nonetheless, although they may not be the most pleasant people to live with, they can be quite creative.

Very high creative achievers are often monarchic with respect to their work. The top creative achievers—people like Freud, Picasso, Faraday, Einstein, Brahms, and many others—reached the pinnacle of achievement precisely because they were so hard-driving. As Gardner (1993) points out in his analysis of creative geniuses, however, the cost of such achievement can be substantial in the context of life as a whole. Other people may be ignored or forcefully pushed aside. And the person often ends up living a life that is noticeably unbalanced.

Not everyone is as strongly monarchic as some of the greatest of the creative achievers. For example, we know a student who tends toward the monarchic. At different times in his life, his passion is focused in different directions, but there usually seems to be something that is consuming almost all of his attention. The past few years this something has been computers, and so the student has come home and started working almost immediately on the computer. Sometimes it will be late in the night before he will remember that, yes, he does have homework to get done. Other times he'll just forget the homework.

An interesting point about monarchic people is that they rarely see themselves as monarchic, because they usually love whatever it is they are monarchic about rather than seeing it as work. Others, however, may realize very quickly that these monarchics find time for little else beside the object of their passion. Thus the monarchic person may need someone else to point out this tendency to him or her.

If, as a parent, you have a monarchic child with the potential for creativity, then you need to be thinking about how you can help your child channel his or her monarchic style constructively. For example, the child may love some extracurricular activity, but unless the child reaches the level of achievement in school necessary to pursue that activity in a meaningful way, he or she may never be able maximally to capitalize on his or her interest.

In the case of the student mentioned earlier, his parents were concerned because he was spending so much time with the computer. One marking period, when the boy's science grade was lower than he had hoped, the father went in to talk to the teacher about what could be done to improve his son's grade in this subject. The father was surprised to learn that the science teacher was only vaguely aware of the boy's interest in computers and didn't see how it tied in with the science instruction that she was giving. The father therefore suggested that the science teacher try to capitalize on the boy's interest in computers in science, and, to her credit, she did just that. The teacher showed the boy how to combine his interest in computers with other interests in science, and up went the boy's science grade.

The general principle of capitalizing on the interest of a monarchic person applies in any area of interest to children. For example, many children don't want to read; the boy described above didn't. But at the time he wasn't reading, he was keenly interested in sports. His parents bought him sports novels, and suddenly the boy became a reader. After he lost some of his enthusiasm for sports novels, he stopped reading again. He just wasn't excited about what he was reading in school. But buying him computer books and mystery novels got him reading again. The point is that the monarchic style can be maladaptive if not channeled properly. Channeled well, it can actually enhance rather than detract from success.

THE HIERARCHIC STYLE

1. When undertaking a task, I like first to come up with a list of things the task will require me to do and then to assign an order of priority to the items in the list.
2. Whenever I engage in a task, it is clear to me in what order of priority various parts of it need to get done.
3. When writing, I tend to emphasize the major points and to deemphasize the minor ones.

People with a hierarchic style tend to take a balanced approach to problems. Unlike monarchic people, they can easily and happily deal with multiple tasks and goals simultaneously and, moreover, are comfortable assigning priorities for getting done the various things that need to get done. When there are multiple goals to be achieved, a hierarchic person will set up a hierarchy of goals, recognizing that some goals may not be fulfilled as well as others, and that degree of fulfillment should be a function of the importance of a given goal. Hierarchic people generally do not believe that the ends justify the means, and are more self-aware, tolerant, and flexible than are monarchic people.

Most creative people are hierarchic, and this style usually serves them well. The reason is that almost no one has the luxury of being able to be creative all the time, and hence a person needs to have a sense of when it is time to invest his or her resources maximally and when it is not.

Hierarchical people range in extremity. One of us once worked with a consummately hierarchical employee. When she would come into the author's office, she would often have a list of things to get done. The items on the list were rank-ordered by priorities. One day the employee came in with what looked like a much longer and more structured list than usual. Asked what it was, she responded with some embarrassment that she had created a list of her lists and activities within each list.

Hierarchical people do better in many jobs, and in school, than those with other stylistic forms, because they effectively set priorities for what they need to get done. They are also likely to realize that not all problems are equally important and worth spending the time on to solve creatively.

THE OLIGARCHIC STYLE

1. When there are competing issues of importance to address in my work, I somehow try to address them all simultaneously.
2. I sometimes have trouble setting priorities for multiple things that I need to get done.
3. Usually when working on a project, I tend to view almost all aspects of it as equally important.

People with an oligarchic style are characterized by multiple, often competing, goals of equal perceived importance. They are good at finding competing approaches to solving problems and at seeing a variety of alternative decisions they can make. Unfortunately this tendency to see all sides of a problem can lead them to indecision and goal conflict, so that they can have trouble getting things done and decisions made. People who never seem to have enough evidence to decide one way or another are likely to be characterized by the oligarchic style. Although they are flexible, tolerant, and often self-aware, they have trouble setting priorities and sometimes make decisions unnecessarily complex.

The oligarchic style is not ideally suited to creative performance. In writing creatively an author needs to know what ideas to emphasize and what ideas to play down. Oligarchic people have trouble making the decision, and when they do, don't always make it so well. When doing creative artwork, you need to focus on some aspects of what you are drawing or sculpting and deemphasize others, again difficult for the oligarchic person. In business, decisions need to be made, and time is money: Delaying too long so that more and more information can be sought can often result in tremendous costs due to lost opportunities. By the time the decision is made, the competition has already edged ahead. In science, knowing the important issues from the less important ones is key to optimizing on one's ability to do creative research. Thus, an oligarchic person may have the abilities and knowledge to do creative work, but be held back by a style that impedes the optimal use of the abilities and knowledge.

THE ANARCHIC STYLE

1. When I have to start to do some task, I usually do not organize my thoughts in advance.
2. When thinking about an issue that interests me, I like to let my mind wander with the ideas in whatever which way.
3. When talking about issues that interest me, I like to say things just as they occur to me, rather than waiting until I have organized or censored my thoughts.

The anarchic stylist is someone who takes a more or less random approach to problems. The person's thoughts and actions seem to be motivated by a potpourri of needs and goals that are often difficult to sort out, for the anarchic person as well as for those who have to live or work with him or her. The person's thinking may seem to be muddled, and he or she to be driven by what seem like inexplicable forces. Anarchics often seem unclear as to their goals and means, or liable to the extent that today's goals and means are history by tomorrow. They may be politically ultraleftist at one point in their lives and then ultrarightist at another, without being particularly bothered about it. The reason is that they are asystematic—eschewing systems of any kind—and so when they stay with a system, it is only for the short period of time in which it is convenient and a means to what often seems like a hazy end.

Because anarchics don't work well within most systems, they often find themselves outside them. Hence anarchics are most at risk for antisocial behavior. They often end up on the fringes, socially and politically. Revolutionaries whose behavior makes no sense at all to the large majority of those in society are likely to be anarchic in their style.

With regard to creativity, the anarchic style is a mixed bag. On the positive side people with this style tend to be receptive to multiple and diverse cues in the environment—much like an antenna that extends out in different directions and receives many different signals in rapid succession. Thus anarchic people can be in a position selectively to encode stimuli that other people might miss, and to let diverse ideas cross-fertilize each other. On the negative side, however, they do not always have the discipline that is necessary to translate wide-ranging thoughts into a creative product.

Although we tend to think of creativity in terms of divergent thinking and openness to new experience, there is a perhaps less discussed side of creativity that requires tremendous self-discipline, self-organization, and self-control. Few people are Mozarts, who can just sit down and spin out an almost flawless creative product. Most people need to work hard at developing and redeveloping their ideas. And without the self-discipline to do this reworking, a person may never translate potentially creative ideas into a creative product. Anarchic people often need someone to channel them in ways that enable them to harness the creative potential that their style may enable them to display, given the right circumstances.

Levels of Mental Self-Government

THE GLOBAL STYLE

1. I like to do projects in which I don't have to pay much attention to details.
2. In any written work I do, I like to emphasize the scope and context of my ideas, that is, the general picture.
3. Usually when I make a decision, I don't pay much attention to the details.

People with a global style prefer big issues and tend to eschew and often to ignore details. They are idea-oriented conceptualizers who like to think abstractly. They are good at seeing the forest, but sometimes ignore the trees. Dr. Benoit Mandelbrot, the mathematician who originated fractal geometry, prefers the global style when first confronting a problem: "One should never, in my opinion, when first crossing new territory, worry about fine tools and about clean argument" (Lubart, personal communication, 1990). If you were crossing a jungle, you would take crude tools like a machete and an axe, rather than a fine tool like a clarinet screwdriver. The global style is a key one for creative thinking. Often a creative solution can be obtained only by extracting oneself from the details and taking a look at the big picture.

THE LOCAL STYLE

1. I like problems that require engagement with details.
2. In carrying out a task, I am not satisfied unless even the nitty-gritty details are given close attention.
3. When writing I like to focus on one thing and to scrutinize it thoroughly.

People with a local style prefer details and tend to be more pragmatic, concrete, and often down-to-earth than people who display a global style. Sometimes local stylists are susceptible to not seeing the forest for the trees.

Local people can be creative but they tend to be creative in the small. Often, they are not the movers and shakers but rather those who fill in the gaps in thought and action left by the movers and shakers. If you ever want to see the epitome of creative ideas in the small, go to a scientific convention or read a scientific journal. Most of the research described will be at least somewhat creative but narrow in the scope of the problems with which it deals. Similarly, in the business world, there are the people who form start-up companies and twenty years later are supervising the same five to ten people they supervised when they started; and there are others who have built worldwide conglomerates. For example, Ross Perot made much of his money from the realization that although many businesses had computers, most of them didn't really know quite what to do with them or how to exploit them in a maximally effective way. But providing data-processing services before others provided them enabled Perot to get an edge on the firms that started providing such services later. The problem with local stylists is that they often don't see the big issues that underlie what they do or should be doing.

Ideally a creative person would be more global than local, but not wholly global. In most creative work there are at least some details to be attended to. The writer or the artist may need the grand conception, but he or she also has to get the details right, whether of a novel, a poem, or a painting. Similarly a scientist may come up with grand theories, but then he needs a way of dealing with the specifics that emanate from that theory.

People who are strongly global or local can sometimes be particularly effective if they work with someone who complements them. For example, a global scientist might pair up with a local collaborator. By sharing responsibilities, their whole effort might be considerably better than what either of them could achieve individually. For such a collaboration to work, the global and the local person need to respect each other's styles. The global person needs to recognize his or her need for someone to attend to the details, whereas the local person needs to recognize his or her need for someone to attend to the big picture.

The Scope of Mental Self-Government

THE INTERNAL STYLE

1. I like to be alone when working on a problem.
2. I like to avoid situations in which I have to work in a group.
3. To learn about some topic, I would rather read a well-written book than participate in a group discussion.

A person with an internal style tends to be introverted, task-oriented, aloof, socially less sensitive, and interpersonally less aware. She usually prefers to work alone rather than in groups. Thus her best creative work will be done when she is left to work alone, without having to deal with other people in collaborative or other group-type situations.

THE EXTERNAL STYLE

1. Before I start on a project, I like discussing my ideas with some friends or peers.

2. I like to work with others rather than by myself.
3. I like talking to people about ideas that occur to me and listening to what they have to say.

External people tend to be extroverted, people-oriented, outgoing, socially sensitive, and interpersonally aware. They like to work with others; hence they will generally do their best creative work when working in a group rather than by themselves.

Note that internal versus external styles do not, on the average, yield differential levels of creativity. Rather, they yield different styles through which creativity can be expressed. In working with employees, students, children, or others, one of the best things you can do to help them express their creativity is to help them find the right working conditions, including whether they should be left alone or be facilitated through interaction with a group.

Although much creative work is solitary (for example, the work of the artist, the mathematician, the theoretical physicist, the novelist, the poet, and so on), there are many opportunities for creative work in groups as well (for example, business executives, dancers, advertising agencies, and so on). We believe that parents and schools need to place more emphasis than they often do on teaching children to work together in groups. In the real world much of the time, people have to work with others or at least be responsible to others for what they do. Relatively few people in the world of work have the luxury of having to please only themselves. Hence, the sooner children learn how to work with and cooperate with others, the better off they are likely to be later in their lives.

Orientations of Mental Self-Government

THE LIBERAL STYLE

1. I like to do things in new ways, even if I am not sure they are the best ways.
2. I like to avoid situations where I am expected to do things according to some established way.
3. I am comfortable with projects that allow me to try unconventional ways of doing things.

A person with a liberal style (also called "progressive") likes to go beyond existing rules and procedures. This person prefers novelty, likes to maximize change, and seeks ambiguous situations. The person has the potential for creativity if he or she can channel that preference for novelty into a preference for novelty of high quality. Simply wanting to sweep out the old in favor of the new is not sufficient for doing creative work.

Some people like to do new things, but really don't care about whether what they do is creative or not. Sensation seekers, for example, are constantly looking for new thrills and are likely to have a liberal style, but they will not necessarily channel the style in a way that is at all creative.

In general we would expect a correlation between the legislative and liberal styles. In other words, on the average people who are legislative would be expected to be liberal, and vice versa, but there is no necessary relation between the two. In principle someone could be legislative and prefer to make up the structure of a task but choose to do so in ways that are minor variations of past practices.

BOX 7.1

Alternative Conceptions of Thinking Styles for Creativity

The theory of mental self-government described in this chapter provides one perspective on thinking styles. In this box we will consider alternative theories. In particular, we will look at creativity-relevant styles from Carl Jung's theory of types and Michael Kirton's adapter-innovator styles.

In Jung's (1923; Myers & Myers, 1980) theory of types, sensing and intuitive styles of perception are proposed as most relevant to creativity. Sensing types, who are less creative, rely more on external information, focus on "the realities of a situation, . . . work with what is 'given,' . . . They prefer to use proven procedures and are careful with detail." In contrast, intuitive types, who are more creative, concentrate more on "meanings, relationships, and possibilities that go beyond the information from [the] senses. Intuitive types look at the big picture and try to grasp the overall patterns" (Myers-Briggs Type Indicator-Form G report form, 1987, p. 2). The sensing and intuitive types are related theoretically to the local-global and conservative-liberal styles of mental self-government described in this chapter.

Empirically, creative samples show a strong preference for intuitive thinking (Myers & McCaulley, 1985). In one study by Hall and MacKinnon (1969), all forty architects (100 percent) whom peers related as highly creative showed a preference for the intuitive style of thinking. In a matched control group of architects only 61 percent preferred the intuitive over the sensing type.

Another converging theory of style is Kirton's (1976) distinction between adapters and innovators. Adapters seek problem solutions that involve adjustments or incremental modifications while maintaining basic structures. Adapters work within a paradigm; innovators seek to restructure fundamental elements, and this concern with fundamental change involves innovators in global aspects of a task. Both adapters and innovators favor some change but vary on the extent to which they are progressive in terms of mental self-government progressive-conservative styles. Research studies demonstrate moderate correlations between a preference for the innovative style and scores on divergent-thinking tests of creativity (Isaksen & Puccio, 1988; Masten & Caldwell-Colbert, 1987; Mulligan & Martin, 1980; Torrance & Horng, 1980).

THE CONSERVATIVE STYLE

1. I like to do things in ways that have been shown in the past to be correct.
2. When I am in charge of something, I like to make sure to follow the procedures that have been used before.
3. I like to participate in situations in which I am expected to do things in a traditional way.

People with a conservative style like to adhere to existing rules and procedures, to minimize change, and to avoid ambiguous situations. They prefer familiarity and working within the constraints that have been set up in the past. In general their adherence to the ways of the past can interfere with their finding creative paths in their work and in their lives.

It is important to realize that when we refer to liberal and conservative styles, we are referring to ways of thinking, not to political ideologies. Within any given political ideology, people can be more or less eager to try new things and to think in new ways.

Some Empirical Findings about Mental Self-Government

In empirical studies of the theory of mental self-government in classroom as well as in other settings, some interesting results have emerged (Sternberg, 1994; Sternberg & Grigorenko, 1993).

Measuring People's Styles

Studies by Sternberg and Grigorenko (1993) were not limited to the self-report measure illustrated above for each style. A theme we try to stress in this book is that no one measure of a construct is wholly adequate. No single test can fully assess a person's creativity, intelligence, or, relevant to our present discussion, range of styles.

In a first additional measure beyond the self-report questionnaires, rather than ask students simply to characterize themselves in general, we ask them what they do or would do in specific situations. Here are a couple of examples of the kinds of questions we use.

1. When I am studying literature, I prefer:
   a. to make up my own story with my own characters and plot [legislative style].
   b. to follow the teacher's advice and interpretations of authors' positions, and to use the teacher's way of analyzing literature [executive style].
   c. to evaluate the author's style, criticize the author's ideas, and evaluate characters' actions [judicial style].

The words in brackets do not appear in the actual measure. A second type of problem asks about stylistic preference beyond a school setting:

2. You are the mayor of a large northeastern city. You have a city budget this year of $1 million. Below is a list of problems currently facing your

city. Your job is to decide how you will spend the $1 million available to improve your city. Next to each problem is the projected cost to eliminate the problem entirely.

In the space, list each problem on which you will spend city money and how much money you will budget for that problem. Whether you spend money on one, some, or all problems is up to you, but be sure your plan will not exceed the $1 million available. Whether you spend all the money to solve one or a few problems or divide the money partially to solve many problems is up to you.

   a.   Drug problem ($1 million)
   b.   Roads ($250,000)
   c.   Landfill ($250,000)
   d.   Shelters for the homeless ($500,000)

Scoring was done in a way to elicit the forms of mental self-government. A monarchic person tends to spend all the available money on a single problem. A hierarchic person has a prioritized distribution for spending the money. An oligarchic person distributes the money roughly equally across problems. And an anarchic person has no system at all.

In a second additional measure we have children's teachers evaluate their styles. For example, a teacher would be given a statement like, "S/he likes to evaluate her/his own opinions and those of others," and would characterize each of the students in her class on a 1 to 9 scale. Although we have not used this measure in employer-employee situations, it would apply equally well.

In a third additional measure we ask teachers to evaluate their own teaching styles. For example, they might be given a statement like, "I agree with people who call for more, harsher discipline, and a return to the 'good old ways.'" This statement measures the conservative style.

What have Sternberg and Grigorenko found, using measures such as these?

RELATION OF STYLES TO INTELLIGENCE
Although we believe styles contribute to creativity, we believe them to be relatively independent of intelligence. Data collected with Marie Martin confirm this hypothesis. In these data none of the styles correlated significantly with IQ, grade point average, or SAT verbal score. There were three

significant correlations with SAT math score (the judicial, global, and liberal styles all correlating positively). Thus styles do not appear to be strongly related to intelligence.

TEACHER STYLES

One of the motivations for this work was Sternberg's view that teachers vary in styles, and that what happens to children in the classroom very much depends on teachers' styles. In a study looking at eighty-five teachers in four different schools (an urban public school, a Catholic parochial school, a traditional private school, and a very progressive private school), we found that teachers do differ in styles, and that there are certain trends.

One trend was across grades taught. Teachers at the lower grades tended to be more legislative and less executive than are teachers at the upper grades. There are at least two possible interpretations of this result, either or both of which may be correct. The first interpretation is that people with more legislative and fewer executive tendencies are attracted to the lower grades. The second interpretation is that in the upper grades, teachers do not have the luxury of being legislative because they are more straitjacketed in terms of what they must teach in order to prepare students for statewide and national exams. Whatever the interpretation, the results fit our own experience that teachers in the lower grades tend to be more exploratory and encouraging of creative exploration on the part of students than are teachers at the upper grades.

A second finding was with regard to teacher age. Older teachers tended to be more executive, local, and conservative than did younger teachers. The combination of these three styles is what we refer to as the "authoritarian triangle," because these three styles in combination tend to suggest a rigid and usually noncreative attitude toward life. The results thus suggest that, on average, younger teachers would be more encouraging of creativity than older ones. Again there are two possible interpretations of this result, either or both of which may be correct. The first interpretation is that as teachers become older, they grow more authoritarian. The second is that the age effect is due to a cohort effect: Teachers who grew up in the earlier part of the century are simply more authoritarian than teachers who grew up in the later part of the century. Whatever the cause, the findings suggest more tolerance and probably encouragement of creativity among the younger teachers. We cannot emphasize enough, however, that these are group trends, and for any group trend, there will be many individual exceptions.

A third trend was that science teachers tended to be more local than did teachers in other subject areas, and humanities teachers more liberal. The latter result did not surprise us, because teachers of the humanities constantly expose themselves to new and different philosophical ideas in their teaching; a liberal way of living would follow naturally. The finding regarding science teachers however, is disappointing, although consistent with our experience working with teachers in the schools. Science teachers often have the idea that learning science consists of the memorization of small and isolated bits. One of our children's science teachers once commented that, although he encourages science projects, when it comes to testing, he measures what they "really" know—namely the so-called facts. The problem with this attitude is that children are exposed to a concept of science that is quite different from what science is really about, which is in large part broad ideas. Children with a global style may be turned off to science, whereas ultimately they may have the most to contribute.

Finally we decided to look at the relation between teachers' styles and the schools in which the teachers taught. We had noticed way back that not just students and teachers but schools themselves seem to have different profiles of styles. Some school seem to be conservative, others liberal. Some seem to encourage legislative, style, others a conservative one. Some encourage group exploration (external style), others only individual work (internal style). In order to see whether teachers tend to match the styles of the schools, we had a rater characterize each of the four schools for seven of the styles on the basis of information obtained from catalogs, faculty and student handbooks, statements of goals and purposes, and curricula. For six out of seven styles, we found statistically significant matching between teachers and schools. In other words either teachers tend to gravitate toward schools that match their profile of styles, or else they tend to become like the schools they are in—or, more likely, both. People tend to try to find jobs in environments that are compatible with how they think; at the same time they become like the environments they are in. This last point is important, and will be discussed further in chapter 10. You should choose carefully the environment in which you place yourself or your child, because eventually you tend to become like that environment, stylistically and in other ways as well. If you place yourself or your child in an environment that discourages creativity, you are likely to suppress whatever creative tendencies either one of you may have. Just as "we are what we eat," so "we are where we live and work."

In a second study Sternberg and Grigorenko found some further effects of styles. This study looked at the styles children have and how these relate to teacher styles.

A first finding was that firstborn children tend to be less legislative than later-born children. Again this finding is consistent with past literature suggesting that first-born children tend to be more accepting of societal norms and mores, whereas later-born children tend to be more rebellious. The finding does not necessarily suggest that younger children will be more creative, but it does suggest that they have a style conducive to creativity. Specifically, later-born children may be more rebellious with respect to the established order for doing things in a given domain of life or work.

A second finding was that students tend to match their teachers in their profile of styles. This finding provides further evidence for the importance of role modeling and socialization, and highlights the notion that we should be careful of the environment into which we place ourselves or our children, because we become like our environments.

An issue that is sometimes raised is whether it is best for children to have teachers who match them in styles or who are different. On the one hand children might seem more compatible with teachers whose styles match theirs. On the other everyone has to learn to work with people who are not just like them. We believe that the critical variable is not so much whether styles match, but whether teachers and students alike can be flexible with regard to the differences that they encounter in other people's styles. A teacher, for example, can't match every student in styles. But the teacher can teach in a way that allows children to express their styles to maximum benefit. The key is flexibility on the part of the teacher.

This principle is true regardless of subject matter. For example, in literature, students can listen to lectures and take short-answer tests on what they read (executive tasks), but they can also write poems and short stories (legislative tasks), or write critiques of novels and plays (judicial tasks). Similarly in history children can learn the facts and dates (executive tasks) but can also imagine what they would do if they had to make major government policy decisions of the past (legislative tasks) or analyze the strengths and weaknesses of such policy decisions by major leaders (judicial tasks). In science children can learn the major facts of a discipline (executive tasks), but they can also invent theories and design experiments (legislative tasks) or evaluate the strengths and weaknesses of experiments done in the past (judicial tasks). Our point, quite simply, is that any subject matter can be taught in a way that benefits all students, regardless of their styles.

Originally a major motivator for our work in the schools was this question: Do students have an advantage if their styles match those of their teacher? Stated in another way: Do teachers tend to evaluate more positively those students who are like themselves? We evaluated the styles of twenty-eight teachers and their students, spread out over four schools. We found that in fact teachers evaluated more positively those students who matched them in styles. The matching effect could be considered unfair, because it is independent of ability or even of achievement. It merely suggests that we tend to value more highly others who are like ourselves. It also suggests that children placed in the classroom of someone with a very different pattern of styles may be unfairly disadvantaged.

We also found that teachers tended to overestimate the extent to which

---

TABLE 7.1

Thinking Styles and Instructional/Evaluational Assignments

Style Emphasized, by Type of Prompt		
Executive	*Judicial*	*Legislative*
Who said?	Compare and contrast	Create
Summarize	Analyze	Invent
Who did?	Evaluate	If you
When did?	In your judgment	Imagine
What did?	Why did?	Design
How did?	What caused?	How would?
Repeat back	What is assumed by?	Suppose
Describe	Critique	Ideally?

students matched their own styles. In other words not only do people evaluate more positively others who are like them; they also overestimate the extent to which others *are* like them. The problem is that teachers may not teach to a variety of student styles because they assume that the students are all more or less like themselves.

Teachers and parents alike can examine what sorts of styles they foster in their children by examining the kinds of prompts they use in their interactions with children. Table 7.1 shows a list of typical types of prompts used and the styles they engender. Ideally one would use a combination of prompts so as to encourage the development of all three styles simultaneously.

In conclusion, we have argued that thinking styles are a key ingredient of creativity. To buy low and sell high, you need to go against the crowd, and to go against the crowd, you need at least some of the legislative and liberal styles. You are likely to go against the crowd in more significant ways if you have a global style, and to choose better in which particular ways to go against the crowd if you have some of the judicial style. A monarchic person may be fabulously creative if he or she directs his energies toward creative work, or not very creative at all if whatever turns him or her on is an uncreative pursuit. A hierarchic person is more likely to find a balance in life among tasks that offer possibilities for creativity and other tasks that don't. An anarchic person tends to set his or her own path, but often does not have the self-discipline and organization effectively to exploit this tendency in a creative way. It is not enough just to look at abilities and knowledge; you need to look also at how people direct their abilities and knowledge.

The Role of Personality
in Creativity

Whether a person *can* buy low and sell high in the world of ideas does not fully determine whether he or she *will*. One of the main reasons that many potentially creative people (those who can) rarely or even never demonstrate their creativity (thereby not becoming those who will) is that they do not have the necessary personality traits.

Personality can be thought of as a preferred way of interacting with the environment. In the early part of the century, theorists tended to view personality as relatively stable across different kinds of situations, setting up grand theories of personality by which they tried to characterize the dimensions of personality traits along which people vary. Personality theorists took different approaches to the task. Some, like Freud (1908), sought to understand personality in developmental terms: Personality developed as a function of the resolution of (or failure to resolve) conflicts in childhood. Trait theorists such as Cattell (1971) or Eysenck (1983) concentrated more on identifying just what traits people have, from the time they are quite young to the time they are quite old. Today most theorists would agree that people have a set of more or less stable traits, at the same time that they now recognize that how these traits manifest themselves in the environment reflects an interaction between the person on the one hand and the situation on the other. In other words a person who is not usually "aggressive" can be made so by environmental circumstances that are sufficiently provocative, such as having been wronged by another on numerous occasions, the presence of high temperature, the

205

opportunity to have revenge, possession of a means by which to act aggressively (that is, by which to punish a transgressor), and so on.

Before we begin our discussion of personality, we feel obliged to make one remark that is critical of some of the work that has been done in the field of creativity. On the one hand there are investigators who have concentrated very strongly on the personality side of creativity, almost to the exclusion of the cognitive side, which we discussed in the earlier chapters (for example, Barron, 1969; MacKinnon, 1962b). For the most part these investigators acknowledge the importance of cognitive processing in creativity, but simply choose to focus on the personal side. On the other hand even more investigators have concentrated very strongly on the cognitive side and have basically ignored the personal side altogether (for example, Johnson-Laird, 1989; Langley et al., 1987; Weisberg, 1986). They seem to believe that creativity can be understood wholly as a cognitive phenomenon, without taking into account at all the personality traits of creative people. For them a complete model of creativity would specify exactly what mental processes a person uses when he or she thinks creatively.

We believe that these investigators are seriously mistaken in their exclusive preoccupation with the cognitive side of creativity. Cognitive processes may be sufficient for a person to be creative once or twice, at one stage of life or another. But they are not sufficient for a person to be creative over a lifetime, or even over any extended period of time. Buying low and selling high requires going against the crowd, and even if you have the ability to do so, over the long haul you *won't* do so unless you have the requisite personality traits. For example, consider Joel Glickman's experience in toy design (Lawson, 1994). He designed K'nex, color-coded plastic pieces that allow children to build sophisticated models. The K'nex system, which rivals Lego and is considered one of the most imaginative recent entries to the toy market, is manufactured at Glickman's own plant, and sales are expected to double in the second year of national distribution. However, he was initially turned down by major toy companies and attributes his success to his "bison" personality that can withstand a great deal of discouragement. Some of the potentially most creative people never realize their potential because they lack perseverance or other creativity-relevant personality traits: They "buy high" simply because it is easier to conform.

The wholly cognitive models, therefore, may apply to creativity in a laboratory or in a rarefied environment where people are simply left to their own devices to do as they wish without any external interference whatsoever. The only problem is that virtually no one lives in such specialized environments, and hence to realize the creative potential within us, we need the personal as well as the cognitive side of creativity.

When we speak of personality traits here, we are referring to relatively stable dispositions, yet ones that can change with environment and certainly with time. People do not have a fixed personality that is carved in stone from the time they are born. Rather, dispositions with which they may well be born interact with the environment to produce a set of more or less stable personality traits. These traits are at least partially under a person's control. In other words any of the traits that we are about to discuss can be developed if a person really sets his or her mind to it. Thus if you do not have the attributes that constitute a creative personality, you can develop them in yourself. Anyone can. What are these attributes?

Perseverance in the Face of Obstacles

Sooner or later *all* creative people encounter obstacles to the expression of their creativity. What if Paul Klee had stopped painting in 1910 when a gallery owner displaying his work wrote saying that visitors disliked it and it was unsuccessful (Ray & Myers, 1986)? The obstacles may be external, or they may even be internal ones that people generate themselves. But nothing is more certain than the fact that those who engage in creative work will eventually encounter obstacles.

The reason is that when you buy low and sell high, you go against what others are doing. And given human nature, people are not just going to relax and smile while you do it. Rather, they will try to get you to join their team, and if you don't want to, they will treat you the way they would any member of a hostile force: When you go against the crowd, the crowd turns on you.

As a mentor to many students, one of the authors makes a point of telling them that the difference between people who succeed in being creative over long time periods and those who are flashes in the pan is not in whether they encounter obstacles but in whether they persevere in the face of those obstacles. The flashes in the pan give up the first or second time the going gets tough, whereas the truly creative people forge ahead.

One of us had the good fortune to learn this lesson early. As an elementary school student, his test anxiety had resulted in low scores on intelligence tests. So in seventh grade, at age thirteen, when he had the opportunity to do a science project, he did his science project on intelligence testing. For the first time he entered the adult section of his hometown library, and to his surprise he found a book containing the Stanford-Binet Intelligence Test, a test widely used for the measurement of intelligence in children and adults.

He decided that it would be good practice to give the test to some of his classmates, one of whom was a girl in whom he had a romantic interest. Though she did extremely well on the test, the relationship didn't— and the author learned a valuable lesson: If you want to break the ice with a member of the opposite sex, giving the person an intelligence test is probably not the way to go.

The second classmate to whom he gave the test was a young man with whom he had been in the Cub Scouts. Continuing his run of bad luck, however, it turned out that the classmate had a deep-seated psychological problem: He was a fink. After the author gave the classmate the test, the fellow told his mother what had happened. Apparently finkism is inherited, because the fellow's mother then told the junior high school guidance counselor. And it appears that finkism is contagious as well, because the guidance counselor then told the head psychologist of the school system, who was not amused.

During the author's social studies class period, he was called down to the guidance office to meet with the psychologist. The psychologist bawled him out, ending with the admonition that if he ever brought the book into school again, the psychologist would personally burn it.

This—not the best way to launch a career in psychology—is what we mean by an obstacle. The psychologist was definitely not interested in the author's continuing his line of inquiry into intelligence testing and was making a powerful statement to this effect. (He did suggest that if the author was so interested in intelligence, he could study it in rats. To this day the author wonders if the psychologist was offering himself as a subject!) The prospects were bleak, and they are of the kind that often discourage people from pursuing one interest that really excites them and push them to another that excites them less. But the author made a decision: If the psychologist was making such a big deal about the whole thing, it must be precisely because it *was* so interesting. (If it had been of no consequence, the psychologist would not have bothered to come to the school and spend fifty minutes bawling out a thirteen-year-old.) So the author decided to continue to study intelligence, but he went underground and studied it in secret. Only his parents knew (and supported him too). As we said, the question is not whether you are going to encounter obstacles—it's whether you have the fortitude to overcome them.

In business Solomon Price's ability to overcome obstacles earned him the title "father of the wholesale-club industry" (Landrum, 1993). In Fed-Mart, his early business venture, Price fought outdated laws that increased the cost of products to the end consumer. In 1975, when Fed-Mart had become a successful mass-merchandising chain, Price sold it and stayed on in the company. However, he was fired less than a year later and began to look for new opportunities. Price noticed that small retailers were not buying wholesale supplies in the most efficient, cost-effective way. He had the idea that if he could concentrate on selling a limited number of items and eliminate as many cost factors as possible (like credit cards), he might be able to give small retailers quality products at a bargain price. After his first year Price was operating in the red, but he didn't give up. Rather, he opened his Price Club to a broader audience such as government groups and the self-employed. Price also had the innovative idea to make shoppers pay an annual fee to shop at the Price Club. Eventually, through his perseverance, Price's cut-rate selling philosophy, which traded amenities for cost reduction, gained the interest of the general public.

Other examples and statements regarding the importance of perseverance in creative work are shown in box 8.1.

Our view regarding the key importance of persevering in the face of obstacles has several implications. It is important, we believe, to recognize these implications because they will confront you, one way or another, in your own attempts to be creative.

A first implication is that both the very best and the very worst work is likely to be met with rejection. In any field the worst ideas are rejected because they are quite simply bad. But the best ideas are often rejected, too, not because they aren't good per se, but because they go against the crowd. Wendell Garner, a distinguished professor at Yale, once commented that his most creative papers were often turned down by several journals before they found a home.

BOX 8.1

Perseverance

Vincent van Gogh, in a letter, wrote the following description of his work: "When I have a model who is quiet and steady and with whom I am acquainted, then I draw repeatedly till there is one drawing that is different from the rest, which does not look like an ordinary study, but more typical and with more feeling. . . . The first attempts are absolutely unbearable. . . . If you see something worthwhile in what I am doing, it is not by accident but because of real intention and purpose" (quoted in Ghiselin, 1985, pp. 46–47).

Benoit Mandelbrot spoke of the need for perseverance in an interview (Lubart, personal communication, 1990). His accomplishments with fractals "took an incredible amount of time." For example, his landmark paper on multifractals took *six years* to publish. Similarly, when constructing the famous Mandelbrot set, he had to go through literally thousands of drawings.

In a survey of 710 inventors (Rossman, 1931), perseverance was the most frequently mentioned characteristic needed for success. In line with this result, Nathaniel Wyeth, the inventor of the plastic soda bottle, speaks of how he was able to utilize his initial failures and achieve multiple insights because he persevered: "You have to have a tremendous amount of patience and not give up easily. Even when a problem has been bugging me for weeks or months, I would go to work every morning with a good, clean slate and feel that I was starting fresh—using my failures and the knowledge of things that wouldn't work, as a springboard to new approaches. If I hadn't used those mistakes as stepping stones, I would never have invented anything. I would have said, 'Well, if it doesn't work the first time, forget it'" (quoted in Brown, 1988).

Philip Roth describes his perseverance when beginning a book: "I type out beginnings and they're awful, more of an unconscious parody of my previous book than the breakaway from it that I want. . . .

I often have to write a hundred pages or more before there's a paragraph that's alive. Okay, I say to myself, that's your beginning, start there. . . . I'll go over the first six months of work and underline in red a paragraph, a sentence, sometimes no more than a phrase, that has some life in it, and then I'll type all these out on one page . . . that's the start of page one" (quoted in Plimpton, 1986, p. 271).

Rejection also confronted Randall Skalsky as he worked on his now accepted and acclaimed interpretation of the frieze on the ancient Roman vase known as the Portland Vase (Honan, 1992). Through a series of insights into the symbolic meaning of different portions of the frieze and connections to Roman poetry, Skalsky suggested that the real meaning of the frieze, which has been debated for centuries, is that a love match is not always of heaven's making and may lead to a tragic end. Initially Skalsky met with rejection from prestigious members of the scholarly community and numerous journals. For example, the editor of *Archaeology* said that Skalsky's paper had "no merit whatsoever," and an expert on antiquities at the British Museum said that his interpretation "did not even pass the first hurdle." But Skalsky did not back off, and his work was eventually published. Now it is predicted that Skalsky's work will "completely reorient the study of Roman glass" by viewing Roman art as visual poetry.

When you have an idea that goes against established ways of seeing things, often the reaction of those who review these ideas is that yours just can't be right. If you ever need to apply for a grant to fund some kind of project, you will see what we mean. The very best grant proposals are often turned down because the evaluators just can't see outside the existing paradigms that are used to study or work on whatever problem the grant proposal addresses. Sometimes people find themselves toning down the proposals and trying to make them sound less controversial, just so that they can get the funding to do what they really want.

A second implication of our view is that, over time, a lot of creative people will disappear into the woodwork for good, never to do anything creative again. Why? Because when they can't take the heat, they get out of the kitchen. Often the rewards for creative work are rather minimal, at least in the short term. In educational research and development, for example, you don't get paid more if you have really creative ideas. In fact, if you go against existing ways of seeing things and can't get your grant proposals funded, you may find yourself out of a job. The short-term payoffs are for going with the crowd; this is especially so if you are young and if to advance you need to be in the good graces of whoever is managing the crowd. As a result there is a terrific temptation just to follow what everyone else is doing. So people sometimes do something creative, get burned, and then decide to "play the game." Others may try the creative route two or three times before they finally decide that it just isn't worth the hassle. Sooner or later the large majority of people simply decide that it isn't worth the grief to go their own way.

Sometimes the difficulty you face is more fundamental than the obstacles people put in your way. Rather, the difficulty lies in the fact that the problem is a really tough one to solve. Many of us are familiar with how many failures Edison had before he found that tungsten worked well as a filament for an electric light bulb. And anyone who has worked in science knows that in order to get an experiment to work, you often have to do seemingly countless "pilot experiments" to refine your techniques and make them viable. Ultimately there is no substitute for sheer perseverance in creative work. Kim (1990) notes that failures are to be expected in creative work; failures point out flaws or gaps in understanding. Failures help people to "prune" their problem-search tree. In fact Kim suggests a "principle of accelerated failure: When the cost of failure is low, fail quickly and often." Obviously a person needs perseverance to follow this principle—to keep trying after repeated failures, and to learn from those failures.

Up to now we have talked about external obstacles, and many of the obstacles people face are in fact external. You can see such obstacles almost any day just by reading the newspaper. Anytime a politician proposes doing something in a new way, opposition rises immediately from those who "know" that things can never change. In education it is extremely difficult to bring about change, because so many people feel that the way things have always been is the way that they must be. Otherwise, why would they have been the way they are? But not all obstacles are external: Sometimes they come from within oneself.

Internal obstacles can be of several kinds. One kind is the mental block, which relates to our chapter on the role of intelligence. You can get stuck in one way of seeing a problem. By approaching the problem several times, however, you increase your odds of finding a new, useful insight. Another internal obstacle is internal rigidity. You may find yourself not only uncomfortable questioning old ways (the conservative style referred to in the previous chapter), but actually unable to get yourself to defy authority. You have always been taught to accept that things are done in a certain way, or that they are viewed in a certain way, and you cannot break out of the mold yourself. So you become rigid in your adherence to a way of thinking, and when you are on the verge of seeing things in another way, you stop thinking. Before blaming external obstacles, therefore, you need to ask yourself whether there are obstacles in yourself that are proving to be barriers to creative expression.

Willingness to Take Sensible Risks

Overcoming obstacles often requires a second personality characteristic—namely the willingness to take sensible risks. In choosing to study intelligence secretly, for example, one of the authors risked the wrath of the school psychologist had the man found out what the author was doing. Often you may be told that you would be well advised not to follow a certain path that might bring you into conflict with an entrenched establishment.

As we discussed in chapter 3, we socialize our young in a way that discourages sensible risk taking. But to buy low and sell high, you virtually always have to take a risk. In the market an investor who buys an unpopular stock risks losing his or her shirt. In the world of ideas, when you present an idea that goes against the crowd, you, too, are risking your "shirt." But in order to do something really creative, and something that makes a difference to the world, you have to take that risk. In 1959 Kazuo Inamori, a twenty-seven-year-old ceramics engineer, quit his job and began to start his own company. He obtained forty thousand dollars from private investors and began one of Japan's first companies funded by venture capital. Inamori convinced Texas Instruments to let his company produce "ceramic microchip packages" for the Apollo project in 1967. Inamori's company, Kyocera Corporation, met the initial challenge and now makes diverse products such as ceramic circuitry for jet control systems and "bioceramic bones [that] the body won't reject" (Watanabe, 1990b, p. D-1).

Just as nobody ever got rich or even well off by placing their money in low-interest passbook bank savings accounts, so has no one ever gotten rich with ideas by always going for the safest options. One of the authors once found himself in a conversation with a well-known but not particularly distinguished psychologist. This psychologist bragged to the author that in her entire career she had never had an article turned down or a grant proposal rejected. Although the author was supposed to be impressed, he wasn't. If you have never had any of your ideas turned down—whether by a boss, a granting agency, a journal or magazine, a company, or whatever—then the one thing you can be sure of is that you are not taking risks. People who play a very safe game may feel content that they never receive rejections. But you can be quite certain that they are not the people who are making the most creative contributions.

In chapter 3 we also discussed different kinds of risks, the effect of problem framing, and risk aversion. Now we will expand on the issue of risk taking by describing research that links creative performance with risk taking. John Glover provided some early evidence on the topic; in one study (Glover, 1977), eighty-four undergraduates completed the Torrance Tests of Creativity (paper-and-pencil tests involving divergent thinking) and a Choice Dilemma Questionnaire (CDQ) that measures risk-taking tendencies by asking people how they would respond to hypothetical situations that involve financial, physical, or mental risk taking in work or daily life.

All the participants in his study completed the tests both at the start (pretest) and end (posttest) of the experiment. However, one group of participants, those in a "critical conditions" format, experienced a group discussion between the pre- and posttest of the risks involved in the Choice Dilemma scenarios. Glover found from this study that a group discussion of the risks in a situation led the individuals to be more willing to take risks. This is called a "risky-shift" effect. Group discussions of a topic, in general, have been found to lead people to become more extreme in their own opinion on an issue but not necessarily to change their basic view.

As evidence that the risky shift occurred for the people who engaged in a discussion of the CDQ scenarios, these participants' posttest CDQ scores showed greater risk taking compared with pretest levels. The people who did not discuss the scenarios showed no change from pretest to posttest.

The risky-shift people also showed significant increases in the originality and flexibility of their responses on the creativity posttests. In other words the discussion procedure experimentally induced a risk-taking state of mind, which led to increased creativity.

In a later study Eisenman (1987) had two hundred men complete tests including a creative attitude questionnaire and a divergent-thinking test (generating unusual uses for bricks). The participants also chose between entering a high-risk, high-payoff contest or a low-risk, low-payoff contest. The main finding was that choice in the contest (high risk or low risk) correlated positively ($r = .34$) with the originality of responses on the divergent-thinking test and on the creative attitude questionnaire.

Building on this early work, we conducted our own study of risk taking and creativity (Lubart & Sternberg, in press). We began by thinking about the "rules" of risk taking in the financial world. Investment in a long-standing company with a record of slow growth involves less risk than investment in a new company that promises fast growth. The new company is unproven, and although the opportunity for larger profits exists, there is also increased uncertainty that profits will materialize.

Analogous to the financial world, most endeavors offer more and less risky alternatives. For creative work the risks tend to be intellectual ones (which carry social and monetary ramifications). An artist, for example, may choose among several projects. Within each project there may be further options for topics, topic development, materials, and style. Typically the choices at each step fall into two risk-payoff options. One option can be labeled "low risk, low payoff," because a high probability of success is usually associated with following a well-worn path. The other option, "high risk, high payoff," offers a chance for great success but the path is treacherous and less traveled.

In our study we examined these risk-payoff options using multiple measures of risk taking and creative performance in drawing and writing. Forty-four adults from the New Haven, Connecticut, area completed creativity tasks, risk-taking measures, and other tests. The creativity measures for drawing and writing involved expanding a title into an actual product (as described in chapter 2). We measured risk taking in three ways: contests, hypothetical scenarios, and a self-report questionnaire.

Two contests provided behavioral measures of risk taking. People were given the opportunity to enter their artwork in one contest and their short story in another. Each contest established two "pools" of work from which the best entries would be selected. One pool was described as high risk and high payoff. In this pool there was one winner of twenty-five dollars. The other pool involved lower risk and lower payoff, with five winners of ten dollars each. The instructions allowed subjects to enter one pool for the drawing contest and a different pool for the writing contest. Based on our judges' ratings, prizes were awarded at the conclusion of the study.

The hypothetical scenarios measured risk-taking propensity in a very different way. Three CDQs assessed risk taking in the artwork, writing, and general life domains. The questionnaires were based on Kogan and Wallach's (1964) work.

Each questionnaire contained twelve hypothetical situations in which people were asked to imagine themselves. Each scenario presented a choice between two courses of action: (a) a high-risk, potentially high-payoff alternative, and (b) a low-risk, low-payoff alternative. People selected the minimum odds for success they would require before pursuing the high-risk option. A sample scenario from the art-domain questionnaire follows:

> You are a potter, making a large vase to be displayed at a craft show. You hope to receive recognition in the pottery guild's magazine which will be doing a feature story on the show. You have two ideas for the vase. Idea A would use a potter's wheel to form a vase with smooth contours that are pleasing to look at. You know that several other potters at the show use the same method, but you feel confident that your vase will receive some recognition for technical skill. Idea B would use a hand-coil method in which you roll clay into strips and piece the strips together. This method yields an unusual, primitive vase. The magazine editors may feature your coil vase because of its uniqueness or they may not even mention it because it could be seen as too far out of the mainstream. Listed below are several probabilities or odds that the coil vase (idea B) will turn out successfully. Please check the lowest probability that you would consider acceptable to make it worthwhile to pursue the coil vase.

The possible odds for success were: 1 in 10, 3 in 10, 5 in 10, 7 in 10, or 9 in 10. A subject could also refuse the risky alternative "no matter what the possibilities" and then would receive a score of 10 out of 10 for that scenario.

Risk taking was further assessed with a biographical questionnaire. People used a seven-point scale to describe their tendencies toward risk in drawing and writing for the overall task, topic selection, topic development, and materials and style used. People were also asked if they would describe themselves as high or low risk takers in the drawing and writing domains.

A separate group of fifteen New Haven subjects judged the creativity of the drawing and writing work with good interrater reliability (.81 for drawing and .75 for writing on a scale of 0 = low and 1 = high).

In agreement with previous research, our findings showed that people were relatively risk avoidant. For example, in the drawing contest, 32 of the subjects chose the low-risk, low-payoff option, in contrast to twelve who chose the high-risk, high-payoff alternative. In the writing contest twenty-nine subjects selected the low risk and fifteen the high. In both cases, the bias toward lower risk was significant.

The main question of interest in our study, however, was whether higher levels of risk taking were associated with higher levels of creative performance. For the drawing contest, people choosing the high-risk, high-payoff option showed an average creativity score of 4.21 (on a seven-point scale), whereas people choosing the low-risk, low-payoff option showed an average score of 3.90. When creativity ratings were obtained from three additional judges with artistic training, the basic results were accentuated: The high-risk group received an average creativity score of 4.36 and the low-risk group's mean score was 2.86. Thus more creative people leaned toward taking more risks.

The scenario-based measures of risk taking also supported a connection between risk taking and creativity. Risk taking on the artwork scenarios correlated significantly with creativity in drawing (correlation = .39). An analysis of the artwork, writing, and general life scenario scores with regard to creative performance on the drawing task tested the extent to which the relationship between creativity in drawing and risk is domain-specific. In other words, does creative artwork depend on how risk-taking someone is in general or just when the person is engaged in artwork? We found support for domain-specificity. Creativity in drawing is related to risk taking in the artwork domain but not especially related to risk taking in writing or general life situations. This finding is consistent with other research on risk taking in various domains. For example, the extent to which a person takes risks with money is not very predictive of the risks taken in physical situations (sports, sex) or in social situations (Jackson, Hourany, & Vidmar, 1972).

In contrast to the scenarios and behavioral contest measures of risk, self-report items showed little relationship to creative performance. Only one item that assessed "overall" risk taking in drawing related to creative performance (correlation = .34).

In summary we found some support for the hypothesized link between risk taking and creative performance in the drawing domain. The artwork scenario measure of risk taking showed this relationship most clearly. In the writing domain no significant results were obtained. However, examination of the writings produced by people who scored in the top 20 percent and bottom 20 percent on the writing scenario risk-taking measure suggested an interesting trend: We believed the stories of the high risk takers to be more unconventional than those of the low risk takers. We had three additional peer judges rate unconventionality and found a significant difference in the ratings for high risk takers (mean = 4.00) versus low risk takers (mean = 3.11). As mentioned earlier, an investigation of the stories suggested that the unconventional stories did not receive high creativity ratings, on average, because of the controversial issues with which they dealt.

Willingness to Grow

Hard as it may be to have even that first creative success, many people eventually pull it off. After a fair amount of effort (or, if they are lucky, not so much effort), a person receives recognition for something creative he or she has done. It might be anything—an idea at work, a book, an invention, a business plan, or whatever. If you have that success, the rewards may well finally come pouring in.

One of the questions we have sometimes asked ourselves is why there are so many "one-idea" people, who have that first creative success but then never do anything really creative again. For example, the majority of Ph.D.s never do another major piece of scholarly work after their dissertations. Many companies come and go because after their first idea for an innovative product, they can't keep up with changing tastes in the market and come up with more different and innovative ideas. Other companies come up with an innovative idea, but the trick is to update it.

For example, during World War II the Breyer Molding Company made industrial plastic parts for the military. At the end of the war the company was able to capitalize on a chance event because, in part, it was willing to grow into new areas. What happened was that the Master Crafter Clock Company ordered plastic parts, including plastic horses, to go on its clocks. When, instead of paying for the order, the clock company told Breyer to keep the horse molds, Breyer turned a sour deal into an opportunity. Breyer went to the F. W. Woolworth Company and began to sell plastic horses. Over time Breyer continued to develop new models of horses, capturing in plastic famous horses, different breeds, and horses that starred in movies or featured in stories. Today Breyer is known for its hand-painted model horses, which are considered collectibles and sell about a million each year. To go with the horses, the company also makes a line of accessories and publishes a magazine for collectors. Thus the company has adapted and grown in new directions as the world and market needs have changed.

Another example of a company that has not fallen into the "one-idea" trap is CRM, which owns Nordic Track. The original product (produced before CRM bought the company), the Nordic Track cross-country skier, was enormously successful. Indeed, from a single model, the company spun off a number of alternative models varying in price, quality, and features. But the market for cross-country skiers almost certainly has a limit. So over time the company developed other products, such as a rowing machine, a bicycle, and so on. In developing these products, the company tried to maintain the same quality that had characterized the earlier cross-country ski machine. Clearly a company does not have to get locked into a single successful idea.

Given what would seem to be the obvious advantages of branching out, why would anyone stay with just a single idea or product? Oddly enough, there are various pressures that drive people to stay with a single creative idea or product, rather than to expand beyond it.

First, there is fear of failure. A person who has had some success and has acquired a reputation now wants to retain that reputation. But what if he or she was just lucky? Or what if the next idea just simply isn't as good as the last one? The thought of a failure following a success is enough to scare almost anyone. The successful person imagines the embarrassment of a flop, and *voilà!* may find him- or herself staying with that first idea.

Second, there is actually good statistical reason to be worried about failure following success. Statisticians refer to an effect called "statistical regression toward the mean." Roughly speaking, when a case occurs (such as your highly creative idea) that departs substantially from the mean of a distribution of observations (the average quality of your ideas), subsequent cases (your next ideas) are likely, by chance alone, to be closer to the mean of the distribution than was the first observation.

What does regression to the mean signify in practice? Some examples may help clarify the concept. Consider three of them.

One example is what we call the restaurant effect. Did you ever go to a restaurant for the first time, find the food to be really outstanding, and then decide to revisit the restaurant? People often find that the food is not as good the second time. They then find themselves wondering whether the chef has become complacent or the food has gone downhill. In fact, the successive visits provide an example of regression toward the mean. If the restaurant was really outstanding the first time, chances are it won't be as good the next. Similarly, if the restaurant was extremely bad the first time, chances are that it would be better (closer to the mean) the second time, if you were to go back.

Similarly baseball and football players who have outstanding first years in the major leagues almost never quite repeat their great performance the second year, although they may continue to play quite well. And as a third example, parents with very high IQs tend to have children with somewhat lower IQs, whereas parents with very low IQs tend to have children with somewhat higher IQs. All these are examples of statistical regression effects—of movement toward an average level of performance.

The implication for creative work is rather straightforward. For statistical reasons alone, if you have one exceptionally successful creative idea, it is quite likely that your next will not meet with quite as much success. The problem is, though, that you can't succeed if you don't try! And, moreover, not every idea has to be your best one—which leads us to a third internal factor that keeps people back.

Third, some creative people are or become perfectionistic and, as a result, need to get an idea just right before they let go of it. On the one hand it can be counterproductive to let ideas go too soon, as discussed below. On the other holding on to an idea and trying harder and harder to perfect it may actually result in your losing credit for it. For example, Charles Darwin held on to his idea about the theory of evolution for so long that someone else, Alfred Wallace, eventually formulated the same idea. In other cases you may lose credit altogether, or your career may go so slowly that you never even are given the opportunity to have other creative ideas. For example, a young university professor who publishes only one "perfect" article may lose his or her job after a few years, resulting in the loss of opportunity to follow up on further ideas, at least at that institution.

Fourth, people who have a creative idea that goes against the established ways of doing things sometimes then become part of a new establishment themselves. The problem is that once you have a creative idea and that idea is accepted, you start to receive various kinds of rewards for it. You may get a patent, publications, money, speaking tours, appearances on radio or television, write-ups in newspapers, and so on. Also you may be able to keep producing minor spin-offs of your original idea, which keep bringing you some rewards. Eventually the person who once bought low acquires a vested interest in staying just where he or she is. The person becomes corrupted by success, becomes part of the establishment, and stops functioning creatively. He or she never sells high!

Fifth, others may interfere with your creativity more effectively than you ever could yourself. Once people slot you, often it pains them to see you change. We see this phenomenon in interpersonal relationships: People view themselves as forming a relationship with a particular person who is a particular way. When one person changes, even if it is in the direction of growth, it is often upsetting to partners who are used to their partner's being a certain way. Similarly people are often threatened by change in the relationship as a whole—again, even in the direction of growth. The result is that the relationship may never evolve in creative ways because of pressure from one or both partners for things to stay the way they are.

In the world of work it is often quite difficult to establish yourself in a new endeavor once you have become well known in another. A good example is acting, where actors can easily become stereotyped and unable to find roles that do not fit the stereotype—not necessarily because they could not play other roles, but rather because people have just become so used to seeing them in one kind of role that they can't find the flexibility to see the actors in another.

One of the most extreme examples of this typecasting was George Reeves, an actor who played Superman in the 1950s television series by the same name. On the one hand Reeves was extremely successful in the role. On the other hand after the series ended, Reeves had enormous difficulty finding other acting jobs. He was told that he was so typecast as Superman that he just wouldn't fit any other role. In despair he eventually committed suicide. Although not everyone ends up in such an extreme position, the problem is by no means unique: Once people perceive you in certain working roles, it is often hard to get them to perceive you any other way.

As another example Bill Estes, a world-renowned psychologist on the topic of learning, described how typecasting occurred in his own work. In a lecture on perception, an area that differed from the one in which he had established his reputation, Estes began with an unusual prologue: He said that he wanted the audience to know that the work he was about to describe had been funded by himself. Although he had applied for grant funding to do the work, he had been turned down. How could a granting agency turn down such a famous psychologist in his most productive years, particularly when the research he proposed was of excellent quality?

Estes told the audience that with the rejection had come a summary of the critiques of his proposal, basically saying that the agency would be happy to fund him to continue his work on learning but that it didn't really know if Estes could conduct research in perception. And without such a track record on his part, the agency didn't want to take the risk of funding him. As soon as Estes wanted to move on to a new field, therefore, people were right there to try to stop him. Ironically, then, the very people who presumably want you to propose creative research (funding agencies) often don't want to fund you if you want to do something really creative. Estes funded the work himself, was very successful with it, and later gained renown in the field of perception as well as that of memory. But it wasn't easy.

One of the authors had a similar experience in his own career. Some time ago he decided that he would like to expand his research enterprise beyond the study of intelligence. He had some ideas about how to study love, and so started a research program on the nature of love. Naively he thought that people would be impressed that he was expanding his work and that he was not locked into the study of just a single phenomenon. More typical reactions were ones like: "I guess he's running out of ideas about intelligence." "Sounds like he's getting a little soft in the head." "Looks like he's having personal problems." And the best was: "Obviously he wants to be another Dr. Ruth!"

The work ended up being rather successful, leading to several books and even an article in the top theory journal in psychology, which had not, to our knowledge, ever previously published an article on love. But it was an uphill battle and, to a large extent, still is. It's not easy to move on, but if you want to stay creative throughout your life and not be just a one-idea person, you have to be willing to grow, even if there are strong internal and external pressures to stay where you are.

Tolerance of Ambiguity

We discussed above the danger of perfectionism—of holding on to work until the opportunity is lost to have the maximum impact for your creative contribution. At the other side of the continuum is the person who is in too much of a rush to come up with his or her creative idea. Sometimes the problem is impulsiveness: The person just finds it hard to hold back. More often, we would argue, the desire to rush out with the contribution stems from a different psychological basis: an inability or unwillingness to tolerate ambiguity.

Tolerance of ambiguity refers to the capacity to withstand the uncertainty and chaos that result when a problem is not clearly defined or when it is unclear how the pieces of the solution are going to come together. When you do creative work, groping along in unclear situations is commonplace. You can go through long periods of time in which you are trying to get the idea but it just doesn't quite emerge, or emerge the way you would like it to. For example, if you are trying to get an idea for a new business product, you may have a sense of what consumers want but not quite have it right—and know that you don't. If you are trying to write a novel, you may have the novel sketched out but find that there are gaps in the plot that you just can't fill. If you are trying to draw something, you may find that there are parts of it that you just can't visualize clearly. And if you are doing scientific work, you may find that you can't quite design an experiment the way you would like to, or that you cannot quite make sense of the data you collected in an experiment. Even relationships, when they are in transition, are ambiguous.

Specific examples of tolerance of ambiguity can be found in the work of many creative people. In regard to his novels *Night Rider* and *At Heaven's Gate* Robert Penn Warren says, "What I want to emphasize is the fact that I was fumbling rather than working according to plan and convictions already arrived at" (quoted in Plimpton, 1989, p. 8). Similarly William Maxwell, a writer and fiction editor, describes writing a novel: "The thing creeps along slowly, like a mole in the dark" (quoted in Plimpton, 1986, p. 44).

In the eighteenth century Antoine Lavoisier, a founder of organic chemistry and biochemistry, had very imprecise measuring tools. As a result he worked with "messy," ambiguous data and had to decide which observations were meaningful and which were not. According to a historian of science (Holmes, 1985), Lavoisier "lived with incoherence" for long periods. For example, in his work on oxidation and combustion, he was forced to live for two years with contradictory characterizations of air as either a single changeable substance or a composite of several basic substances.

Ambiguity is uncomfortable and anxiety provoking. As a result people strive to resolve it. Moreover, the pressure for resolving ambiguity is often not completely internal. Often your employer or your partner in a relationship puts as much or more pressure on you as you do on yourself. The employer may need to get the new product out. The spouse may be uncomfortable not knowing how you really feel about him or her. The publisher may want the novel tomorrow and not next year. From all sides, therefore, you may be experiencing pressure to get the damn thing— whatever it may be—over with.

The problem is that, to optimize your creative potential, you (and others) need to be able to tolerate the discomfort of an ambiguous situation long enough so that what you produce is the best or close to the best of which you are capable. Any number of products have come onto the market—cars, books, pens, or whatever—that just weren't quite ready. If the company had waited just a bit longer, it might have gotten the product right. Sometimes in business situations a competitor steps in and does get it right. The result is that what could have been a stunning success becomes a modest one, or even a failure.

A notable example of a situation in which what appears to have been an unwillingness to tolerate ambiguity may have resulted in a costly loss of credit is described in *The Double Helix*, by James D. Watson (1968). A number of different teams were hot on the trail of the discovery of the structure of DNA. Several of them were close, but none had it quite right. According to Watson and Crick, the first to publish an article on the helical structure of DNA was not they themselves but rather Linus Pauling. When Watson and Crick first saw Pauling's article, their initial reaction was one of disappointment that someone had beaten them to the punch. But as they studied the published structure carefully, they realized that it couldn't be quite right. On the other hand the helical idea seemed quite promising. Eventually Watson and Crick were able to bootstrap on Pauling's idea and to come up with the idea of the double helix.

If Pauling had tolerated ambiguity just a little longer, he might have been the first to discover the correct structure of DNA. In a later reflection on the discovery of DNA, Pauling describes the ambiguous X-ray diffraction photographs of nucleic acids that were available to him. The evidence could be interpreted to support a two- or three-stranded helix. Pauling writes, "I am now astonished that I began work on the triple helix structure, rather than on the double helix. . . . The triple-chain structure apparently appealed to me, possibly because the assumption of a three-fold axis simplified the search for an acceptable structure" (Pauling, 1980, p. 152).

Openness to Experience

Why is it that some people always seem to come up with new ideas and others never do? As you have probably gathered, the reasons are many and varied. But certainly one of them is the difference we observe in people's openness to experience. Some people seem always to be sticking out their antennae in every direction: They seek new experiences; they ask questions; they wonder about the world. Other people close themselves off and thereby deny themselves the opportunity to be creative. Carl Rogers, a psychologist who helped found the humanistic movement in psychotherapy (1976), saw openness as one of the key aspects of creativity and contrasted relatively open individuals with those who were psychologically defensive— protecting themselves from potentially disruptive new experiences.

According to Costa and McCrae (1985), open individuals are people who are curious about both their inner selves and the world in which they

live, and willing to experience things that others close off. Costa and Mc-
Crae distinguish among six kinds of openness. First, openness to fantasy
refers to people's willingness to explore their inner mental worlds and let
their minds wander. Second, openness to aesthetics refers to people's willingness to appreciate and value a variety of kinds of artistic expression.
Third, openness to feelings refers to people's willingness to accept their
own emotions, both positive and negative. Fourth, openness to actions
refers to people's willingness to try new activities. Fifth, openness to ideas
refers to people's intellectual curiosity and willingness to try on new ideas
for size. Finally, openness to values refers to people's willingness and readiness to reexamine the fundamental values on which they base their lives.

Many creative people have gained a wide array of experiences because
they were open-minded and later drew on these experiences for inspiration. For example, Marc Davis, an animator for Walt Disney Studios who
has worked on *Snow White, 101 Dalmatians*, and other productions, has
commented on how his experiences living in the Deep South—watching
the rides of the Ku Klux Klan, seeing snakes and alligators in Florida—
and later experiences in New Guinea, have shaped his work. "My creativity . . . comes out of that personal experience. I'm not afraid to go places,
I'm not afraid to meet people, and I think this is a very important thing"
(Lubart, personal communication, 1990). Being alert to the world around
you, and asking how it can inform your creative world, can be one of the
best ways to get creative inspiration. Box 8.2 describes research that links
aspects of creativity with openness to experience.

Belief in Yourself and the Courage of Your Convictions

The last of the personality attributes we discuss—belief in yourself and
the courage of your convictions—is one that comes in two parts, each
complementing the other. Stanford Ovshinsky, an inventor who demonstrated the usefulness of amorphous semiconductor material, describes
how he needs these very personality attributes for his creative work:

> You must not be afraid of being alone. A lot of people may have good
> ideas and see different pathways and never have the courage to go
> against the crowd. Maybe they can't fight in defense of something that

---

BOX 8.2

Research on Openness to Experience

McCrae (1987) conducted an investigation as part of the Baltimore Longitudinal Study of Aging. A total of 268 men (average age, 48.4 years) completed tests of thinking skills. These tests required participants to generate multiple ideas, associations, or outcomes when presented with a starting idea or question. At a later time the participants completed personality measures, which included questions about openness to experience. In addition peers and spouses gave personality ratings for the participants.

The divergent-thinking score correlated significantly with self-reported openness ($r = .39$), peer-rated openness ($r = .40$), and spouse-rated openness ($r = .29$). When educational background, age, and vocabulary knowledge were statistically held constant, openness was still related to divergent-thinking performance.

In another study Schaeffer, Diggins, and Millman (1976) had 106 college students describe their creative activities and complete personality scales. The openness measure assessed aesthetic sensitivity, unusual perceptions, openness to theoretical ideas, use of fantasy information, and openness to unconventional views of reality. Creative activities in the domains of art and writing correlated significantly with the openness scale for both men ($r = .51$) and women ($r = .67$).

Finally Uhes and Shaver (1970) examined openness from another angle. They gave 316 high school students the Rokeach Dogmatism Scale and a divergent-thinking test to measure creativity. Dogmatism, which can be considered an opposite trait to openness, correlated negatively ($r = -.29$)—as expected—with the originality of the students' responses on the divergent-thinking test.

---

they believe in or persevere against great odds. A lot of people don't want to do that. Why should they go through that? I can't speak for other inventors, but I know that what has been important for me has been the ability to stand on my own and not cave in because other people don't agree with me. (Quoted in Brown, 1988, p. 164)

In some of the interviews that we conducted, the same basic personality traits also came up: Mike Thaler, author of children's riddle books, spoke of "believing in himself" and trusting his own judgment over that of others (Lubart, personal communication, 1990): If "you care what everyone else thinks . . . you're not going to create anything." Anne Hamburger, founder of En Garde Arts Theater Company, spoke of her "tenaciousness"—she doesn't take no for an answer (Lubart, personal communication, 1990).

And Donald MacKinnon (1970), who has conducted research on creativity for many years, describes personal courage—"courage of the mind and spirit" (p. 32)—as the core of a creative person. This courage includes the strength to stand aside from the crowd and to be in conflict with it as necessary.

Betty Emerick, who founded the Fair Street Nursery School in Kingston, New York, in 1950, is an example of someone who had the personal courage to pursue an idea that became her lifework. "Emerick recalled that . . . people thought the idea of a nursery school would never fly in this community where most mothers were full-time homemakers. 'They didn't believe that anyone would want to send their children to school so young, but they were wrong' and the idea caught [on] rapidly" (Harding, 1994, p. 3). Her school, one of the earliest cooperative nursery schools (involving parents in the classroom), became a model for numerous others. According to Emerick she pursued her idea because she loves children, had a personal motivation to be a teacher, and strongly believes that "learning is and should be fun."

When you are buying low and selling high, you are bound to encounter some naysayers and have some failures in getting your ideas accepted. New ideas are often challenged simply because they threaten the status quo. And, just by the luck of the draw, sometimes your failures will be strung out in a rapid succession of acts without intermission. When you get such a string of failures, often accompanied by damning criticism of your work, it is hard not to get discouraged. But all creative people become discouraged at times, even if they have skins as thick as coconut shells.

In our own cases we have both experienced these strings of failures in getting our ideas accepted. There have been times when we thought about giving up—finding another area of research or even another occupation. Why keep going on in a field where people seem to love to dish out gratuitous criticism, and to make it as personally offensive as possible? Perhaps they don't mean to—but it often seems that they don't even have to try. The difference between the people who lead creative lives and those who do not is probably not in whether they ever question their ideas and think about giving up—probably almost all of them do—but in whether they actually do cave in to the crowd. The question is not whether you have failures but whether you believe in yourself, have enough courage of your convictions, and are able to bounce back from failures.

It is interesting to look at some of the research that relates belief in oneself and courage to creative work.

BOX 8.3

Studies on the Role of Personality in Creativity

Research with a cluster of personality traits supports the notion that creative work involves belief in oneself and the courage of one's convictions.

Several studies have been conducted, for example, examining how much people are willing to conform their own opinion to group norms. During the test a person sees stimuli on a screen. The stimuli could be two lines, for example, of different lengths. The individual is told to judge which line is longer, and to respond after the other participants have responded. During the critical trials all the other participants respond with an answer that is clearly incorrect. The conformity score is the percentage of trials in which the person goes along with the group's incorrect answer.

People who are judged as highly creative by their peers conform consistently less often to the group's opinion than do people judged as less creative. For example, high-creative industrial research scientists conformed 10 percent of the time, whereas low-creative scientists conformed 18 percent of the time. In a different study, with college students, the high-creative group conformed 23 percent of the time and a control group conformed 41 percent of the time. Creative people are unwilling to agree with a crowd that is clearly wrong.

Another line of research shows a link between creativity and the personality traits of self-assertiveness, self-sufficiency, dominance, and independence:

—MacKinnon (1962b) studied high-creative and low-creative architects. Self-assertiveness scores correlated .34 with peer-rated creative performance.

—Using a sample of 740 chemists and psychologists, Chambers (1964) found that creative research scientists were significantly more dominant and self-sufficient than noncreative control scientists.

—A study with fifty-six professional writers focused on independence of judgment (Barron, 1963). Thirty of the writers were nominated as creative by English and drama professors. The other twenty-six writers were nominated as successful and productive but not particularly creative. Creative writers had an average score of 16.20 on the independence-of-judgment scale, compared with an average of 11.69 for successful writers, and an average of 8.12 for the general population.

—Also, concerning independence of judgment, Ochse (1990) has reviewed many research studies and finds that creative people can be independent in three ways. First there is emotional independence. Creative people tend to be reserved, withdrawn, or introverted. Second there is intellectual independence. Creativity is marked by autonomy and self-sufficiency in thinking about a problem. Third there is independence from society's standards. Creative people do not feel bound by conventions; they are nonconformers.

In closing it is important to remember that we may see or hear about creative people only at the height of their success. But in almost every case they have had to believe in themselves to get where they are. Some creative people never even have much acceptance of their work while they are alive.

When you are buying low and selling high, there may be many periods in which it seems that no one believes in you. For this reason it is critical that you believe in yourself. At times your own belief in yourself may be the only thing that keeps you from despair. But if you have it, and the courage to fight for what you believe in, you have the chance to make a difference with creative work.

The Relation of Motivation
to Creativity

Several years ago the senior author's son, Seth, decided that he wanted to study the piano. The author was delighted, because, as it happens, he plays the piano himself. He likes the instrument and liked the idea of his son learning to play it. Unfortunately even the best-laid plans do not always work out well. In short order Seth stopped practicing. His piano teacher was not oblivious to this fact and suggested that Seth either start practicing or stop taking lessons. Shortly thereafter Seth quit. Though the author was disappointed, to say the least, at the same time he knew that he was facing behavior in Seth that countless parents were facing in their own children.

Several months later Seth asked to start trumpet lessons. The author snapped: "We've already been through this, Seth, and we both know what's going to happen. You're going to quit. So why even bother to start with the lessons?" Seth was disappointed, but after a few unsuccessful pleas he dropped the subject.

A few hours later the author found himself wondering why he had responded so harshly to his son. On the one hand Seth might well quit again; no one could be sure. On the other perhaps the piano wasn't a good fit for Seth, and the trumpet would be. At this point the author had several insights about factors that had motivated his own behavior. At the same time he discovered firsthand some of the ways parents and teachers can squelch children's motivation to grow in new directions.

The author's first realization was that he was still annoyed that Seth

233

had quit the piano. Yet we need to realize that not every endeavor that we undertake will prove to be one that gives us pleasure, presents the kind of challenge we like, or enables us to achieve competence in a way that suits us. We've got to realize that for every "hit"—for every endeavor that a child (or an adult) really enjoys—there may be any number of misses. We can't expect always to find the hits on the first try.

The second realization was that subconsciously the author had been pleased that Seth had taken up the piano because the author himself is a piano player. He liked the idea of his son following in his footsteps, and he was especially pleased when his son originally suggested of his own accord that he take up the piano. Thus he was doubly displeased when Seth quit the piano, because at some level Seth's quitting was not just a rejection of the musical instrument but a rejection of himself, the father.

The author was not alone in his desire for his son to follow in his footsteps. Every year the author meets premed or prelaw undergraduates at Yale. When the author asks them why they are preparing for a certain program, some of these students admit that it is because their parents want them to, and after all, their parents are footing the bill. Now it is a fair guess—for reasons to be discussed in more detail later—that these students may indeed have the ability to be competent at whatever occupation their parents have selected for them. But at the same time it is a fair guess that none of them will ever truly excel in their endeavor, or at least excel creatively, unless they decide for themselves that what they are doing is what they truly want to do.

The senior author is not unsympathetic to these students. When he was an undergraduate, his mother had her heart set on his becoming either a doctor or a lawyer. Because the author didn't take the necessary premed courses, law would have been his mother's option of choice. Instead he went to graduate school in psychology—disappointing. But when the author received his Ph.D., his mother pointed out that the president of Rutgers, the state university of New Jersey, near where he had grown up, had advanced degrees in both psychology and law. It wasn't too late, therefore, to go to law school and get that second degree. But that's not the way things turned out, and the author went on to be an assistant professor of psychology at Yale.

When, five years later, the author was tenured, his mother's reaction was, "Now you've shown yourself that you can succeed as a psychologist.

So now is the time when you ought to go back and get that law degree." Well, the author still doesn't have the law degree, nor did he ever enroll in law school, despite his mother's efforts.

As parents, we frequently hope that our children will follow in our footsteps. Sometimes this desire is conscious; other times it is not. But it is perfectly normal to hope that one day our children will grow up to be like us. The problem is that they are *not* us, and we cannot fairly expect them to be. Our goal should be to help them maximize their *own* potentials and interests, not those we wish they had that happen to correspond to ours. Helping your children find things that they love to do means finding what is right for them, not what is right for you—it means finding out what suits their motivations, not yours.

The author's third realization was that just as he liked the idea of Seth's being a pianist, he disliked the idea of Seth's being a trumpeter. Playing the trumpet was not on the author's "approved list" of activities.

We usually convey to our children what our approved list is, although our communication may be subtle. Indeed, we may not even know that a certain activity is or is not on it until our child suggests that he or she do the activity. And it makes good sense that we have such lists. Who would defend a parent who allowed his or her child to take drugs just so the child could "find her own path"?

A problem arises, however, when items are not on our approved list not because anything is intrinsically wrong with them but rather because they just don't happen to fit our image of what we always wanted our child to be. That was what happened in Seth's case. There was really nothing wrong with his playing the trumpet, other than that the author couldn't imagine any kid of his doing it.

So Seth was allowed to start the trumpet, did very well with it, and became first trumpet in the school band. Eventually he moved on to other things. But the author learned that kids need to find what is right for them, and not what is right for their parents' image of them. People do their best and most creative work when they actualize their own interests, not those of their parents or other elders or even peers.

Parents need to remember not only that children do their best when they pursue their own interests, but also that children do their best when they learn how to motivate themselves rather than always having their parents motivate them. Psychologists have long recognized that children do best when parents give them an occasional shove, but not when the parents constantly push the children to succeed (see, for example, Elkind, 1981). In a time when most American big-city children are competing even for entry to private kindergartens, it is easy for parents to find themselves in the role of pushing and then pushing some more. But the problem is that the children of parents who are always pushing never learn to push for themselves.

The year one of the authors went to Yale as an undergraduate was a lucky one for his (public) high school: Six students matriculated at Yale. But even as an entering freshman, he noticed something interesting about the classmates who went with him: Though all of them were good students, their performance in college was inversely proportional to how much the students' parents had pushed them at home. Why? Because those children had never learned to push for themselves.

The author sometimes cites this observation as the basis for an idea that he refers to (with tongue in cheek) as the "laxative principle of motivation": People who always take laxatives become dependent on them—they can't push for themselves. Similarly, children whose parents always push them become dependent on their parents for their motivation. When these children then leave home, they are at a loss as to how to motivate and organize themselves. Thus we need to help children along every now and then, but we need to help them develop motivation from within rather than try constantly to provide it for them. We do so by showing why activities are exciting or at least worthwhile and by emphasizing the pleasure or value of the activities themselves rather than the extrinsic rewards for doing them.

What Is Motivation?

What, exactly, is motivation anyway? Motivation is the driving force or incentive that leads someone to action. Basically it's the nature and strength of your desire to engage in an activity. Someone with a strong desire is referred to as highly motivated, while someone with a weak desire is referred to as less motivated.

Researchers on motivation commonly distinguish between two basic kinds of motivation: extrinsic and intrinsic. Extrinsic motivation comes from the outside. You are extrinsically motivated when you do something in order to realize some gain that has little or nothing to do with the activity in which you are engaged. Basically the activity is a means toward an end. Thus, a student who works hard to get A's in school, an artist who makes a painting to win a prize in competition, or a worker who puts in long hours to earn a lot of money, would be characterized as extrinsically motivated. And of course people who invest in the financial markets tend to be driven by monetary profit, clearly an extrinsic motivation. In contrast, intrinsic motivation comes from the inside. You are intrinsically motivated when you do something because you enjoy doing it, because you gain personal satisfaction, or because the activity is meaningful for its own sake, without regard to external rewards. People who write novels, even though they may never be published, or who paint because they love to paint, are intrinsically motivated. Such people do what they do because they want to do it, for the sheer enjoyment of the activity itself.

Intrinsic Motivation and Creativity

In terms of the investment theory, to be creative you have to want to buy low and sell high and at some level enjoy doing so. Someone can give you intellectual arguments as to why you should follow your own instincts and separate yourself from the crowd, but unless you really want to, your efforts to do so are likely to be tentative and half-hearted. Creative people are those who consciously and purposefully decide to follow their own path. They do it because they want to, not because someone makes them.

Surgeon-inventor Julian Henley puts it this way: "Some people derive pleasure out of playing golf. Some people derive pleasure out of eating. When I get involved in a project, I can stop eating, and golf doesn't come near. There's something intrinsic to being able to take an idea and build it into a reality. That whole process—the process in itself is almost like a hobby" (Lubart, personal communication, 1991). Creative people enjoy what they do—like a hobby. To them it's not work.

The research literature supports the importance of intrinsic motivation for creativity. Hill (1991) found that the quality of creative writing was significantly related to whether the subjects were writing for enjoyment. Amabile (1983) found that children who enjoyed writing poems produced significantly more creative poems than did those who were motivated only to please their teacher. Hennessey, Amabile, and Martinage (1989) found that children could actually be trained to focus on intrinsic motivation, and that when they did, they showed increased creativity. In this study intrinsic motivation training consisted mainly of watching a videotape of children discussing intrinsic reasons for doing schoolwork. The creative task was collage making, with a panel of teachers serving as judges of creativity.

Why is intrinsic motivation particularly beneficial to creative performance? We believe that intrinsic motivators focus a person on a task. Essentially the motivational goal, or "the gold at the end of the rainbow," is almost fused with the task itself. For example, the intrinsic motivation of enjoyment is fulfilled by actually engaging in task performance, such as the act of painting or writing. This is the most powerful link of a motivator with a task. For extrinsic motivators, by contrast, there is a clear separation between the motivational goal and the task.

Extrinsic Motivation and Creativity

Over the years a large literature has grown up on the relation between extrinsic motivation and creativity, and its message has been, in a nutshell, that extrinsic motivation is to creativity what strychnine is to orange juice.

A number of experimental findings are consistent with the notion that extrinsic motivation poisons the creative wellsprings. For example, Kruglanski, Friedman, and Zeevi (1971) found that when thirty-two high school students were asked to complete two creative tasks (writing a story and generating a title for it), the work of students who were promised a reward for being in the study was less creative than that of students who were not promised a reward. Amabile et al. (1986) similarly found that when 115 children varying in age from five to ten were asked to tell stories, those who were promised rewards were less creative than those who weren't.

More results along this line were obtained with college students. In a study by Hill (1991), mentioned above, whereas enjoyment in creative writing was positively correlated with the quality of the product, motivation to get good grades and motivation to achieve recognition were negatively correlated with product quality. And in another study college students who wrote poems before and after thinking about extrinsic reasons for writing showed decreased creativity on their second poems (Amabile, 1985). These studies are representative of many that have suggested a negative relationship between extrinsic motivation and creativity.

Why should extrinsic motivation undermine creative performance? The typical explanation is a variant of one proposed by Hennessey and Amabile (1988b), who have suggested that extrinsic motivation focuses people on goals rather than on paths to attaining these goals.

There is a tendency with extrinsic motivation to take the fastest, most direct route to accomplish a task—more often than not an obvious, well-traveled one. Some research supports this idea. For example, people who tried to solve an insight problem (see chapter 5) with the promise of a monetary reward performed significantly worse than did people who worked without the goal of a reward. The reward condition showed more cases in which the problem solver could not conceive of using the materials (for example, a matchbox) in a nontypical way.

Basically extrinsically motivated people don't care much how they get where they are going, so long as they can get there fast and receive the reward that comes with getting there. For example, one of the authors once signed a book contract for which he received a substantial advance. He was initially very excited about the book, but as he started work on it, he found himself thinking more and more about the advance he would get when he had completed half the manuscript. After a while he was focusing more on the money than on the book.

The author's experience with the book is an example of a general phenomenon that has been uncovered in the literature on motivation: Extrinsic motivation can undermine intrinsic motivation. Studies by Lepper, Greene, and Nisbett (1973) and others have further shown how extrinsic motivators can undermine intrinsic motivation. Schoolchildren who undertook a task in order to win a "Good Player Award" lost much of their intrinsic motivation as a result of focusing on the award.

This effect can be seen in even the most pedestrian of situations. Several years ago the nine-year-old son of one of the authors volunteered to cut the grass. Great—the author sure didn't want to cut it himself! And Seth loved cutting the grass, for reasons that will perhaps forever remain a mystery. After a while, though, the author began to feel guilty that his son was cutting the grass and receiving no compensation for it. So he decided to pay Seth a nominal sum—one dollar—each time he cut the grass. The son was grateful, and that was the end of that.

The next summer the author asked his son if he would be cutting the grass again. Seth said, "Sure, but this year I'm charging two dollars." Although the author explained that inflation had not yet reached 100 percent, and a compromise was reached, he nevertheless realized that he had become a victim of a mechanism on which he had frequently lectured. Seth had originally offered to cut the grass because he enjoyed doing it. As soon as he was paid, however, he began to perceive himself as doing it for the money. Eventually the extrinsic motivator took over from the intrinsic one, and Seth forgot that he had ever enjoyed cutting the grass.

The story may have a bit of charm when its protagonist is a boy cutting the grass. It loses its charm, however, when we consider the effects of the extrinsic motivators that we regularly infuse into our school and work environments. Grades are a central part of schooling from the moment children start school. And grades are an extrinsic motivator par excellence.

Grades almost certainly undermine creativity. Children quickly learn that the main criterion for receiving a high grade is not creativity per se but rather pleasing the teacher. That is the name of the game. Pleasing the teacher to receive the A crowds out creativity and everything else to become the major goal of school work. The children rarely learn to enjoy the work they are doing simply for its own sake.

When the senior author arrived as a professor at Yale, he was a bit distressed about what he discovered to be the typical student attitude. Students seemed to be doing the bare minimum they needed to do to get an A, and nothing more. Moreover, when they asked questions, they were much more likely to ask about requirements—what would be tested and how they would be graded—than they were to ask questions about the material they were supposed to be learning. Their focus, in other words, was on the grade, not on learning of the material that lay behind the grade. Most certainly they were not focusing on going beyond the given information in creative ways.

Although the author was distressed, he realized that the students were not to blame: They were just playing the game that they had been taught to play by their teachers, classmates, and probably parents. They did not create the system in which they were working. At best they were relatively innocent participants in a game whose rules they had not invented.

The problem in the university extends as well to the workplace. In the worker's desire to please the power structure and obtain the concomitant rewards, creativity can quickly get lost in the shuffle. People find themselves spending less and less time thinking about what they are doing but more and more about the impression their work will make.

Both students and workers face another obstacle—namely time. Although we sometimes read about flashes of creative inspiration, the truth is that creativity takes time. And people today find themselves with so much to do that they often simply don't have time to think about problems creatively. If we want to encourage people to think creatively, we need to do so in a way that gives them the time to do so. Often this means deciding on what the important things are that need to be done, and then assuring that these things are done creatively and well.

Another Look at Intrinsic and Extrinsic Motivation

Some things in life are black and white, but not that many. The relation of intrinsic and extrinsic motivation to creativity is one of the things that isn't. Although early research painted a picture of intrinsic motivation as the good guy in the script and extrinsic motivation as the bad guy, the truth has proved to be more complex.

In a review of the literature Ochse (1990) listed some of the motivators that have been found to be particularly salient for creative people. She suggested eight such motivators: (a) the desire to obtain mastery over a problem or to overcome ignorance, (b) the desire to achieve immortality through work, (c) the desire to make money, (d) the desire to prove oneself—both to oneself and to others, (e) the desire to attain recognition, (f) the desire to attain self-esteem, (g) the desire to create a thing of beauty, and (h) the desire to discover an underlying order in things. Some of these motivators, such as the desire to obtain mastery, are clearly intrinsic; others, such as the desire to make money, are clearly extrinsic. And some are just difficult to characterize. When people are trying to prove themselves, they are not necessarily focusing on enjoyment of the task, but they are not focusing on external rewards either. Ochse's list suggests that both intrinsic and extrinsic motivators can motivate creative people, and that some motivators don't fall neatly into either group.

Years earlier Rossman (1931) had asked 710 creative inventors what motivated them to invent. The top five motivations for their work, from most to least frequently mentioned, were: (*a*) love of inventing, (*b*) desire to improve, (*c*) financial gain, (*d*) necessity or need, and (*e*) desire to achieve. Again, intrinsic motivation clearly came out at the top, but you can see some of those extrinsic motivators right there in that top-five list. In a study of patent winners Bennett (1943) also found that economic incentives were powerful motivators of creative work by the inventors who won patents.

As a case in point, Paul McCready describes his motivation for designing the first human-powered plane to fly a one-mile, figure-eight course, an aviation first, for which he won the Kremer Prize. McCready invented a special glider, the *Gossamer Condor*, which now hangs in the National Air and Space Museum in Washington, D.C. McCready says the prize money (£50,000), established by British industrialist Henry Kremer, combined with debt that he had to pay off, led him to work on the problem: "I felt that I didn't have the time to mess with such things, but I had this strong economic motivation to take an interest in man-powered flight, so I charged around trying to figure out a way to solve it" (quoted in Brown, 1988, p.2).

Studies of creative business executives (for example, Adams, 1986b) have found that all the really "bad" extrinsic motivators aren't so bad when it comes to motivating creative work by people in business. Adams has found that money, recognition, awards, and publicity are all effective motivators for creative work in business. Money in particular often leads people to see risks as worth the gamble.

Extrinsic motivators may have gotten something of a bad rap because creative people are embarrassed to admit that they are extrinsically motivated. For example, Ochse (1990) notes that although Edgar Allan Poe originally stated that he wrote to satisfy his taste and love of art, and that he didn't care about what others thought of his work, he later admitted that he lied—that he loved fame and doted on it. Certainly Poe was not alone.

Investigators of creativity have therefore begun to reformulate their ideas about what motivates creative people. Sure, intrinsic motivation is the key, but extrinsic motivation is not necessarily a plague. For example, Hennessey and Amabile (1988b) have suggested that certain extrinsic motivators, such as fame and fortune, may not interfere with creative work. Some people can be driven by extrinsic rewards yet maintain their task as the real focus of their attention.

More recently Amabile (1988) suggested that although extrinsic in the absence of intrinsic motivation may undermine creativity, extrinsic combined with intrinsic motivation may actually enhance creativity. One idea is that intrinsic motivators are particularly important in the early problem-formulating, idea-generation stages of work on a task. And extrinsic motivation is particularly helpful in the laborious phase, when the product needs to be fleshed out with all the details (Amabile, 1988).

In our own view intrinsic and extrinsic motivation are often highly interactive, and can work together rather than in opposition to each other. What many highly creative people do is find a way in which they can be paid and otherwise rewarded for doing what they love to do anyway. Thus creative scientists go into research positions in universities and corporations because such positions enable them to exercise their creative bent at the same time that they make a living doing so. Entrepreneurs often create businesses or other environments in which they can do what they love. Authors may enjoy writing, but most would prefer gaining enough income from their writing so that they can write full-time, precluding the necessity of having to work at a steady job that allows them to write only on the side when they can find the time. In short, people often try to shape their environments in a way that will enable them both to be creative and to get rewarded for being so.

Staying Motivated

Almost anything can become boring if you do it enough. The first time you write a mystery story you may gain great enjoyment from it, and perhaps the second and the third times as well. Perhaps the fiftieth time there will be less challenge and less excitement. And you may find yourself falling into a formula that is predictable not only to you but to your readers as well. For example, as mystery fans ourselves, we often find that after we have read a number of stories by a given author, it becomes easier to predict who did it because there are certain clues that tend to be giveaways in a particular author's mysteries.

When you become bored you lose your intrinsic motivation and therefore find it harder and harder to maintain your creativity in what you are doing. Creative people are therefore constantly seeking new challenges so they won't become jaded in their work. As discussed in the preceding chapter, they have a desire to grow, and when they fulfill this desire they maintain the intrinsic motivation they need to do creative work. For example, Benoit Mandelbrot has moved from field to field to stay interested in what he does, and also to avoid focusing on what he has done instead of what he would still like to do.

We try to do the same. For example, when the senior author began his career as a psychologist, he studied human intelligence. He imagined himself spending his career studying pretty much the same topic. But in the twenty years he has been doing research at Yale, he has branched out into many other diverse topics as well, including creativity, styles of learning and thinking, conflict resolution, nonverbal communication, love and close relationships, language, reading, management, leadership, and wisdom, to name just a few. In part he has branched out in order to stay interested and fresh in the work he does.

People in a variety of occupations use the same strategy. Teachers switch the grades they teach or the approaches they take to teaching. Executives take on new projects and switch to new companies and higher-level jobs in order to face new challenges. Writers branch out into new kinds of writing, and artists into new kinds of art. Pablo Picasso is an excellent example of an artist whose development never stopped; his style showed a continual creative evolution over the course of his career. In contrast, people who start with one thing and pretty much end up doing the same thing may continue to do a competent job, but often their competence is not matched by their creativity. We know a scientist who has been studying the same problem for close to twenty-five years and who shows no sign of changing what he works on. He is well known in his work, but basically for the work he did twenty years ago. If your goal is to create rather than to stagnate, you need constantly to be seeking new challenges in the work you do.

Other Kinds of Motivation Involved in Creativity

Although we have concentrated on intrinsic and extrinsic motivation up to now, other kinds of motivation have also been found to be related to creativity; these additional motivators also tend to focus a person on the task rather than on the ultimate rewards. We consider now some of these other kinds of motivation.

A first kind is achievement motivation. People vary in their need to achieve—to perform to a high standard of excellence (Maddi, 1965)—and the level of this need is related to creativity.

In an interesting study DeCharms and Moeller (1962) examined children's books that were widely used from 1800 to 1952. They scored how much the motive to achieve was emphasized in a selection of books from roughly each twenty-year period. The content of the children's books can be taken as a marker of a society's concern with achievement in general during a given period of time. The investigators also computed the number of patents awarded per capita during every twenty-year period. The amount of achievement imagery in children's books and the number of patents followed a similar pattern over time. Both increased rapidly from 1800 to 1900; continued at a steady, high level until approximately the depression (1929), and then showed declines to 1950, the end of the period studied. For example, in the early 1800s there was, on average, one page containing achievement imagery out of twenty-five in children's books and approximately ten patents issued per million population. Around 1900 there were eleven pages (out of twenty-five) containing achievement imagery and seventy patents per million people. In the period during and after the depression, the average number of pages containing achievement imagery dropped to four (out of twenty-five) and there were fewer than fifty patents issued per million population, on average. The correspondence between achievement imagery and the number of patents shows a rank-order correlation of .79, which indicates a strong and significant relationship.

In general higher need to achieve is related to creativity, but only up to a certain point. Once people pass an intermediate level in the need to achieve, there is evidence that they actually become less creative (McClelland, 1962). McClelland reports on a study by Stein of forty-five industrial chemists in which it was found that the most creative chemists were somewhere in the middle of the distribution of all chemists with respect to the need to achieve. Other work by McClelland also supports this notion.

Why would creative people be high, but not too high, in the need to achieve? The reason probably is that people with an exceedingly high need to achieve start to focus so much on the ultimate outcome and the recognition that they will get for it that they divert their attention away from the creative processes that would be needed to attain that outcome.

Thus, these very achievement-oriented people are very reward- rather than task-oriented. Their focus on ends rather than means hinders rather than helps their creativity.

Creative people also seem to be self-actualizers: They want to make the most of themselves that they possibly can (Rogers, 1976). Aaron Copeland, the composer, highlights this motive through an analogy with eating: "Why do you eat? You're hungry. . . . It's the hunger that stimulates you to eat. It's the same thing in art; except that, in art, hunger is the need for self-expression" (quoted in Rosner & Abt, 1970, p. 271). Creativity is a means to achieve self-actualization.

Further, creative people tend to be motivated to organize their work and their lives. Often their creative work is a way to impose order on what they originally believe to be chaos. Arthur Miller, author of the famous play *Death of a Salesman* wrote, "For myself, it has never been possible to generate the energy to write and complete a play if I know in advance everything it signifies and all it will contain. The very impulse to write, I think, springs from an inner chaos crying for order, for meaning, and that meaning must be discovered in the process of writing or the work lies dead as it is finished" (quoted in Cole, 1960, p. 275). For composer, lyricist, and playwright, Stephen Sondheim, composing involves organizing music and designing the rhythm, harmony, and words to fit together like pieces of a puzzle: "Art tries to make order out of chaos, not just the chaos of the world, but the chaos of your own feelings and your own discombobulations" (Kakutani, 1994, p. 31).

Creative people also have at least some need for novelty and a simultaneous need to fight boredom. Isaac Bashevis Singer wrote: "I get up every morning with a desire to . . . do some creative work. . . . When I find a person who [has] lost this desire, such a person is almost dead" (quoted in Rosner & Abt, 1970, p. 235). For many creative people, including Singer, their need for novelty is found through a kind of aesthetics. They want to create something that is new but that is also beautiful.

In sum motivation is an important part of being creative. Creative people are motivated by the desire to do something that sets them apart—by the desire to buy low—and to keep doing such things again and again—to sell high. They don't rest on their laurels: They are interested in what they will be doing today and tomorrow, not in what they did yesterday. They are virtually always people who love what they do—and thus are intrinsically motivated—at the same time that they are far from oblivious to extrinsic motivators. Although they do what they do for love of it, they are rarely averse to receiving recognition and compensation for what they have done. A key point is to remain focused on your current problem-solving process rather than to concentrate on the ultimate rewards you may receive.

The kinds of motivations we have discussed are relatively domain-specific, meaning that a person is not either "motivated or not." Rather, the person may be highly motivated in one particular pursuit and have absolutely no motivation in another. Part of capitalizing on your creativity is finding what you love to do, and finding a way to make it your lifework, or at least a part of it. You cannot force someone to be motivated to do something, but you can encourage them to give something a try. Often something that is tough and perhaps even tedious at first—perhaps music or art lessons—can become engaging once the person reaches out beyond the bounds of duplicating what others have done and starts extending them. The power of creative motivation lies in anyone and everyone; the hardest part is often to find it and to find a way to make it a part of your life.

Motivating Creativity: Implications for Educational and Business Settings

Here are some implications of the ideas in this chapter for education:

1. *Deemphasize grades, which are a salient extrinsic motivator.* It is important to be aware, however, that attempts to deemphasize grades may meet with student resistance. Students may simply not believe that grades are not important because they are so used to grades. Also the students may fear that their work will now be evaluated by looser, more subjective criteria.

2. *Make creativity an explicit part of the assignment to show that creativity is valued.* For example, one of the authors once structured an assignment for a psychology class at Yale that made creativity 50 percent of the grade and research knowledge the other 50 percent. The students who had previously been turning in highly competent but mundane work suddenly became creative. Of course a range of creativity was exhibited, but every student made some noticeable creative effort.

3. *Give verbal recognition for creative work.* Praise for creative work signals that this type of effort is valued and may further motivate creativity.

This praise may occur in a private comment to a student or during a public review of students' work. A related way to praise creative work and subtly motivate creativity is to use outside examples of creative work as part of teaching material.

4. *Encourage students to submit their work to external shows or contests*. One of us remembers instances in his high school art classes when the teacher announced that the class's paintings would be displayed at a local bank. This opportunity for a wide audience (rather than only the teacher and one's peers) motivated students to push their work for both creativity and technical skill.

5. *Attempt to use a combination of motivators*. For creativity some students may respond well to grades, others to praise, others to opportunities for competition; still others may find the task material intrinsically interesting and not need extra motivators. Indeed, adding extrinsic rewards (for example, a prize) when people are already intrinsically interested in a task may enhance the motivation to be creative for some people but can undermine it for others.

And here are some implications for business:

1. *Know the person you are trying to motivate*. For example, some people respond well to monetary incentives; others thrive on praise and recognition. It is important to keep in mind that what may serve to motivate one person may demotivate others. For example, a monetary award for creative work could stimulate worker-A but cause worker-B to focus on the "dangling carrot" to the detriment of creativity (and the team effort).

2. *The effectiveness and use of monetary awards for motivating creativity needs to be reexamined*. Monetary awards are common in business. For example, Foote, Cone, and Belding Communications, an advertising firm, recently awarded a $25,000 cash prize for the most creative, successful advertising campaign in its agency. A *Chicago Tribune* report (Lazarus, 1993) went on to say that many other agencies give cash awards to recognize top creative work. However, the research and ideas expressed in this chapter suggest that monetary awards, when used consistently, may not always lead to creativity.

3. *In addition to money, there are several possible motivators for creative work in business settings*. Managers can give verbal praise, add notes to an employee's performance record, or give special opportunities that ac-

knowledge creative work. For example, an employee might be given an opportunity to present ideas at a conference (in-house or external) or be allowed to obtain rights on new ideas.

To obtain creative work, you need to design the environment to encourage such work. In the next chapter we consider the relation between environment and creativity.

The Relation Between the Environment and Creativity

Creative people seem without fail to encounter obstacles in the environment to the realization of their creative potential. Creative people often bemoan how such obstacles interfere with their creative work, and theorists of creativity note how environmental impediments can thwart the expression of creative and sometimes universally significant ideas (Amabile, 1983; Rogers, 1976; Torrance, 1967, 1979). It is the rare parent who does not observe the seemingly countless perverse ways in which schools can undermine the creativity of his or her child.

To draw on the investment metaphor, the viewpoint represented above claims that creativity is hindered by a bear market. A bear market for investment, in general, is one that is down and either staying there or expected to get worse. In contrast a bull market is a market that's rising and is expected to continue to do so.

The viewpoint that creativity needs a bullish environment sees creativity as something that is highly delicate and in need of supportive milieu. However, there is a second viewpoint—that creativity actually needs aspects of a bearish environment. This perspective sees creativity as hardy and resilient in the face of adverse environmental conditions, and in need of some but not constant support. Indeed, in the bearish view, creativity even thrives in the face of adversity. To be creative you need an obstacle to push against. Although the first viewpoint is by far the more common one (for example, Amabile, 1983; Bloom, 1985), the second one has been proposed as well (for example, Dabrowski, 1964, 1972).

251

The difference between the two viewpoints is of interest to theorists of creativity, because the two views hold radically different and even opposing predictions about what kind of environment will best stimulate the development of creativity and optimize the interaction between the person and the context in which he or she lives. According to the bull-market perspective, creativity flourishes only in highly supportive and nurturant environments, whereas according to the bear-market model, it not only can flourish in harsh and sometimes repressive environments but may actually be stimulated by them. Whereas most theorists have taken the first point of view (Amabile, 1983; Bloom, 1985; Sternberg & Lubart, 1991b), a few in addition to Dabrowski, such as Eisenstadt et al. (1989), Goertzel and Goertzel (1962; Goertzel, Goertzel & Goertzel, 1978), and Simonton (1988b) have entertained the second.

The difference between the two viewpoints has striking practical implications as well—for child rearing, education, and even professional and business settings. According to the first view, we undermine and perhaps destroy the creative potential of our citizens, and possibly our society, when we fail to provide environments that maximally foster and reward creativity. According to the second, we may actually undermine creativity if we make things too easy or too comfortable for individuals of significant creative potential.

It should be said that there is a third, intermediate point of view between the two described above. This view is that the type of environment that fosters the development and realization of creative potential may depend upon several factors, such as the extent of a person's creative potential, the type of creative potential the person shows, or possibly the field in which the creative person expresses him- or herself. According to this view, the environment that facilitates creative expression interacts with personal and situational variables.

Does Creativity Require a Bullish or Bearish Environment?[*]

Creativity Needs a Bullish Environment: The Traditional View

Two groups of theorists approach the environmental influences on creativity from the bullish point of view. One group, the humanistic theorists, not

---

[*]Spomenka Calic, a postdoctoral fellow working with the senior author at Yale, contributed ideas to this section.

only sees the potential for creativity in everyone but also understands the environment as a crucial facilitator for the unfolding of innate potential for creativity (Maslow, 1970; Rogers, 1976). The ideal environment for nurturing creativity is a social climate free from pressures toward conformity or outside evaluation. However, although the environment itself cannot provide for the creative development of the individual, it can provide an atmosphere for spontaneous growth toward self-actualization. Self-actualization and self-fulfillment are understood by humanistic theorists as naturally creative. The humanistic approach to creativity explains inhibitions in the individual's environment as the main obstruction to the liberation of creative impulses. Totally accepting environments will decrease the need for defense mechanisms and increase creative behavior. The humanists, like Fromm, Maslow, May, and Rogers, developed their understanding of human beings and creativity on a Rousseauesque view of humans as naturally good but degenerated by socialization.

The view of creativity as healthy functioning influenced the development of techniques for enhancement of creativity. Rogers (1976) suggested that it is especially important to remove barriers to creativity from educational programs because an individual will be creative in the environment in which he or she is not evaluated and measured by some external standards. Such evaluation is a threat to almost everyone and creates a need for defensiveness. Gowan (1972), Sarnoff and Cole (1983), Taylor (1972), Torrance (1979), and Treffinger, Isaksen, and Firestein (1982) pointed out that absence of judgment, freedom of expression in childhood, and unconditional acceptance, trust, and love are related to the development of a healthy personality and thus to the development of creativity. Zajonc (1976) concluded that a one-parent home provides an inferior intellectual environment, and that early parental loss is likely to result in intellectual deficits. The more recent theories of creativity, such as Amabile's (1983) componential theory of creativity, although not humanistic, posit a very similar view—namely that external evaluation and control decrease creativity. Withholding judgment, avoiding external rewards, and minimizing social pressure have beneficial effects on creativity. Following this view, researchers and educators have tried to create educational programs that are designed to nurture the development of creative people through a nonevaluative, easygoing atmosphere and through spontaneous expression of creative ideas.

In contrast to the humanistic theorists, who are in favor of naturally and totally accepting environments, the environmentalists look for specific situations that are functionally related to creativity. Like the humanists, environmentalists approach creativity as an outgrowth of favorable conditions in a person's environment. They focus on isolating the important variables in a favorable environment in order to reinforce them and to foster creative behavior. By seeking to manipulate these environmental variables, they take an active role in the environment in order to increase creative production. The environmentalists study desirable and undesirable attributes of social context, especially schools, businesses, and family (see, for example, Bloomberg, 1973).

Torrance (1965) has been a leading researcher typifying this approach. He has provided a variety of advice for teachers on how to increase creativity in students, and has approached the reinforcement of creative behavior by exposing students to training. Torrance's studies have indicated that some conditions, such as restrictions on manipulativeness and curiosity, conditions resulting in fear and timidity, misplaced emphasis on certain verbal skills, overemphasis on success, and lack of resources for working out ideas, can negatively affect development and expression of creative thinking. On the other hand the composition of groups in which thinking takes place, competition, teaching of principles for thinking, and rewarding creative thinking all help children to value their own ideas and thus affect positively the production of creative thinking abilities (Torrance, 1967).

There are various other examples of this approach as well. Ward (1969) found the effects of physical context on how quickly people could generate ideas; Amabile and Gitomer (1984) reported a positive influence on creativity when children had a choice of materials; Koestner et al. (1984) found that creativity decreased when controlling limits were set up. Also, Simonton (1975) pointed out that competition, which increases over the life span in many professional fields, is a negative aspect of the social environment that influences creative performance; Sternberg (1988e), too, concluded that the reward structure of schooling and job settings can be formulated in a way that either fosters or inhibits creativity.

Creativity and a Bearish *Environment: The Dabrowskian View*

In contrast to the bull-market view on the effects of context of creativity, the bear-market approach finds its support in striking themes noticeable through biographical data of creative achievers. Such data include the general emotional climate in the homes of creative individuals, as well as such specific factors as instances of bereavement and other traumas. The childhoods of creative people, although usually rich in intellectual stimulation, are often described as lacking in emotional comfort. Whereas humanistic psychology promoted a widely accepted view that creative persons would come from happy homes and supportive loving parents, research by MacKinnon (1962a, 1970) found that many extraordinarily creative people had suffered traumatic experiences, frustrations, and deprivations during their childhood. Studies by Goertzel, Goertzel, and Goertzel (1978; Goertzel & Goertzel, 1962) found that 85 percent of four hundred eminent people of the twentieth century had come from troubled homes. Similar results were found in studies by Chambers (1964) and Stein (1962).

Albert (1971) and Eisenstadt (1978) reported on a disproportionately high number of eminent people who lost a parent early in life. Research by Roe (1953) on eminently creative scientists supports the hypothesis of early parental loss being related to eminence. The only other groups that suffered approximately the same proportion of childhood trauma caused by loss of a parent were delinquents and suicidal depressives, which implies that the death of a parent may have an influence leading either to adaptive or to maladaptive development (Ochse, 1990).

After reviewing studies on the early development of creative persons, Albert (1978) concluded that the childhoods of such persons were rich in opportunity and encouragement for intellectual development, but poor in emotional comfort. Distress and deprivation are more typical than atypical of the childhoods of eminent people, a finding which does not correspond with the bullish environmental view of the effect of context on creativity.

Thus studies reviewed under the bear-market view do not support Maslow's view of satisfaction of lower needs in the hierarchy as necessary or possibly even as wholly desirable for the development of creativity. Fromm's view of a loving relationship between parent and child, or Rogers's view of unconditional support being necessary for creative development (Ochse, 1990), receives little support. However, the nature of the link between distress and suffering in childhood and creativity needs further research and a firm theory. As Feldman (1988) pointed out, intellectual stimulation and emotional deprivation may produce a genius, but also may produce unsuccessful and unsatisfied people.

Perhaps the most notable example of the bear-market point of view was proposed by the Polish psychologist Kazimierz Dabrowski earlier in this century. Dabrowski understood that unpleasant stimuli are indispensable for the awakening of creativity. Dabrowski saw conflict as neither positive nor negative, but as the reaction of the individual to situations that might ultimately prove to be well-springs of creativity. Unpleasant life experiences, stresses, and anxieties, which may be seen as undesirable from a mental health standpoint, are desirable from the standpoint of Dabrowski's (Dabrowski, Kawczak & Piechowski, 1970) theory of positive disintegration as significant elements for creative development. Case studies of authors such as Franz Kafka and Gerard de Nerval, just to mention a couple of the creative persons Dabrowski (1972) studied, demonstrate the process of interplay among strong developmental potential, emotional traumas, and environmental stresses in producing creative development and behavior.

Bull vs. Bear: A Synthesis

In the above sections, we have considered the general question of environments that facilitate creativity. Clearly an environment that encourages and values creativity is desirable. However, the perfectly bullish environment, in which a person never had anything against which to push, might be imperfect for the development of creativity. The conclusion we draw is that it helps to have a generally favorable environment sprinkled with some obstacles along the way.

Environmental Variables Affecting Creativity

In this section we consider specific environmental variables, and how they have been found to affect creativity. These specific environmental features ultimately contribute to the bullish or bearish nature of the environment as a whole.

Before we start, though, we want to mention that for almost every variable we consider, the research findings seem to be contradictory. Of course, studies differ in their participants, test materials, methodologies, and so on, and so some contradictions are inevitable. But we believe that what is more likely to be happening here is that many variables operate in a nonlinear fashion, meaning that more (or less) of something may be better, but only up to a point. After that point the effect may disappear, or it may actually reverse.

The Context of Work

It appears that an environment rich with stimuli encourages creativity more than an environment that is barren and bare. For example, Ward (1969) found in a study of very young children (of nursery school age) that children preclassified as creative were much more productive in a cue-rich environment (with lots of toys and other stimuli) than in a barren room. Children not preclassified as creative, however, although they benefited, did not benefit as much. Friedman et al. (1978) also found that children benefited from a cue-rich environment, but only if the children were specifically instructed to use the cues in the environment to facilitate their creative work.

The cues do not have to be physical or even visual ones. Ziv (1976) had a large number of tenth-grade students (roughly sixteen years of age) listen to a recording of a comedian before doing creative tasks. Another group did the tasks without listening to the humorous recording first. The participants who heard the comedian were judged to produce more creative work than did those who did not hear the record. A subsequent study (Ziv, 1983) replicated the result with adolescents, this time using cartoon books and short film clips of a comedian in place of the recording. These studies are not flawless in terms of experimental design, because the so-called control groups did not receive any alternative kind of prior treatment—they were just asked to do the creative work. Hence we cannot separate the effects of having any prior task from those of having a humorous prior task. Nevertheless the results make sense, and we are aware of no results that contradict them.

These studies suggest that the kind of relaxed and playful atmosphere introduced by humor is conducive to creative work. We would go one step further and suggest that having a sense of humor can be an important part of creativity. Being creative often requires a person to step back and see things from a perspective that is different, odd, and at times even ridiculous. A humorous perspective meets these criteria. In our own personal experience it is the rare creative person who has not developed a good, if not excellent, sense of humor.

We would conclude on the basis of these studies and our own experiences that a cue-rich environment will generally facilitate creativity more than a barren one. The cues can be visual, auditory, or perhaps even of other kinds (for example, olfactory). In designing environments to foster creativity, however, you need to pay careful attention to the choice of cues. Pedestrian cues (for example, elevator music or conventional posters) do not necessarily contribute to a cue-rich environment. Moreover, we believe that if the cues are too strong, they are more likely to be distracting than facilitating. Having loud, blaring music in the background, no matter how unusual the music, is probably not a desirable way to foster creativity. Having pictures that are highly sexually arousing may also not be the way to go. Ideally one would generally want to choose or design the cues to fit the kinds of creative work being sought.

Task Constraints

One of the problems we have faced in our own work is the question of how many constraints we should place on people when we try to assess their creativity, or when we simply try to give people the opportunity to be creative. For example, we found in a study of creativity that when people were given choices of titles for short stories to write, or titles for artistic compositions, people with a local (detail-oriented) thinking style showed higher creativity than those with a global (big-picture) thinking style—the opposite of what would be predicted from our theory (Lubart & Sternberg, in press). But the result makes sense, because giving a title literally localizes the creative composition within the range of possible options for creative work. If, on the other hand, you give very few or no constraints, people may find themselves unable to do the task. For example, we tried to assess creativity of students taking a psychology course by asking them to come up with their own theory of a psychological phenomenon. With so few constraints, the large majority of people found themselves pretty much at a loss as to where to begin.

Rollo May (1975) probably summed up our own position well—years before we came to it—by recognizing that "limits are not only unavoidable in human life, they are also valuable. Creativity itself requires limits for the creative act arises out of the struggle of human beings with and against that which limits them" (p. 89).

The data regarding the correlation between constraints and creativity are, as usual, mixed. Finke (1990) had adult subjects make creative products under conditions that varied the amount of choice the subjects had. He found that the most creative inventions emanated from people who were given the most limits. The least creative inventions emanated from those who had the fewest limits.

In contrast, Amabile and Gitomer (1984) had young children (ages two to six) make collages using a wide array of materials. One group of subjects was given a choice of materials; the other wasn't. Amabile and Gitomer found that the subjects given a choice of materials were more creative than those who were not. Similarly, Koestner et al. (1984) had children of roughly seven to eight years of age draw pictures of a house in which they would like to live. In one group, the rules of painting were explained, as was the need to keep supplies neat so that others could use them. In another group, subjects were told the same rules, and also that these rules must be obeyed. In a third group, subjects were not told about any limits. Subjects in the group not given any limits were the most creative, whereas those told that they must obey the limits were the least creative.

We would conclude that whether limits foster creativity or not depends on the nature of the limits and their relation to the people involved and possibly on the ages of the people. People are most creative when they are working in a domain that requires them to deal with things that are relatively novel. If the task is too novel, then people don't have enough prior experience to bring to bear to do creative work. If the task is too easy or familiar, then there may be little opportunity for creativity.

In any case helping people realize the extent of their freedom to create is likely to facilitate creativity, whereas impinging on this freedom is likely to impede creativity. Once again it is not just the environmental variables (task restrictions) that must be taken into account but their effects on the people working under them.

Evaluation

Almost all of us have had the experience of trying to be creative while someone is looking right over our shoulder watching us at work. It's not

easy. Steve Wozniak, inventor of the Apple Personal Computer, commented that it's hard to implement an idea you have when everyone is busy
telling you why it won't work. Wozniak stated, with good reason, that
you're probably lucky if you can wait for feedback on a really new idea
until it is pretty far along. Otherwise people will try to nix what you are
doing before you even get a serious start. Such negative reactions are especially likely in fields where there are likely to be a number of false starts
until you get the one that eventually leads to the idea or product you want
(quoted in Brown, 1988, p. 229).

As you might expect, there is evidence that being evaluated interferes
with creativity. But as you can probably guess, too, there is also evidence
for the helpfulness of evaluation. Nevertheless, the seeming contradictions once again will show themselves to be resolvable.

Amabile et al. (1982) had female undergraduates take part in a collage-
making task. Students were either evaluated while they were working,
evaluated after they were done working, watched but not evaluated, or
neither watched nor evaluated. Amabile and her colleagues found that
both having people watch and having people evaluate creative work reduced the creativity of the work. In a second study involving the writing
of haiku, evaluation again interfered with creativity.

Other investigators have observed the same phenomenon. Berglas et al.
(1981) had young children in grades two through six (roughly seven to
twelve years of age) make collages, and they, too, found that evaluation
hurt—in this case even before the students began working and even
though the evaluation was positive! That is, subjects who had received favorable comments on their artwork before beginning the collages produced less creative work than did those who had received no evaluation.

Bob Gundlach, an inventor in the field of xerography, commented that
he discovered early in life that he did his best work when the boss was
out of town, because then he did not have to worry about being evaluated
or intimidated (quoted in Brown, 1988, pp. 108–9). These kinds of subjective comments further suggest that in real-life creative work as in the
laboratory, evaluation can be detrimental to creativity.

As mentioned above the results on the effects of evaluation are mixed.
Torrance (1965) found that children who were told that the one producing the most creative story would win two dollars turned out to be more

creative than children who were told that the most grammatical story would win two dollars. (Note, though, that in this case, both groups were told that they would be evaluated.) Harrington (1975) found that under-graduates who were told that their work would be scored for various aspects of creativity were more creative than those who were not so told. But again there is a big difference between telling students *how* they will be evaluated versus telling them *that* they will be evaluated. Indeed Amabile (1979) found that subjects who were not told that they would be evaluated produced more creative work than those told that they would, but she also found that telling subjects *how* to be creative in their work facilitated their creativity over students who weren't so told.

The results of these studies suggest that when evaluation is perceived as a threat, it usually hurts creativity. However, if creativity is going to be evaluated and subjects know it, it helps them to know on what criteria they will be evaluated. In general people will probably do better work (of almost any kind) if they know on what bases they will be evaluated.

The studies above all look at evaluation by other people. The story for self-evaluation appears to be somewhat different: Self-evaluation can help people by enabling them to spot early creative work that is going off track. Indeed Lubart (1994) has found that early self-evaluation when doing creative writing facilitates creativity more than does later self-evaluation.

Competition

Life tends to throw competitive situations our way, whether or not we seek them out. Studies have diverged in their results on the effects of competition on creativity.

Some studies have suggested that competition facilitates creativity, and indeed countless competitions judged the winner to be the person (or persons) showing the highest levels of creativity. Science contests, invention contests, creative writing contests, and art contests are all examples of such competitions. The Odyssey of the Mind competition, brainchild of Professor Sam Micklus of New Jersey's Glassboro State College (now called Rowan College of New Jersey), is a forty-seven-state creative-problem-solving event (Kahn, 1987). The challenges for different age groups include kindergartners throwing a tea party for imaginary guests, high-school students designing an eleven-inch-high balsawood structure to support six hundred pounds, and a story-writing problem called "Humor from Homer," in which students write their own stories in the style and tone of Homer's *Odyssey*. Competition occurs at the school, state, and national levels.

In an early study of competition and creativity, Torrance (1965) assigned a large number of elementary school children to either a competitive or a noncompetitive condition for making improvements on products. He found that children in the competitive condition generally were more creative than those in the noncompetitive condition. Raina (1968) found that using competition for cash incentives resulted in ninth-grade students doing significantly more creative work than was done by students who were not offered such incentives. Abramson (1976) looked at the effects of competition on creative problem solving and concluded that competition helped, but only for verbal creativity tasks (not for figural or visual arts tasks).

There is certainly everyday evidence to suggest ways in which competition can enhance creativity. In athletics, for example, the competitive spirit is behind most of the creative ideas that people generate in order to win either for themselves or for their team (Brown & Gaynor, 1967). Many athletes find that they perform better in the actual competition than they do when they are just practicing, suggesting again the role that the actual competition plays in encouraging creativity.

Other work, however, has suggested that competition is a mixed blessing. For example, Amabile (1982) had girls ranging in age from seven to eleven make collages under either competitive or noncompetitive conditions. The products created under the competitive conditions were judged as significantly less creative than those produced under the noncompetitive ones.

Other research has also suggested that competition can interfere with creativity. Adams (1968) gave high school students tasks requiring creative thinking. In one group subjects were told only what to do. In another group subjects were told to do well in order to distinguish the group of which they were a member. In a third group subjects were told explicitly that there would be no comparison among groups. And in a last group subjects were told that there would be no comparisons and, moreover, that they should feel free to answer as they wished. Subjects were most creative when told that they would not be evaluated, and to feel free to answer as they wished. Subjects for whom competition was emphasized were the least creative.

Although the results of the various studies would seem to be contradictory, we again believe that some sense can be made of them. Recall from the preceding chapter that people are their most creative when they are motivated, but not hypermotivated, to do well. In other words some pressure (internal or external) is good, but after a certain point pressure interferes with creative production. Competition obviously increases pressure. Whether it facilitates or inhibits creativity, however, is likely to be a function of a person's initial level of arousal. Someone who is not very aroused to begin with is likely to be spurred to greater creativity by competition. On the other hand someone who is already quite aroused may go over the edge when placed in a competitive situation and produce work that is not very creative at all. Thus we need to consider the individual rather than group effects alone in deciding whether competition is a good thing. When deciding whether to enter a competition, or place your child into a competition, you should consider first whether your level of motivation, or that of your child, is already high. If it is, the individual may not need the contest to reach the creative heights. If it is not, the contest may be just the thing needed to bring you or your child to new heights of creative performance.

Another factor that is likely to interact with competition is the difficulty of the task. In general the harder the task a person confronts, the more anxiety he or she is likely to experience. Thus, for very difficult tasks, competition is likely to inhibit creative performance, because a person's arousal level was likely to be high even without the competition. However, if a person tends not be motivated already to do the difficult task, the competition still could enhance motivation. For tasks of easy-to-lower-intermediate difficulty, competition may help by increasing arousal that is likely to be lower without the competitive situation. Note again, though, that the difficulty of the task will interact with the person's natural level of arousal. People at naturally higher levels of arousal (who, on average, tend to be more introverted than extroverted) probably need competition less than people at naturally lower levels of arousal (who, on average, tend to be more extroverted than introverted) in order to produce creative work.

Cooperation

We have seen that competition can either facilitate or impede creativity, depending on circumstances. How about cooperation? What are its effects on creativity?

Exponents of brainstorming (for example, Osborn, 1963; Parnes, 1962) would argue for the value of cooperation. In this technique people are encouraged to generate creative ideas in a group, play off against one another's ideas, and say practically whatever comes to mind, at the same time deferring criticism of others' ideas until the later portion of the brainstorming process. Thus individuals implicitly cooperate in order to enhance the creativity of the group as a whole.

According to Stein (1974) a number of people intervene between the creative work of an individual and the society as a whole, and the full real-ization of a creative idea requires their implicit cooperation. In particular Stein has identified six different groups. One, a "psychic group," allows the creator to discuss new ideas and serves as a source of emotional sup-port. For example, fellow scientists, artists, or members of one's family might all be members of this group. A second type of group is that of the "entrepreneur," the financial intermediary who helps weed out bad or even crackpot ideas. A third group, the "executive or foundation," serves a simi-lar function. This is what funding agencies do, for example, in deciding to fund some creative projects but not others. A fifth group is "transmission agents," people like agents, gallery owners, or journalists who help bring creative work to the public. And the last group is the "public" itself, which makes the ultimate judgments on the creativity of a body of work.

Most people use members of various groups to help them along the way to creative work. For example, many scientists need funding and will therefore have foundations review the quality of the work they propose. To get feedback, scientists often show their proposals to colleagues before submitting them, thereby enlisting their colleagues' cooperation and sup-port. Artists also often seek opinions of colleagues and others whom they respect before exhibiting their work. Authors must enlist the cooperation of a publisher and usually a literary agent in order to bring work from their minds to the general public. The point quite simply is that even work that is individual in its conception usually involves several different kinds of groups before it actually comes before the public.

People would probably be reluctant to say that the cooperation of various groups can hinder creativity, and yet we are convinced that there are cir-cumstances under which cooperation subtly undermines creative work. The most common such circumstances are ones in which members of a professional group will accept and support work only if it conforms to the group's norms. Art, literature, or science that falls too far afield is likely to be rejected and even ridiculed, with the result that when highly creative people seek to ignore or violate the norms of their peer groups, they may find these groups to be distinctly noncooperative. Creative people may be so eager to enlist the cooperation of their peers that their work actually becomes less creative as they try to please them.

Our point quite simply is that if you receive eager cooperation from all groups with which you are involved, you are not thereby guaranteed the most creative products of which you are capable. You need to evaluate not only your work but those who are *evaluating* your work to determine what their vested interests are and to assess to what extent their interests truly correspond to yours.

Home Climate

Certain aspects of the homes in which creative people grew up appear again and again as important to creative development. For one thing the childhood home life of creative adults was usually intellectually stimulating. Homes of creative people often had libraries and parents with a variety of hobbies of an intellectual kind (Ochse, 1990; Simonton, 1984, 1988a). These parents were often well educated, whether through formal schooling or their own self-education efforts.

There is also a tendency for creative people to be firstborns (Simonton, 1984). However, it is probably not being the firstborn per se that results in enhanced creativity, but rather the greater financial and emotional resources that parents expend on firstborns. For example, it sometimes happens that after the firstborn is sent to a school of distinction, there are insufficient financial resources for the second to be sent to the same or a comparable school. It may also happen that the parents devote less time to subsequent children. In any case it appears to be parental investment that provides the key, rather than birth order.

Creative work is sometimes used as an escape from an unpleasant home environment. The child may first start doing creative things as a way of blocking out his or her surroundings. For example, Dean Koontz, author of best-selling thrillers, grew up in a very poor family and used fiction as an escape from his environment. He received little support from his parents, who viewed books as a waste of time.

We believe that it is important for children to learn to be independent, intellectually and otherwise. Parents too often feel compelled to make sure their children have everything and every possible assistance, which we believe does those children no favor. The important thing is to provide children with every opportunity to learn to do and then allow them to do things for themselves.

Role Models

Perhaps the most useful thing parents can give to children is good role modeling. The best way to develop creativity is to watch and emulate creative role models. The same applies to teachers. Often the teachers we remember best, years after we had them as teachers, are those who have served as role models to us. The important thing, therefore, is to provide a creative role model for those you wish to influence.

As an example of role modeling, Stephen Sondheim found a career-shaping mentor in Oscar Hammerstein II, famed lyricist of *Oklahoma* and *Show Boat*. At the age of fifteen, Sondheim left his divorced, angry mother and went to live with neighbors, the Hammersteins. According to Sondheim, "'it was Oscar and Dorothy's saving my emotional life, combined with his teaching me' that made all the difference" (quoted in Kakutani, 1994, p. 31). With Oscar Hammerstein's guidance Sondheim learned how to write songs and express his feelings in song. Sondheim says that his experiences were translated into wanting to create things. A driving force behind Sondheim's work was not success but rather a desire "'to please Oscar,'"—to make him proud.

Although the exact effect of role models on creativity may vary with each case, the evidence for the importance of role modeling is clear. Statistical studies of European and Chinese creators show that the great thinkers of a given generation provide the role models for the next, and the more great thinkers there are in one generation, the more great thinkers there are likely to be in the next (Simonton, 1975, 1988a). Consistent with our earlier comments, however, role modeling can turn negative if the dependence of disciples on the previous generation of role models is prolonged. If the disciples are not able to set their own course, but rather end up imitating their role models, they may actually turn out to be less creative than they might otherwise have been. The point once again is that good role models encourage independence, not slavish imitation.

An interesting study on the importance of role modeling in science was conducted by Zuckerman (1977). Zuckerman studied American scientists who won the Nobel Prize between 1901 and 1972. More than half of the ninety-four laureates (forty-eight to be exact) had themselves worked under or with other laureates, either as graduate students, postdoctoral fellows, or collaborators. In interviews the laureates indicated that their mentors had served as role models from whom they had learned scientific techniques, standards for their work, ways of thinking about problems, taste for what constitutes an important problem, and how the community of scientists operates. The laureates were also more likely to have worked with their award-winning mentors before their mentors won the Nobel Prize rather than after. In science, therefore, you want to pick your distinguished mentor before his or her full distinction is recognized! Sometimes these mentors are not still doing their most active and possibly creative work in the years after they win the prize.

School Climate

Albert Einstein (quoted in Hoffman, 1972, p. 31) criticized traditional education bluntly: "One had to cram all this stuff into one's mind for the examinations, whether one liked it or not. This coercion had such a deterring effect on me that, after I passed the final examination, I found the consideration of any scientific problems distasteful to me for an entire year." Einstein further remarked that it was surprising that the methods of instruction used in schools had "not yet entirely strangled the holy curiosity of inquiry" (quoted in Schilpp, 1951, p. 17).

The notion that schooling inhibits creativity has been shared by many creative people in a variety of fields (see Brown, 1988). In our own experience students often become less able to produce creative work as they progress through school. For example, one of the authors, in working with bright elementary school students, has found that they are often able to produce creative ideas for psychology experiments as well as or better than college undergraduates. It is surely not that the younger children are more creative, but rather that they are more likely to allow themselves to tap their creative resources.

In a nationwide study of 671 college professors nominated for either positively or negatively influencing creativity, Chambers (1973) found that teachers who facilitate creativity conduct classes informally, welcome unorthodox views, allow students to choose topics to investigate, express enthusiasm for what they are doing, and interact more with students outside class. The three most important characteristics of these teachers were that they treated students as individuals, encouraged independence, and served as creative role models. The teachers who inhibited creativity, in contrast, discouraged generation of new ideas, emphasized rote learning, and were insecure or rigid.

Part of the problem in the schools is that teachers sometimes value personal attributes in students that are not facilitative of or that actually inhibit creativity. A study by Torrance (1964) found that traits that teachers valued more than experts on creativity included popularity, social skills, and acceptance of authority. The experts on creativity, on the other hand, valued more highly being a good guesser, independent thinking, and risk taking.

Perhaps the problem goes still further. Work by Giaconia and Hedges (1982) comparing open education, in which children are given more opportunities to explore and set their own individualized curriculum, and more traditional education, which is more rigid, suggests that the open environment that favors the development of creativity may not favor high levels of academic achievement, and vice versa. Thus there may be a trade-off to be considered in setting goals for education.

This trade-off has recently been a point of discussion in the use of textbooks in classrooms (Richardson, 1994). Some schools have begun to allow teachers to spend their textbook dollars on diverse books and materials to create personalized lessons for their classes. One teacher, for example, uses several books about bears to teach her students how to read, write, and count. This relatively open approach to teaching may foster creativity. Other educators, however, support the use of standard textbooks, arguing that they comprise the most cost-effective way to disseminate a basic set of information to a wide audience.

As highlighted by the textbook issue, part of the reason that so many schools discourage creativity may not have as much to do with teachers and principals as with what these individuals are charged with producing. To the extent that society demands high scores on tests that measure academic achievement rather than creative use of knowledge, when the schools emphasize recall of knowledge at the expense of its creative use, they are merely carrying out their intended mission.

Organizational Climate

Taylor (1961) interviewed twelve department heads in ten research laboratories, ten of whom said that the single most important variable underlying creativity was the working environment. Amabile (1988), in a study of 165 scientists engaged in research and development, found that certain variables consistently separated environments facilitating creativity from those inhibiting it. The facilitating variables were (a) freedom and control over work; (b) good management, which sets goals, prevents distractions, and is not overly strict; (c) sufficient resources; (d) encouragement of new ideas; (e) collaboration across divisions; (f) recognition of creative work; (g) sufficient time to think; (h) challenging problems; and (i) sense of urgency for getting work done. Variables inhibiting creativity were (a) poor rewards; (b) poor communication; (c) red tape; (d) lack of freedom; (e) apathy; (f) critical, unrealistic, or inappropriate evaluation; (g) insufficient resources; (h) time pressure; (i) unwillingness to risk change; (j) defensiveness within the organization; and (k) competitiveness.

Creativity is also inhibited, according to Secretary of the Treasury Lloyd Bentsen (former senator and corporate chief executive), when for managers "the measure of achievement and the goals to be reached are as short term as a politician at the next election. Bonuses, salaries, and promotions are too often dependent on this year's increase of profits over last year." Echoing this idea *Business Week* magazine called today's private-sector managers "'business mercenaries who ply their skills for salary and bonus but rarely for vision'" (quoted in Kirby, 1984, p. 46).

Some companies, however, break the typical corporate mind-set and have special divisions that search for or actively foster new ideas. Quaker Oats, for example, has a "new venture group" that seeks out new product ideas (Melia, 1989). Disney Corporation has an "imagineering" group responsible for the creation and expansion of theme parks (Seal, 1990). The original IBM Personal Computer was created by scientists and engineers working in a separate "skunk works" that gave them the freedom from the usual company responsibilities in order to realize their vision.

Companies that are willing to support the unusual are often much more likely to end up with creative new products than are companies with low tolerance for the extraordinary. Nathaniel Wyeth, inventor of the

---

BOX 10.1

The Magic of Disney: A Case Study

Several features of Disney's corporate culture provide a beneficial environment for creativity. As mentioned in the text, Disney has a special division called Imagineering for developing its theme parks. A diverse group, the imagineers come from 130 different disciplines, including artists, writers, engineers, architects, animators, computer programmers, ride-system designers, and finance experts. Walt Disney once said: "Imagineering is the place where we'll take an idea from anybody" (quoted in Seal, 1990, p. 60). "Blue Sky" meetings are held, in which people are encouraged to dream about new attractions and only the sky is the limit.

Disney animator Marc Davis also worked for Imagineering. He contributed to the Haunted Mansion, the Jungle River Cruise, and many other attractions at Disney parks. Davis describes his experiences working on the theme parks: "If you needed some information, there was always someone you could call on" (Lubart, personal communication, 1990). The environment at Disney was one in which people "cross-pollinated" each others' ideas. For example, Davis explains how Joe Grant of the models department would find

---

plastic soda bottle, received support for his work with plastic containers even when the initial efforts were far from perfection (Brown, 1988).

Strict, strong hierarchical organization of a company appears to be negatively related to creativity (Abbey & Dickson, 1983), whereas decentralized authority seems to encourage it. On the other hand a loose hierarchy, where people lower in the totem pole have access to others beyond just their immediate superior, may serve well for the development of creative ideas. It is especially important that people within the organization have others with whom they can share new ideas, even when those ideas are still half-baked.

In any enterprise most people want to be right in the center of the action, working on the hot topics with the right people in the right places. Yet there is some evidence that—at least in science—marginality may fa-

some obscure French cartoonist who had a special style and bring it to other people's attention.

Walt Disney himself provided a role model for innovative risk taking. Nine years after *Steamboat Willie* (1928), which launched Disney's career, *Snow White* came out. People called the project Disney's folly; a full-length feature cartoon had never been done before. People even said it would "ruin your eyes," but Disney was courageous enough to try. Today Disney leadership stresses the need for risk taking, pursuing "great" ideas, and high quality (Seal, 1990). And there is an acknowledgment that this level of accomplishment requires both "a hell of a lot of effort, [and] a hell of a lot of money" (Seal, 1990, p. 92).

The April 1994 opening of the Broadway show *Beauty and the Beast* presented Disney with both a new risk and an exciting opportunity for further creative expression. It was one of the most expensive productions ever to come to Broadway, a challenging theatrical proving ground. The dare was whether a show featuring a multitude of special effects like computer-driven "sorcery" (for example, thirty-four candles popping up in sequence) and a story geared especially to families could do well on Broadway. Disney illustrates an environment that offers stimulating people, needed resources, creative role models, and a corporate culture that takes risks.

cilitate creativity, whether of the professional or even of the personal kind (for example, in new-immigrant groups) (Simonton, 1988b). Being in a marginal field may have the advantage of letting a person propose ideas that are not widely held without immediately incurring the wrath of a large professional establishment accustomed to thinking in a certain way. Marginality doesn't always help, however, at least not when the marginality is physical: Evidence suggests that for those in the arts, being further away geographically from cultural centers is a distinct disadvantage.

Societal Ambiance

Finally there is the level of the society as a whole. Arieti (1976) has proposed nine features of societies that he believes encourage creativity among their members: (a) support for creative work (for example, patrons of the arts); (b) openness to cultural stimuli; (c) stress on becoming rather than being (the society seeks growth); (d) free access to media; (e) freedom; (f) exposure to diverse stimuli (for example, to other cultures); (g) tolerance for and interest in diverging views; (h) interaction of creative persons (for example, to build on one another's work); and (i) incentives and rewards for creative work. Societies that empower individuals to work toward the future and leave them free to do so reap the benefits of their worldview in the enhanced creativity of their members. A culture such as that of the United States, which values self-sufficiency, individualism, and risk taking, may do more to enhance ultimate creativity than some schools do to suppress it.

Anthropological research further indicates that societies can influence creativity by channeling it into some domains or specific forms of work but not others, or into some socially specific groups but not others (Lubart, 1990). For example, the Ashanti, a West African group, encourage creativity in the carving of secular objects but discourage it in carving objects with religious motifs (Silver, 1981). The Yoruba, who also carve figurines, treat the ear and human face in a standardized way but allow creative variation in the hands, the costume, the arrangement of figures in a larger composition, and the ritual items. In Samoa, Margaret Mead reported, dance is an activity in which creativity is allowed: "Dance [is] seen as an area of culture in which the relative positions of child and adult, high status and low status, even sane and mad could be reversed" (Mead, 1959, p. 224). Finally, an interesting example of culture promoting creativity in specific social groups comes from the early-twentieth-century American West. For the Omaha Indians, tradition dictated that there was "but one way to sing a song," and ritual weeping occurred if a song was incorrectly sung (Colligan, 1983). New melodies could be introduced, however, by males in the elite medicine societies, who conceive of them on vision quests. Some findings using historical data on particular societies and institutions, and their effects on creativity, are shown in box 10.2.

Creativity as an Interaction Between the Individual and the World

Creativity does not exist in a vacuum. A person or a product is judged as creative by others. What one organization or society views as creative, an-

---

BOX 10.2

Politics and Creativity

Dean Keith Simonton has conducted a series of studies on creativity using historical data. His research indicates that the political environment of a society in one generation affects the amount of creativity observed in the next. Consider two aspects of the political environment: political fragmentation and political instability.

Political fragmentation, which may indicate cultural diversity, refers to the number of independent states that exist during a generation (a twenty-year period). One hundred and twenty-seven generations of European creators (700 B.C. to A.D. 1839) were studied. Creative accomplishments across a wide range of domains (such as literature, music, visual arts, and science) tended to increase as the amount of political fragmentation in the previous generation increased.

Political instability is another variable of interest. It can be measured, for example, by the number of political assassinations, coups d'état, and contested power claims that occur during a generation. The relationship between this environmental factor and creativity for 127 generations of European history is a negative one. Political instability in one generation inhibits creative work in the following generation.

---

other may view as pedestrian or even awful. For many centuries Sandro Botticelli was considered to be a painter of little talent, and it wasn't really until the nineteenth century that art critics began to reevaluate his work in a favorable light (Csikszentmihalyi, 1988). The importance for genetics of the work of Gregor Mendel was not recognized until well after Mendel's death (Csikszentmihalyi, 1988). And although Johann Sebastian Bach is now considered to be one of the greatest composers of all time, his work did not receive the appreciation now bestowed on it until well after his death (Weisberg, 1986). The first submarine was invented by a Dutchman in 1620. It was able to hold twelve sailors, contained bottled oxygen for breathing, and was propelled by oars that could be used underwater. The invention was ignored, and the inventor ended up as the proprietor of a pub in his later years (Grudin, 1990).

Sometimes people are remembered for reasons other than those they intended. Arthur Conan Doyle believed his serious work to be his nonfiction, and wrote his Sherlock Holmes stories for profit and pleasure. George Washington Carver's work improved the lives of poor farmers, and his efforts expanded agriculture in the United States, but he is best remembered for helping the peanut industry (Briggs, 1990).

Finally, we sometimes remember people for things that were shunned during their own times. Galileo was condemned as a heretic, and many other scientists were seen as crackpots in their time. In the 1951 satirical film *The Man in the White Suit*, the invention of what appears to be an indestructible fabric is regarded as a threat by virtually all who learn of it. Manufacturers see the fabric as a threat to their sales, unionists as a threat to their jobs. The movie ends "happily," however, when the chemicals in the fabric eventually prove to be unstable and the suit falls apart (Grudin, 1990). To be creative you need to buy low and sell high, but often the reaction you receive from your environment is one of feeling threatened rather than supported.

We conclude this section by emphasizing the importance of finding an environment in which you can capitalize on and be appreciated for your own creativity. Some years ago the senior author had a very talented graduate student. The student received two job offers, one from a highly prestigious institution, the other from a good but less prestigious institution. The only problem was that the highly prestigious institution did not seem to be one that particularly valued the kind of creative work the student did, whereas the less prestigious institution did seem to be such a place.

The author, in what was probably the worst advice he ever gave anyone, recommended that the student take the prestigious job, because if he didn't he would always wonder whether he could have made it there. Unfortunately the student took the advice. He did all right, but probably not as well as he would have done at the other place. There is a lesson to be learned: Find the environment that rewards what you have to offer, and then make the most of your creativity and of yourself in that environment.

Creativity at the Organizational Level

Up to now we have considered creativity at the level of the interaction of the individual with the environment. But we can consider creativity at the level of the organization as well. Certain organizations seem to be creative themselves and to foster creativity in their members. Other organizations are stagnant and repulse creativity at every opportunity. One of us has provided a theory of organizational environments as they foster or discourage creativity (Sternberg, in press), which we describe here.

The theory requires that one ask three questions about an organization—a school, a business, a government agency, or whatever—in order to assess its encouragement of creativity. The three questions are:

1. How much desire is there for actual creativity in this organization?
2. How much desire is there for the *appearance* of creativity in the organization?
3. What is the self-esteem, or opinion of itself, of the organization?

If, for convenience, we respond to each of these questions with a value that is either "low" or "high," then we end up with eight different kinds of organizational environments with respect to their encouragement of creativity. The argument here is that the eight kinds of organizational environments differ rather dramatically in their encouragement of creativity. Of course, no organization need be a pure case: It may be a mixture of kinds of environments. Moreover, although one would certainly not want to claim that these are the only possible kinds of environments with respect to creativity, they do appear to encompass some of the major types.

Support of creativity can be of two basic kinds: surface-structural or deep-structural. (Of course there is an underlying continuum here, which we have dichotomized for the sake of convenience.) Surface-structural support refers to the extent to which creativity is encouraged in work but not necessarily in spirit. Low-level creativity is tolerated so long as nothing fundamental about the organization and its workings is called into question. Surface-structural support of creativity allows change, but only within the context of the organization as it exists. Deep-structural support refers to the extent to which more profound creativity is supported. Here, even ideas that might challenge fundamental tenets of the organization are allowed expression. The environment of an organization depends primarily on desire for actual change, and secondarily on desire for appearance of change and self-esteem.

Contexts may sometimes be at least partially domain-specific. In other words, one part of the organization may fall into one category, another part into another. Moreover, an organization may allow creativity in some domains but not in others.

TABLE 10.1

The "Mineralogical" Theory of Support for Creativity

Description of Organization	Desire for Actual Change	Desire for Appearance of Change	Self-Esteem	Resulting Support for Creativity	
				Surface	Deep
Rusted Iron	L	L	L	L	L
Granite	L	L	H	L	L
Amber (with Internal Insects	L	H	L	ML	L
Opal	L	H	H	ML	L
Cubic Zirconium	H	L	L	ML	L
Slightly Imperfect (SI) Diamond	H	L	H	MH	ML
Lead	H	H	L	MH	ML
Diamond in the Rough	H	H	H	H	H

Note: L = Low;   ML = Medium low;   MH = Medium high;   H = High.

Each of the eight types of organizational environments is depicted in terms of a different kind of mineral. Table 10.1 summarizes the theory.

Alternative Organizational Environments

The Rusted-Iron Organization

The Rusted-Iron Organization is low in desire for actual change, desire for appearance of change, and self-esteem. The mood of the organization is despondence; its self-image is that "we're lost; we're hopeless." Typical self-statements of this organization are: "We were once okay, but now we're long gone"; "We're beaten down with bureaucracy from one side, and stale customs from the other"; and "We just try to get through the day."

Various signs indicate a Rusted-Iron Organization. Among these signs are an entrenched bureaucracy, apathy, a decayed physical plant, staff burnout, lack of follow-through on agreements, indifference to clientele, and lack of resources. The prognosis for creativity in an organization showing these signs is poor: The likelihood of both surface-structural and deep-structural support of creativity is low.

The Granite Organization

The Granite Organization is low in desire for actual change, low in desire for appearance of change, but high in self-esteem. Its mood is one of smugness. Its self-belief is that "we're sure and solid like the Rock of Gibraltar. Change would only chip away at us." Typical self-statements are: "We may not look great, but we're solid and durable"; "This is an organization that works"; and "We keep our employees in line."

Some signs of a Granite Organization are a traditional organization, emphasis on appearances, pride in always having done things the way they're now being done, and grim staff attitude. The prognosis for this organization, like that for the Rusted-Iron Organization, is poor: Both surface-structural and deep-structural support of creativity is low.

The Amber Organization (with Internal Insects)

The Amber Organization is low in desire for actual change, high in desire for the appearance of change, and low in self-esteem. Its mood is one of frustration; its self-belief is that "we're internally flawed. To change would destroy our very core and us with it." Thus, though the Amber Organization believes that it has internal flaws, if they were to be removed, it would result in the destruction of the organization, just as removing internal insects from amber would destroy the amber. Typical self-statements are: "We know we've got problems, but you just can't beat the system here"; "Moving the organization ahead is like moving a graveyard anywhere"; and "The core is rotten: Management hasn't budged in years."

Some signs of an Amber Organization are an inured and often aging management team, obvious structural flaws in the way the organization works, hyperstability in the face of dissension, and inaccessibility of the power structure. The prognosis for surface-structural support of creativity is medium low, and the prognosis for deep-structural support is low.

The Opal Organization

The Opal Organization is low in desire for actual change, but high in desire for appearance of change and high in self-esteem. Its mood is one of self-righteousness. Its typical self-belief is that "when you're the best,

you've got to put your efforts into staying that way." Typical self-statements are: "Anywhere you look, creative new things are happening";
"We're the best in the business"; and "Look at this production plant" (or
data-processing facility or whatever).

This organization is like an opal, in that if you look at it from different
perspectives, it looks different and as if it's changing when, in fact, it's always the same. And the power structure of the organization believes that
changing the organization, like changing an opal, is likely only to make it
worse. It fares best when left alone.

Signs of an Opal Organization are typically affluence, a shiny physical
plant, many (often unused or ill-used) resources, slickness of management, clear emphasis on appearances, high salaries, and surprising lack of
mission. The prognosis for surface-structural support of creativity is moderately low; the prognosis for deep-structural support is low.

The Cubic Zirconium Organization

The Cubic Zirconium Organization is high in desire for actual change but
low in both desire for the appearance of change and in self-esteem. The
mood of the organization is fraudulence: As with a cubic zirconium, no one
wants observers to know that it's fraudulent, so observers are kept at a distance. Its self-belief is that "We're a fraud; we can't let outsiders get too close,
lest they find out." Typical self-statements are: "We can't have outsiders disrupt our operation"; "You can see yourself that things are fine here. Thanks
for stopping by"; and "We don't do research here; we make money."

Signs of a Cubic Zirconium Organization are resistance to scrutiny, a
history of no research and development, descriptions that emphasize
show rather than substance, and employees who are reluctant to talk to
outsiders. The prognosis for surface-structural support of creativity is
moderately low; the prognosis for deep-structural support is low.

The Slightly Imperfect (SI) Diamond Organization

The Slightly Imperfect (SI) Diamond Organization is high in desire for actual change, low in desire for the appearance of change, and high in self-
esteem. Its mood is one of denial. Its self-belief is that "If only we could
get rid of X, we'd be really good." (X is a different thing in different organi-

zations, but it is the scapegoat for the organization's woes.) The organization is like a slightly imperfect diamond in that it has, from its own point of view, one not easily visible flaw, which it would just as soon deny if it could. Typical self-statements of the organization are: "We're pretty damn good, although we've got this X to deal with"; "If it weren't for X, we'd be number one"; and "We try to keep X in line, ha-ha."

Signs of a Slightly Imperfect (SI) Diamond Organization are praise of the system coupled with veiled digs at X; deflection of probing questions about X; attempts to deny the problem of X; but subtle hints, despite generally favorable signs, that something is wrong. The prognosis for surface-structural support of creativity is moderately high, and for deep-structural support is moderately low. Indeed, if the problem of X can be successfully dealt with, the organization may be in an excellent position to change.

The Lead Organization

The Lead Organization is high in desire for actual change, high in desire for appearance of change, but low in self-esteem. Its mood is one of superstitiousness. Its self-belief is that "We need a quick way to turn lead into gold." The organization has an almost alchemical or magical view that some quick fix will turn it into the kind of organization it wants to be. Typical self-statements are: "We'll give you a month to show what you can do"; "We can give you an hour per week"; "We need quick results here"; and "We want change, not research."

Signs of a Lead Organization are impatience, magical thinking with respect to possibilities for change, lack of interest in understanding interventions, lack of understanding of organizational problems, and an emphasis on doing, not planning. The prognosis for surface-structural support of creativity is moderately high, and that for deep-structural support is moderately low. If one can get the self-esteem of the organization up, so that it is not forced to resort to superstition, the prognosis can be excellent.

The Diamond-in-the-Rough Organization

The Diamond-in-the-Rough Organization is high in desire for actual change, desire for appearance of change, and self-esteem. Its mood is one of hopefulness. Its self-belief is that "We've got the raw material here to be really great, and we're going to be." Examples of self-statements are: "We can make this work and we will"; "We're on the way up"; "You can help us be what we want to be"; "There'll be problems but we can overcome them"; and "We want to be great."

Signs of a Diamond-in-the-Rough Organization are willingness to devote resources such as time and money to change; playfulness; accurate recognition of strengths and weaknesses; and receptiveness. The Diamond-in-the-Rough Organization views itself in just this way—as a diamond that has a great deal of value but needs to be shaped and formed. Often it will seek outsiders to help it do so. The prognosis for surface-structural change and for deep-structural support of creativity is high.

Examples of the Various Kinds of Organizations

To many of the readers of this book, at least some of the types of organizations described will be familiar. Nevertheless it may be helpful to illustrate some of these types. We use examples taken from encounters we've had while serving as consultants to organizations in efforts to encourage change within those organizations. "Irontown" was a Rusted-Iron Organization. For starters it was extremely difficult to find out where in the bureaucracy of the Irontown organization district one should make a contact to find anything out. Eventually we made a contact, however. The contact person, who was from the corporate headquarters, did not seem to have much enthusiasm for meeting with us, but agreed to do so. Inexplicably the meeting was later canceled by a secretary. After yet another cancellation, the meeting finally took place. However, the official we contacted did not show up. The people who did show up seemed to be minor functionaries without much understanding of (or interest in) how the organization worked. We did make some progress in the meeting, however, and both sides agreed to make some preparations for a future meeting. This meeting took place, but it was as though the first meeting had never happened: There had been no follow-through on the part of the organizational personnel. Moreover, they seemed to have only a foggy recollection of the first meeting. This time we tried specifying in writing what each team would do in order to facilitate interaction with the organization. The next meeting was canceled. When we eventually met again, once more nothing had happened. We discontinued contact with the organization after this meeting.

Consider another example. "Granite Academy," a parochial school that drew its students mostly from a blue-collar ethnic population, had a reputation for regimentation but also for giving students a fine education. We had no trouble making contact with the proper officials and met with them promptly. The officials listened politely to our presentation for a suggested intervention. They seemed interested and asked several questions. They told us that they would get back to us.

They did so the next day. Their decision was that they did not really want a research and development project in the school. They informed us that they had found what we had to say interesting, but that they felt their school wasn't in need of fixing so there was no point in fixing it. It had been clear all along that they really did have high confidence in what they were doing, and that it would take hard persuasion to get them to change. Obviously our persuading hadn't been hard enough. In this particular case the questioning attitude we sought to instill in the students was in direct conflict with the presuppositions of the school and many of its personnel. The emphasis in the school was on rote memorization of both secular and religious content, and the successful student was one who spit back the facts—or what would often seem to some to be opinions, rephrased as facts. It would have been difficult to get this school to change, given its Granite culture.

Whereas Granite Academy saw itself as a bastion of traditional values, Opalessence saw itself as being at the forefront of modern organizational science. This organization had a high budget for technology, a high budget for consultants, and some of the highest salaries in its field. Located in a well-heeled town, Opalessence was generally considered to be among the best organizations in its area of manufacture. The organization welcomed consultants as much as organizations ever do—but almost exclusively for one- or two-shot consultations. They were interested in the consultation as part of their image rather than as a vehicle for change. Moreover, the consultation pattern was one of one-shots. This month might be on productivity, the next on competitiveness, the next on management-employee relations, the next on government regulation. The organization paid good money to bring in nationally known consultants, but there seemed to be little follow-through. Again one had the feeling that the organization was more concerned about the appearance of for-ward-looking programs than it was about any real change. And indeed, the organization did not appear to be changing much. Rather it rested on a fine reputation and on putting a lot of money into giving itself the image it wanted.

As a last example consider Diamond City. Diamond City was compara-ble in size to Opalessence, but its attitude toward creativity was very dif-ferent. Whereas Opalessence wanted only one-shot, brief consultations, Diamond City wanted only consultations that brought with them some real chance of creative change in the organization. The organization en-couraged us to get involved not only with management but also with the employees. Our program became sort of a community effort, and we would occasionally get calls from interested people about the program and what they could do to support it. The program lasted five weeks and was among the most successful we've done. The combined support of all aspects of the organization make this the kind of experience any consul-tant would like to have.

Creativity does not just happen in an organizational context. Some orga-nizations actively encourage creativity, but many do not. We found that the level of creativity at any level of the organization depends not just on hiring creative people but on providing an environment that supports creativity.

Putting It All Together:
The Creative Spirit

In this book we have discussed six resources for creativity: aspects of intelligence, knowledge, thinking styles, personality, motivation, and the environment. Linking all these resources is a single concept: Buy low and sell high. To be creative you need to buy low and sell high in the world of ideas, much as an investor buys low and sells high in the world of securities or other investments. But although almost everyone knows that she should buy low and sell high, few people do it. Why? We believe that it is because to buy low and sell high, you have to (*a*) generate the options that other people don't think of, and recognize which are the good ones (intelligence); (*b*) know what other people have done in your field of endeavor so that you will know what they are not doing or have not yet thought to do (knowledge); (*c*) like to think and act in creative and contrarian ways, and see the forest from the trees in your creative endeavors (thinking styles); (*d*) be willing to take risks and overcome the obstacles that confront those who buy low and sell high, and to continue to do so throughout the course of your life (personality); (*e*) not only like to think and act in contrarian ways, but have the drive actually to do so rather than just to think about it (motivation); and (*f*) work at a job, live in a country, or be in a relationship to others that lets you do all these things (environment).

As an illustration of the confluence of resources often needed to yield creativity, consider Gray Wolf and the story of Roger Rabbit. As a child during the depression, Wolf was engrossed by comic books and used the local smoke shop and soda fountain as his library (Morgan, 1990). After college Wolf became a copywriter at an advertising agency and wrote short stories in his spare time, often rising at 4 A.M. to write. One Saturday morning, while watching television, Wolf had a selective-encoding insight. In describing the experience, Wolf says, "I wasn't too taken with the programs but the commercials had cartoon characters like Tony the Tiger, Snap, Crackle and Pop, and Cap'n Crunch coexisting with real kids and nobody thought it was odd. I thought, wow, what an interesting concept" (D'Emidio, 1990, p. 7).

For nine years Wolf worked to transform his insight into a novel that combined real-life characters with animated ones. The manuscript, however, was rejected by more than one hundred publishers, who said there was no market for "adult fantasy." They said that even if it were *Gulliver's Travels* or *Alice in Wonderland*, it wouldn't sell now either. Finally an editor at St. Martin's Press saw the value of the book and lobbied for its publication.

As luck would have it, Disney Studios was looking for a bold new film script using animation at that time. The fit was right and Wolf's novel eventually became the hit movie *Who Framed Roger Rabbit?* Wolf's creative success centered on a selective-encoding insight. However, his background knowledge and experiences, perseverance, and support from the environment (an editor at St. Martin's and then managers at Disney) were important contributing resources in this creative case.

To be creative you need to have a lot of things going for you, and it's not always easy to find them. On the other hand a consistent theme of this book is that it is largely (although not totally) in your power to create the resources that will enable you to have creative accomplishments. The toughest resource to optimize may be the environment, but you need to remember that often in life you do not have to adapt to a stifling environment. You can try to shape it to be closer to the environment you would like to have, or if that fails, you can try to find yourself another environment— another place to live, another place to work, or even another relationship.

Although many psychologists like to quantify things—assigning numbers wherever they can—it is important to realize that your creativity is not just a sum total of the availability of the six resources: The resources aren't even additive. If you were without any intelligence it wouldn't matter what other resources you had—you could never truly be creative. Neither could you be creative if you knew absolutely nothing about the field in which you wanted to work, or hated to do creative work, or were simply unwilling to take even the slightest risk. If you are at or close to the "zero level" on any of the resources, your chances of being creative are practically nil.

At the same time you can certainly compensate for less of some resources with more of others. The desire to work creatively can often compensate at least in part for an environment that is not particularly supportive of creative work—and as we have seen, most environments aren't. A willingness to see things in new ways can sometimes compensate for a lack of detailed knowledge about a field, and indeed, we have seen that the most creative people in a field are not necessarily those who know the most.

Of course, increasing the level of one resource to compensate for another works only up to a certain point, because some resources, such as knowledge, can actually turn detrimental for creativity if the level becomes too high. Finally, in terms of a confluence of resources for creativity, we suggest that some resources can combine interactively to enhance creativity. In other words the co-occurrence of optimal levels of some resources, such as risk taking and motivation, may contribute an extra boost to creativity beyond the simple effects of the two individually. This is one more instance where the whole is greater than the sum of its parts. In our research we found a case of this interaction: With regard to creativity in writing, two resources—knowledge and intellectual ability—interacted to enhance creativity in a multiplicative way.

In sum, the resources work together to yield creativity. Some adequate level of each resource is required. Beyond the minimum level a high level of one resource can compensate for a low level of another. And the resources can combine interactively to enhance creativity beyond the simple effects of each isolated resource.

People are not born creative; rather, creativity can be developed. You can choose to live creatively—to make buying low and selling high a habit. Some basic steps creative people take—and you can take—lead to creative performance:

1. *Redefine problems. Don't just accept what you're told about how to think or act.* For creative people there are relatively few givens. In their lines of creative endeavor they make questioning traditional assumptions a way of

life and are constantly looking through and around problems, not just directly at them. Redefining problems is an ability, but in order to exercise this ability, you first need an attitude—not accepting things as being a certain way just because you're told they are. Sometimes the major thing holding people back is not that they can't see problems in new ways but that it never occurs to them to do so. Creative people, in other words, intentionally decide to buy low and sell high—to walk away from and often ahead of the crowd.

2. *Look for what others don't see. Put things together in ways that others don't; and think about how past experiences, even ones that may initially seem irrelevant, can play a part in your creative endeavors.* To buy low and sell high you constantly have to be looking in the environment for the clues that will tell you what unpopular ideas are likely to go somewhere, and that means looking for clues where others don't. Creative people also look for novel ways to combine the inputs they gain from the environment. They see analogies to past experiences that other people don't see or don't even try to see.

3. *Learn to distinguish your good from your poor ideas, and pay attention to their potential contribution.* A person may be fabulously generative of ideas, but not every idea he or she has will be among the best. You need to go beyond generating ideas to distinguish your good from your bad ideas. If you don't, you may find yourself coming up with ideas that are not only "selling low" now but are likely to continue to do so for the indefinite future! You also need to pay attention to whether a given idea has the potential really to make a difference to a field or the world, and to whether you should invest further to pursue an idea.

4. *Don't feel that you have to know everything about the domain in which you work before you are able to make a creative contribution.* Many people falsely believe that to be creative in an endeavor they have to know absolutely everything about it. We have argued in this book that often the most creative contributions are made by people who know something about a field, but not all or even practically all that there is to know. In fact, as we have seen, too much knowledge can interfere with the creative process. People with a lot of knowledge are sometimes unable to see problems in a new way.

Good investors are not always those who know the most about the available stocks, but rather those who know something and, more important, are alert and know where they should focus their attention. Creative people are the same way.

5. *Cultivate a legislative, global style*. Creative people not only have the ability to come up with ideas—they like to do this kind of work. Any number of people have the ability but not the desire to be creative. To buy low and sell high you have to want to do it.

Stemming from another style dimension, many people are "creative in the small." They have new and possibly even useful ideas, but they are ideas at the level of details. There is nothing at all wrong with having such ideas, because much of life is about little things. Moreover, sometimes small ideas combine eventually to yield the big ones. However, we suggest that those with a global style—people who usually look at the large picture—tend to have a better chance at an overall novel solution to a problem. Of course, the ability to shift between global and local levels, as well as the ability to shift among other styles that a task requires, is also important.

6. *Persevere in the face of obstacles, take sensible risks, and be willing to grow*. To be creative you need to recognize that you will face obstacles. You can't defy the crowd and then expect it to ignore you. More likely it will try to get you to join it. And if you don't, the crowd is likely to throw up an obstacle course in your way. The question is not whether a creative person will face obstacles, but rather whether he or she will have the perseverance to overcome them. The creative person, also like the good investor, must be willing to take risks and to go beyond his or her first creative idea and generate others. We have also discussed the importance of openness to new experiences, tolerance of ambiguity, and having the courage of one's convictions.

7. *Discover and tap into your intrinsic motivations*. Good investors happily spend many hours—and usually days, weeks, and months—poring over information. Creative people are almost always ones who love what they do; they do not work at a task because they have to do it. To be creative find what really turns you on and then do it. Extrinsic motivators can be either beneficial or detrimental for creativity. We suggest that a key point is whether a person concentrates more attention on the ultimate reward or instead on the task itself.

8. *Find or create environments that reward you for what you like to do*. To be creative you need to construct your environment in such a way that it will reward you for what you like to do. And if you can't shape your present environment to do so, you need to consider finding a new environment that will reward you. Environments typically contain elements that are both bullish and bearish for creativity. We discussed such environmental features as task constraints, competition, and home, school, work, and societal climate.

9. *Resources needed for creativity are interactive, not additive*. To be creative you need at least some of the appropriate resources. Although you can compensate for lack of some resources with more of others, compensation works only up to a point. A person who is below certain levels of intelligence, knowledge, willingness to take risks, intrinsic motivation, or whatever, is unlikely to be creative, no matter how much of other resources he or she may have available. For example, at the time this chapter was being written, there were serious internal conflicts in Somalia and Bosnia. No matter how adequate a person's internal resources, the minimal environmental resources in these countries make it unlikely that someone living there will be in a position to produce lasting works of art or science.

10. *Make a decision about a way of life that fosters creativity*. Many of the resources needed to be creative become available when a person decides to *make* them available. Although the ability to redefine problems is not a matter of decision, openness to redefinition of problems is. To redefine a problem you have first to be willing to look at it in new ways. Similarly willingness to take risks, to overcome obstacles, to grow, to tolerate ambiguity, and to see the forest instead of the trees (global versus local style) are all, in large parts, resources a person can have if he or she decides that they are important to have. Our point, quite simply, is that the major obstacle to creativity often is not in the environment but in the way a person looks at the world. If you decide to look at it creatively, you can rather quickly improve the chances of having creative ideas.

Implications and Extensions

Our view of creativity has some implications that go beyond the theoretical, and we discuss some of these implications here.

GIFTEDNESS, ESPECIALLY CREATIVE GIFTEDNESS, IS NOT A "UNITARY ENTITY"

Some schools have "gifted programs," whereby certain children are identified as gifted in general and then placed in special classes exclusively for the gifted. In some school districts there are even special schools open only to those children who receive high scores on entrance tests. For example, New York City has some schools of this type that are rather well-known across the country, such as Hunter High School, Stuyvesant High School, the Bronx High School of Science, and Music and Art (now named LaGuardia High School of Music and Art and Performing Arts).

But we saw in chapter 2 that creativity tends domain-specific. The correlations of rated creativity of creative products are not zero across domains, but they are low to moderate. And our findings are no exception in this regard.

Runco (1987) found correlations that averaged only .19 when performances of 228 children in grades five to eight were compared across seven domains (writing, art, music, crafts, science, performing arts, and public presentations). Isaacs (1978), studying eminent creators, noted that although there are examples of so-called Renaissance men, like Leonardo da Vinci and Benjamin Franklin, they are far more often the exception than the rule.

Gray (1966) listed 2,400 eminent Western creators in various fields who worked between the years A.D. 850 and 1935. Creators were categorized in ten different fields (architecture, sculpture, painting, printmaking, dramatics, poetry, fiction, nonfiction, philosophy, and musical composition). Only 17 percent of the total sample were listed as eminent in more than one domain, and only 2 percent spanned domains that are distant from each other (such as musical composition and philosophy, in contrast to sculpture and painting, which would be viewed as relatively close domains).

The implication is clear: To talk about such a thing as "general creative ability" simply does not fit the best data available. This is not to say that people potentially could not be creative in a variety of domains, but in the world as we know it people generally show their highest levels of creativity only in one domain (or a small number of related domains).

We have argued elsewhere that intelligence is similarly relatively domain-specific (for example, Sternberg, 1985a, 1988e), meaning that although people can certainly be intelligent in more than one way, there are many different ways of being intelligent, and the same people are usually not maximally intelligent in each. A better model for assessing creative giftedness therefore would be to find the area (or those areas) in which a person excels and help him or her realize as fully as possible his or her giftedness in those areas. Consigning a person to the "nongifted" group pretty much labels the person in a way that discourages and ultimately may suppress the creative contribution that the person might have made.

THE MOST HIGHLY CREATIVE PEOPLE MAY BE SO NOT BECAUSE THEY HAVE MORE OF
ANY ONE RESOURCE BUT BECAUSE OF THE CONFLUENCE OF RESOURCES
Many cultures, including the North American and Western European ones, tend to accept a linear model of the relation of ability to performance. The more a person has of some ability or some kind of knowledge, the better he or she will perform. The investment approach, however, belies the linear model.

The relation between some of the resources and creativity is anything *but* linear. For example, we have seen that very high levels of knowledge may actually interfere with creativity. Moreover, too high a level of extrinsic motivation can actually paralyze a person in his or her attempts to produce creative work, because the person can become reward focused. According to Dabrowski (1967), the ideal environment for creativity is not one that always encourages and rewards creative work but one that throws its shares of obstacles in the way of the creative person, so that he or she has something to push against. Our point is simply that the investment theory argues more for a balanced conception of creativity. A person is most likely to be creative when there is a balance among the resources needed for creativity, not when he or she is at or near the top on one resource, irrespective of the others.

Our view suggests that what appear to be qualitatively higher levels of creativity in some people may not be qualitative jumps in some abstract creativity scale but rather synergistic confluences of resources. The person who is good at redefining problems but executive in thinking style, or who is intrinsically motivated but unwilling to take risks, will not make the qualitative leap to creative greatness. The person who does, however, may do so as a result of having an above-average level of ability, some knowledge about a field, legislative and global styles, willingness to surmount obstacles and take risks and grow, intrinsic motivation, and a supportive environment. In other words the qualitative leap may be a synergy among resources more than it is a super-high level of any kind of creative skill.

THE BEST PREDICTOR OF FUTURE CREATIVE BEHAVIOR IN A DOMAIN IS PAST CRE-
ATIVE BEHAVIOR IN THAT DOMAIN
Psychologists tend by nature to be interested in prediction, so perhaps it is not surprising that they have invented tests to predict creativity, such as the Torrance tests (Torrance, 1974). But the data we have reviewed, and our own data as well, suggest that domain-general tests of fairly trivial kinds of creativity (for example, thinking of unusual uses for a paper clip) are not likely to be the best predictors of future creative performance. Rather, the best predictors of future creative performance are likely to be past creative performances of the same kind.

In the world of art and of musical composition, readiness for various kinds of training has traditionally been assessed via portfolios of products. The person has demonstrated his or her creative potential by showing past creative performances. In our opinion this "portfolio" view ought to be extended to all domains. And indeed there is a strong movement toward testing in this direction (for example, Resnick & Resnick, 1992). Instead of relying on fairly trivial tests to make our decisions about creativity, or on interviews that may not measure creativity at all, we should assess past creative performances.

FOR THE MOST PART CREATIVE PERFORMANCE IS NOT NOW BEING ASSESSED AT ALL
In fact relatively few institutions seriously assess creativity. A few years ago, one of the authors reviewed his children's report cards and found that even in early elementary school, where creativity is often most rewarded, there were no checkoff boxes for creativity. Later schooling is no different: A child could be the most creative in the class in one or several areas, without its being recognized on his or her report card. And businesses are the same way. In fact the creative person is often "rewarded" by being let go for not fitting in rather than being given a promotion or bonus for having a creative idea.

The tests used for various kinds of admissions—college, graduate school, law school, business school, or whatever—do not measure creativity, nor do they claim to. Yet creativity is essential for outstanding performance in any of these fields. Similarly most of the tests given in schools seem if anything to discourage creativity in one way or another. They may discourage it through a limited multiple-choice format or through scoring of essays and short-answer tests that reward only anticipated answers and not those that go in new and unexpected directions. We need to build mechanisms that reward creativity in our society rather than those that let it go unnoticed or actually punish it.

WHAT IS VALUED AS CREATIVE DIFFERS ACROSS TIME AND PLACE

We stated in chapter 10 and emphasize again that no one thing is creative in everyone's eyes. We suspect that the large majority of people who try to do creative work encounter frustration primarily because there are so many possible environments, and the probability of finding just the one that will maximally reward what a given person has to offer is likely to be low. Thus people need to be assertive in trying out different environments, searching for an environment that rewards what they have to offer. They may or may not find it, but the chances are good that they will have to search for *it*, rather than those in it searching for *them*.

THE NATURE OF CREATIVITY CHANGES WITH AGE

Bamberger (1986) and others have noted that what is rewarded as creative at one age is different from what is rewarded at another. A child prodigy in music or mathematics, for example, is not gifted in the same way that an adult musician or mathematician is likely to be. A person may reach the heights of childhood performance but never make the transition to being actively creative as an adult. Even in adulthood the nature of creativity may change with age (Gardner, 1993; Gruber, 1986). For example, Gardner found that earlier creative works tend to be more brash and daring, whereas latter ones tend to be more integrative. Arieti (1976) proposed that younger creative people tend to show more spontaneity, intensity, and heat than do older ones. Cohen-Shalev (1989) has suggested that artistic creativity in old age may involve (a) a rejection of formal perfection; (b) more emphasis on the subjective than on the objective; (c) lessening of tension and dynamics; (d) even tonality and muted color; and (e) more emphasis on unity and harmony. In writing, he suggested, creativity in older age may involve (a) an increasingly introspective approach; (b) more passivity; (c) more formal ambiguity; and (d) an increased focus on the meaning of one's life and of living with old age and coping with the approach of death (Beckerman, 1990; Lehman, 1953; Wyatt-Brown, 1988).

With regard to the level of creative work, other research has suggested that people in various disciplines produce their most creative work at different ages. For example, a review by Simonton (1991) suggests that mathematicians tend to do their most creative work very early, whereas those in other sciences peak later. Those in the social sciences and humanities peak still later. We do not report ages here because we are not confident that there is truly any consistent "peak." Most creative people go through periods of waxing and waning in their creative enterprises, and the kinds of contributions they make may vary with age. Thus we are slightly skeptical of work that seems to value just one kind of contribution, rather than look at all kinds of contributions a creative person can make.

The practical implication of all this work, however, is that a person ought to be open not only to new creative contributions but also to new *kinds* of creative contributions. In addition to the age effects described thus far, there is a general tendency for the quality and quantity of creative work to decline slowly after age forty or fifty. However, it is important to note research by Simonton (1988a), which shows that the overall reduced creative contribution of older people is not due to their being less capable of highly creative work but simply to their doing less work. The proportion of "hits" remains the same, but as the number of attempts decreases, so does the number of creative products.

Several age-related changes can occur in the resources for creativity that we have been describing throughout this book. These can affect the quantity of work that people produce (and therefore its quality) as well as the type or style of work. For example, intellectual processes are believed to slow down to a small extent with age (decreasing the quantity of work), but there is increased dialectical thinking, which may account for the increased formal ambiguity in older creators' work (Berg & Sternberg, 1985; Cerella, 1990). Older creators recognize the difficulty and often impossibility of arriving at any one "truth" in their work. They also know that knowledge can become outdated with age. However, new knowledge is added about old age itself, which may explain some of the shifts in topics of work with age. Thinking styles may shift toward the conservative pole, which would decrease the tendency to produce new work. Personality changes with age have been documented, showing declines in risk taking, tolerance of ambiguity, perseverance, openness to new experience, and self-esteem (Abra, 1989; Botwinick, 1984; Jaquish & Ripple, 1981). In particular elderly people in research situations often choose to avoid problems that involve risk; this trend continues even if they successfully solve the first problems they are given (Okun & Di Vesta, 1976). This risk aversion with age may limit willingness to try new work, decreasing the number of attempts at being creative. In terms of motivation there are built-in career patterns, namely retirement, that decrease incentives for creative work in the workplace after a certain age (somewhere between fifty and seventy). Finally, changes in the social environment can affect creativity over the lifespan.

For example, as you grow older, the number of demands on your time increases. Often you are asked to take administrative or leadership roles that take time away from the creative work you were able to do earlier (Bjorksten, 1946). In fact, for older people one of the main challenges to staying creative may be finding the time. Often such time is found only if it is actively sought, and if allowances are made in one's schedule to ensure that the time will be there for creative work.

Also, there can be changes over time in standards for creativity. Each generation will have a somewhat different view of exactly what is novel (Romaniuk & Romaniuk, 1981). Products that an older person might consider novel could very well be deemed ordinary by young judges who grew up with such products. This generational shift is especially possible in domains that change rapidly, such as advertising. In fact, in our own research, we found that as people moved away from the average age of the group of judges, the advertisements that they produced were judged less and less creative, even though the judges were unaware of the producers' ages (Lubart & Sternberg, in press).

THE BEST WAY TO FOSTER CREATIVITY IS TO PROVIDE CREATIVE ROLE MODELS

Ultimately, what people are most likely to remember from their schooling or any kind of training is the role modeling they received. One of the authors, for example, does not remember a whole lot of his high school biology course, but remembers very well the way his biology teacher thought about scientific problems. Similarly the most important things he learned from his graduate advisors were about the value of important problems, the value of not accepting what you are told just because you are told it, the value of having an audience to listen to you, the value of working hard even in the face of adversity, and the value of staying ahead of the pack. In other words the most important things we learn are often those that are not directly taught.

If you want your own children or the people with whom you work to be creative, you can prescribe no course or set of exercises that will help them more than being a role model of creativity yourself. We learn to take sensible risks and to fight obstacles by watching others doing these things, not just by reading about risks and obstacles or by solving little problems in a creativity course. Too often the teacher of courses on creative thinking wants students to do what they are told. The most likely outcome is that people will do what they see the role model do. We can create a creative generation of children by being for them what we would like them to be.

Epilogue

The following story is adapted from the novel *The End of Eternity* by the late Isaac Asimov.[*] Although Asimov spun the story for his own purposes, it so well illustrates the major points we have tried to make in this book that we retell it here as our epilogue.

The inhabitants of the distant future realize that they are living with a paradox they must resolve somehow if they are to assure the continuance and continuity of their world. The paradox is that, although everyone knows from recorded history that the formulas for time travel were formulated in the twenty-fourth century by a distinguished mathematician, it is nevertheless impossible that these equations could have been formulated by him or anyone else in the twenty-fourth century because the mathematics that one would need in order to formulate these equations simply was not yet available. Therefore on the one hand all records pointed to the brilliant mathematician as the formulator of these equations; on the other hand he could not possibly have formulated them.

A comparable scenario would be if all our written records indicated that the formulas for the atomic bomb had been developed, say, in the twelfth century. The mathematics, science, and technology needed to come up with these equations could not possibly have been available in the twelfth century, yet our history books stated that it was indeed in that century that the equations were developed.

The people of the distant future realize that they must somehow intervene to keep history on track, and that this intervention, although not recorded in the history books, must take place. If the mathematician does not somehow get the necessary advanced mathematics, he will not be able to formulate the equations, and because much of the future world as they know it exists as the result of interventions by time travel, the failure of the mathematician to develop the equations will presumably result in the future's changing, meaning that the future inhabitants' very existence could be snuffed out at any time.

Finally they realize that there is only one way in which they can resolve the paradox. They must send someone back to the twenty-fourth century to teach the great mathematician the mathematics he will need in order to develop the equations. In other words they need to complete the circle. By sending someone back to teach the mathematician, he will then have the background he needs in order to formulate the equations that will enable their very existence as they know it.

They select someone to go back, but the person they select is no great shakes. Let's refer to him as the technician. There is no need to send back someone extremely valuable to the future society, especially because no one knows exactly what will happen to the fellow when he goes back. All they need is for someone to go back to teach the mathematician what in the distant future is fairly basic mathematics, and then for this someone to get lost. His job will be done as soon as he has prepared the mathematician for the great work that lies ahead of him.

So the technician receives some basic training for what the twenty-fourth century should be like, so that he will be able to be assimilated into the earlier society, and then he is sent back. The mission on its face seems fairly routine, although of course it is extremely important. The technician arrives and, as you may have guessed, things immediately start to go very wrong.

The first thing that goes wrong is that the great mathematician turns out to be a hermit, and no one knows where he lives or even exactly what he looks like. But the technician eventually finds the mathematician, although now time is running out, because the date of the great discovery is getting ever closer, and no one expected the technician to have such difficulty in locating the mathematician.

Then the second thing goes wrong. The great mathematician proves to be something of—well—a jerk. He doesn't want to have anything to do with the technician or with the math the technician offers to teach. But after much effort the technician insinuates himself into the mathematician's presence and convinces him to learn the math. So now it appears that the worst is over.

But finally the third and worst thing goes wrong. One day the great mathematician, out walking on the mountain where he lives, falls and is killed. The technician, who had viewed his work as done as soon as he taught the mathematician the mathematics he would need, realized that he had made a serious mistake: On the date that the mathematician was supposed to have formulated the equations for time travel, he would not have done so, and all future history from that point onward would be changed. The technician's error was perhaps the greatest of all time, causing the snuffing out of the existence of the entire future as it otherwise would have existed.

The technician becomes very depressed, but he realizes he must do something. And then he realizes that he has to redefine the problem. Instead of leaving it to the great mathematician, now dead, to develop the equations for time travel, he somehow has to do it himself. But he is no mathematical genius. In fact, he has a very good basic knowledge of math but certainly is no great whiz in the subject. But the only hope is for him to use what abilities and knowledge he has to formulate the equations.

Essentially he takes the creative path. He works on a big, important problem and really puts himself into it. Time is running out; moreover, he faces enormous obstacles because he does not have available to him the experts and future technology that would have made his task relatively easy. He has to grow emotionally and intellectually, taking on a challenge he never imagined it was in him to take. He risks the future of the world on being able to do the work himself. And although he does not have supportive colleagues in his environment to work with him, neither does he have the distractions and minutiae that can interrupt and interfere with creative work. Finally, in the nick of time, he is able to develop the equations.

So what does he do? He leaves the isolation of the mountain, and tells the press and the whole world first that he is the great mathematician and second that he has formulated the equations for time travel, which he is giving as a gift to the world. Because no one knew what the mathematician looked like, people believed the technician, so that it went down in the history books that on the appointed date in the appointed place the great mathematician presented the equations.

But the technician feels depressed. He has perpetrated an enormous fraud on history. What will go down in the history books will just not be true. But then he has one further realization, with which we will leave you:

There was never any fraud at all. In fact it was always meant to be that he, the technician, saying he was the mathematician, would formulate the equations. Because from the standpoint of history, although not of birth records, he *was* the great mathematician. It was always he, saying he was the mathematician, who had formulated the equations. The circle was thereby completed.

Our point is simply this: It was not the brilliant mathematician who did the marvelously creative work but the erstwhile technician. He was certainly smarter than average and had a better working knowledge of mathematics than the average person. But he was no genius and no mathematical expert. However, with some abilities, some knowledge, a legislative and global style, the willingness to take a risk and to overcome enormous obstacles and to grow, the motivation to give his self-appointed work all he had, and an environment that allowed him to work without distraction, the technician did fabulously creative work. So can we all.

References

Abbey, A., & Dickson, J. W. (1983). R&D work climate and innovation in semi-conductors. *Academy of Management Journal* 26(2), 362–68.

Abra, J. (1989). Changes in creativity with age: Data, explanations, and further predictions. *International Journal of Aging and Human Development* 28(2), 105–6.

Abramson, J. H. (1976). *The effects of non-competitive, individual competitive, and group competitive situations on the verbal and figural creativity of college students.* Unpublished doctoral dissertation, Michigan State University, Ann Arbor.

Adams, J. C., Jr. (1968). The relative effects of various testing atmospheres on spontaneous flexibility, a factor of divergent thinking. *Journal of Creative Behavior 2*, 187–94.

Adams, J. L. (1986a). *The care and feeding of ideas: A guide to encouraging creativity.* Reading, Mass.: Addison-Wesley Publishing Co.

——— (1986b). *Conceptual blockbusting: A guide to better ideas* (3rd ed.). New York: Addison-Wesley. (Original published 1974.)

Albert, R. S. (1971). Cognitive development and parental loss among the gifted, the exceptionally gifted, and the creative. *Psychological Reports 29*, 14–26.

——— (1978). Observations and suggestions regarding giftedness, familial influence and the attainment of eminence. *Gifted Child Quarterly 22*, 201–11.

Amabile, T. M. (1979). Effects of external evaluation on artistic creativity. *Journal of Personality and Social Psychology 33*, 221–33.

——— (1982). Social psychology of creativity: A consensual assessment technique. *Journal of Personality and Social Psychology 43*(5), 997–1013.

——— (1983). *The social psychology of creativity.* New York: Springer-Verlag.

——— (1985). Motivation and creativity: Effects of motivational orientation on creative writers. *Journal of Personality and Social Psychology 48*, 393–99.

—— (1988). A model of creativity and innovation in organizations. *Research in Organizational Behavior 10*, 123–67.

Amabile, T. M., & Gitomer, J. (1984). Children's artistic creativity: Effects of choice in task materials. *Personality and Social Psychology Bulletin 10*, 209–15.

Amabile, T. M., Goldfarb, P., & Brackfield, S. C. (1982). *Effects of social facilitation and evaluation on creativity*. Unpublished manuscript, Brandeis University, Waltham, Mass.

Amabile, T. M., Hennessey, B. A., & Grossman, B. S. (1986). Social influence on creativity: The effects of contracted-for reward. *Journal of Personality and Social Psychology 50*, 14–23.

Arieti, S. (1976). *Creativity: The magic synthesis*. New York: Basic Books.

Asimov, I. (1955). *The end of eternity*. Garden City, N.Y.: Doubleday & Co.

Bamberger, J. (1986). Cognitive issues in the development of musically gifted children. In R. J. Sternberg & J. E. Davidson (eds.), *Conceptions of giftedness* (pp. 388–413). New York: Cambridge University Press.

Barron, F. (1963). *Creativity and psychological health*. New York: Van Nostrand.

—— (1969). *Creative person and creative process*. New York: Holt, Rinehart, and Winston.

Barron, F., & Harrington, D. M. (1981). Creativity, intelligence, and personality. *Annual Review of Psychology 32*, 439–76.

Beckerman, M. B. (1990). Leós Janácek and "the late style" in music. *The Gerontologist 30*(5), 632–35.

Bennett, W. B. (1943). *The American patent system: An economic interpretation*. Baton Rouge: Louisiana State University Press.

Berg, C. A., & Sternberg, R. J. (1985). A triarchic theory of intellectual development during adulthood. *Developmental Review 5*, 334–70.

Berglas, S., Amabile, T. M., & Handel, M. (1981). Effects of evaluation on children's artistic creativity. Unpublished manuscript, Brandeis University, Waltham, Mass.

Birch, H. G., & Rabinowitz, H. S. (1951). The negative effects of previous experience on productive thinking. *Journal of Experimental Psychology 41*, 121–25.

Bjorksten, J. (1946). The limitation of creative years. *Scientific Monthly 62*, 94.

Bloom, B. S. (1985). *Developing talent in young people*. New York: Ballantine Books.

Bloomberg, M. (1973). *Creativity: Theory and research*. New Haven, Conn.: College & University Press.

Botwinick, J. (1984). *Aging and behavior* (3rd ed.). New York: Springer-Verlag.

Briggs, J. (1990). *Fire in the crucible*. Los Angeles, Calif.: J. P. Tarcher, Inc.

Brown, K. A. (1988). *Inventors at work: Interviews with 16 notable American inventors*. Redmond, Wash.: Microsoft Press.

Brown, R. T. (1989). Creativity: What are we to measure? In J. A. Glover, R. R. Ronning, & C. R. Reynolds (eds.) *Handbook of creativity* (pp. 3–32). New York: Plenum Press.

Brown, G. I., & Gaynor, D. (1967). Athletic action as creativity. *Journal of Creative Behavior 2*, 155–62.

Caplow, T., & McGee, R. J. (1957). *The academic marketplace*. Salem, N.H.: Ayer.

Cattell, R. B. (1971). *Abilities: Their structure, growth, and action*. Boston: Houghton Mifflin.

Cerella, J. (1990). Aging and information-processing rate. In J. E. Birren & K. W. Schaie (eds.), *Handbook of the psychology of aging* (3rd ed.) (pp. 201–21). San Diego, Calif. Academic Press.

Chambers, J. A. (1964). Relating personality and biographical factors to scientific creativity. *Psychological Monographs: General and Applied 78*, 584.

——— (1973). College teachers: Their effects on creativity of students. *Journal of Educational Psychology 65*, 325–34.

Clifford, M. M. (1988). Failure tolerance and academic risk-taking in ten- to twelve-year-old students. *British Journal of Educational Psychology 58*(1), 15–27.

Cohen-Shalev, A. (1989). Old age style: Developmental changes in creative production from a life-span perspective. *Journal of Aging Studies 3*(1), 21–37.

Cole, M., Gay, J., Glick, J., & Sharp, D. W. (1971). *The cultural context of learning and thinking*. New York: Basic Books.

Cole, T. (ed.). (1960). *Playwrights on playwriting*. New York: Hill & Wang.

Colligan, J. (1983). Musical creativity and social rules in four cultures. *Creative Child and Adult Quarterly 8*(1), 39–47.

Costa, P. T. Jr., & McCrae, R. R. (1985). *The NEO personality inventory manual*. Odessa, Fla.: Psychological Assessment Resources, Inc.

Csikszentmihalyi, M. (1988). Society, culture, and person: A systems view of creativity. In R. J. Sternberg (ed.), *The nature of creativity* (pp. 325–39). New York: Cambridge University Press.

Dabrowski, K. (1964). *Positive disintegration*. Boston: Little, Brown, & Co.

——— (1967). *Personality-shaping through positive disintegration*. Boston: Little, Brown, Co.

——— (1972). *Psychoneurosis is not an illness*. London: Gryf.

Dabrowski, K., Kawzak, A., & Piechowski, M. M. (1970). *Mental growth through positive disintegration*. London: Gryf.

Davidson, J. E., & Sternberg, R. J. (1984). The role of insight in intellectual giftedness. *Gifted Child Quarterly 28*, 58–64.

DeCharms, R., & Moeller, G. H. (1962). Values expressed in American children's readers: 1800–1950. *Journal of Abnormal and Social Psychology 64*, 136–42.

D'Emidio, S. V. (1990, June). What makes Roger Run? *CableView Magazine*, p. 7.

Dreman, D. (1977). *Psychology and the stock market*. New York: Amacom.

——— (1982). *The new contrarian investment strategy*. New York: Random House.

Einstein, A., & Infeld, L. (1938). *The evolution of physics*. New York: Simon & Schuster.

Eisenman, R. (1987). Creativity, birth order, and risk taking. *Bulletin of the Psychonomic Society 25*, 87–88.

Eisenstadt, J. M. (1978). Parental loss and genius. *American Psychologist 33*, 211–23.

Eisenstadt, J. M., Haynal, A., Rentchnick, P., & De Senarclens, P. (1989). *Parental loss and achievement*. Madison, Conn.: International University Press.

Elkind, D. (1981). *The hurried child: growing up too fast too soon*. Reading, Mass.: Addison-Wesley Publishing Co.

Eliot, T. S. (1932). The function of criticism. In T. S. Eliot, *Selected essays: 1917–1932*. New York: Harcourt Brace.

Emerson, K. (1985, May 5). The creative mind: David Byrne: Thinking man's rock star. *New York Times*, section 6, p. 54.

Eysenck, H. J. (1983). The roots of creativity: Cognitive ability or personality trait? *Roeper Review 5*(4), 10–12.

Feder, B. J. (1992, May 31). Making things stick in the age of plastic. *New York Times*, p. F-10.

Feldman, D. H. (1988). Creativity: Dreams, insights, and transformations. In R. J. Sternberg (ed.), *Nature of Creativity* (pp. 271–97). New York: Cambridge University Press.

Finke, R. (1990). *Creative imagery: Discoveries and inventions in visualization*. Hillsdale, N.J.: Erlbaum.

Finke, R. A., Ward, T. B., & Smith, S. M. (1992). *Creative cognition: Theory, research, and applications*. Cambridge, Mass.: MIT Press.

Frensch, P. A., & Sternberg, R. J. (1989). Expertise and intelligent thinking:

When is it worse to know better? In R. J. Sternberg (ed.), *Advances in the psychology of human intelligence* (vol. 5, pp. 157–58). Hillsdale, N.J.: Erlbaum.

Freud, S. (1908). The relation of the poet to day-dreaming. In *Collected papers* (vol. 4, pp. 173–83). London: Hogarth Press.

Friedman, F., Raymond, B. A., & Feldhusen, J. F. (1978). The effects of environmental scanning on creativity. *Gifted Child Quarterly 22*, 248–51.

Gardner, H. (1983). *Frames of mind: The theory of multiple intelligences*. New York: Basic Books.

———— (1993). *Creating minds*. New York: Basic Books.

Getzels, J. W., & Csikszentmihalyi, M. (1976). *The creative vision: A longitudinal study of problem finding in art*. New York: John Wiley & Sons.

Ghiselin, B. (ed.). (1985). *The creative process: A symposium*. Berkeley: University of California Press.

Giaconia, R. M., & Hedges, L. V. (1982). Identifying features of effective open education. *Review of Educational Research 52*(4), 579–602.

Gilad, B. (1984). Entrepreneurship: The issue of creativity in the marketplace. *Journal of Creative Behavior 18*(3), pp. 151–61.

Glover, J. A. (1977). Risky shift and creativity. *Social Behavior and Personality 5*(2), 317–20.

Goertzel, V., & Goertzel, M. G. (1962). *Cradles of eminence*. London: Constable.

Goertzel, M. G., Goertzel, V., Goertzel, T. G. (1978). *Three hundred eminent personalities*. San Francisco: Jossey-Bass.

Goldstein, L. (1993, Dec. 5). The best-kept secret in Washington. *Washington Post* (magazine), p. W-16.

Goodman, N. (1955). *Fact, fiction, and forecast*. Cambridge, Mass.: Harvard University Press.

Gordon, W. J. J. (1961). *Synectics: The development of creative capacity*. New York: Harper & Row.

Gowan, J. C. (1972). *Development of the creative individual*. San Diego: Robert R. Knapp.

Gray, C. E. (1966). A measurement of creativity in western civilization. *American Anthropologist 68*, 1384–1417.

Gruber, H. E. (1986). The self-construction of the extraordinary. In R. J. Sternberg & J. E. Davidson (eds.), *Conceptions of giftedness* (pp. 247–63). New York: Cambridge University Press.

Grudin, R. (1990). *The grace of great things*. New York: Ticknor & Fields.

Guilford, J. P. (1950). Creativity. *American Psychologist* 5, 444–54.

Hadamard, J. S. (1945). *The psychology of invention*. New York: Dover Publications.

Haensly, P. A., & Reynolds, C. R. (1989). Creativity and intelligence. In J. A. Glover, R. R. Ronning, & C. R. Reynolds (eds.), *Handbook of creativity* (pp. 111–32). New York: Plenum Press.

Hall, W. B., & MacKinnon, D. W. (1969). Personality inventory correlates of creativity among architects. *Journal of Applied Psychology* 53(4), 322–26.

Harding, M. (1994, Apr. 24). School founder still enjoys starting kids off right. *Sunday Freeman* (People), pp. 3, 9.

Harrington, D. M. (1975). Effects of explicit instructions to "be creative" on the psychological meaning of divergent thinking test scores. *Journal of Personality* 43(3), 434–54.

Hayes, J. R. (1989). Cognitive processes in creativity. In J. A. Glover, R. R. Ronning, & C. R. Reynolds (eds.), *Handbook of Creativity* (pp. 135–46). New York: Plenum Press.

Hennessey, B. A., & Amabile, T. M. (1988a). The conditions of creativity. In R. J. Sternberg (ed.), *The nature of creativity* (pp. 11–38). New York: Cambridge University Press.

———— (1988b). Story-telling: A method for assessing children's creativity. *Journal of Creative Behavior* 22(4), 235–46.

Hennessey, B. A., Amabile, T. M., & Martinage, M. (1989). Immunizing children against the negative effects of reward. *Contemporary Educational Psychology* 14, 212–27.

Hill, K. G. (1991). *An ecological approach to creativity and motivation: Trait and environment influences in the college classroom*. Unpublished doctoral dissertation, Brandeis University, Waltham, Mass.

Hoffman, B. (1972). *Albert Einstein: Creator and rebel*. New York: Plenum Press.

Holmes, F. L. (1985). *Lavoisier and the chemistry of life: An exploration of scientific creativity*. Madison, Wis.: University of Wisconsin Press.

Honan, W. H. (1992, March 26). For an answer to a Roman riddle, find Pi. *New York Times*, section C, pp. 15, 19.

Hull, D. L., Tessner, P. D., & Diamond, A. M. (1978). Planck's principle: Do younger scientists accept new scientific ideas with greater alacrity than older scientists? *Science* 202, 712–23.

Isaacs, A. F. (1978). Creativity as manifested in individuals of multiple talents: A preliminary study. *Creative Child and Adult Quarterly* 3(4), 227–45.

Isaksen, S. G., & Puccio, G. J. (1988). Adaption-innovation and the Torrance tests of creative thinking: The level-style issue revisited. *Psychological Reports* 63(2), 659–70.

Jackson, D. N., Hourany, L., & Vidmar, N. J. (1972). A four-dimensional interpretation of risk taking. *Journal of Personality 40*, 483–501.

Jackson, P., & Messick, S. (1965). The person, the product and the response: Conceptual problems in the assessment of creativity. *Journal of Personality 33*, 309–29.

Janis, I. (1972). *Victims of groupthink*. Boston: Houghton Mifflin.

Jaquish, G. A., & Ripple, R. E. (1981). Cognitive creative abilities and self-esteem across the adult life-span. *Human Development 24*, 110–19.

Johnson-Laird, P. N. (1989). Freedom and constraint in creativity. In R. J. Sternberg (ed.) *The nature of creativity* (pp. 202–19). New York: Cambridge University Press.

John-Steiner, V. (1985). *Notebooks of the mind: Explorations of thinking*. New York: Harper & Row.

Jung, C. (1923). *Psychological types*. New York: Harcourt Brace.

Kahn, T. (1987, July 6). Mental agility, not plodding scholarship, gets the gold in the "Odyssey of the Mind." *People*, p. 75.

Kahneman, D., & Tversky, A. (1982). The psychology of preferences. *Scientific American 246*(1), 160–73.

Kakutani, M. (1994, Mar. 20). Sondheim's passionate "Passion." *New York Times* (section 2: Arts & Leisure), pp. 1, 30–31.

Kasperson, C. J. (1978). Scientific creativity: A relationship with information channels. *Psychological Reports 42*(3, pt. 1), 691–94.

Kim, S. H. (1990). *Essence of creativity: A guide to tackling difficult problems*. New York: Oxford University Press.

Kingston, W. (1990). *Innovative, creativity, and law*. Boston, Mass.: Kluwer Academic.

Kirby, M. J. L. (1984). Innovation in government: Problems and possibilities. In A. Charnes & W. W. Cooper (eds.), *Creative and innovative management*, (pp. 41–59). Cambridge, Mass.: Ballinger Publishing Co.

Kirton, M. J. (1976). Adaptors and innovators: A description and measure. *Journal of Applied Psychology 61*, 622–29.

Koestner, R., Ryan, R. M., Bernieri, F., & Holt, K. (1984). Setting limits on children's behavior: The differential effects of controlling vs. informational styles on intrinsic motivation and creativity. *Journal of Personality 52*, 233–48.

Kogan, N., & Wallach, M. A. (1964). *Risk taking: A study in cognition and personality*. New York: Holt, Rinehart, and Winston.

Kotovsky, K., Hayes, J. R., & Simon, H. A. (1985). Why are some problems hard? Evidence from Tower of Hanoi. *Cognitive Psychology 17*, 248–94.

Kruglanski, A. W., Friedman, I., & Zeevi, G. (1971). The effects of extrinsic incentives on some qualitative aspects of task performance. *Journal of Personality 39*, 608–17.

Kuhn, T. S. (1970). *The structure of scientific revolutions* (2nd ed.). Chicago: University of Chicago.

Landrum, G. N. (1993) *Profiles of genius: Thirteen creative men who changed the world*. Buffalo, N.Y.: Prometheus Books.

Langley, P., Simon, H. A., Bradshaw, G. L., & Zytkow, J. M. (1987). *Scientific discovery: Computational explorations of the creative process*. Cambridge, Mass.: MIT Press.

Lawson, C. (1994, Feb. 17). Goo is in the oven, Barbie's at the gym. *New York Times*, p. C-2.

———— (1994, Mar. 20). Music to see and eat by. *New York Times*, (Section 9: Styles), pp. 1, 8.

Lazarus, G. (1993, May 20). FCB puts money on creative work. *Chicago Tribune* (North Sports Final Ed.), Business Section, p. 2.

LeBoeuf, M. (1980) *Imagineering*. New York: Berkley Books.

Lehman, H. C. (1953). *Age and achievement*. Princeton, N.J.: Princeton University Press.

Lepper, M., Greene, D., & Nisbett, R. (1973). Undermining children's intrinsic interest with extrinsic rewards: A test of the 'overjustification' hypothesis. *Journal of Personality and Social Psychology 28*, 129–37.

Lubart, T. I. (1990). Creativity and cross-cultural variation. *International Journal of Psychology 25*, 39–59.

———— (1994). Creativity. In E. C. Carterette & M. P. Friedman (general eds.), *The handbook of perception and cognition*, vol. 12 (R. J. Sternberg, vol. ed.) (pp. 289–332). New York: Academic Press.

Lubart, T. I., & Sternberg, R. J. (in press). An investment approach to creativity: Theory and data. In S. M. Smith, T. B. Ward, & R. A. Finke (eds.), *The creative cognition approach*. Cambridge, Mass.: MIT Press.

Luchins, A. S., & Luchins, E. H. (1959). *Rigidity of behavior*. Eugene, OR: University of Oregon Press.

MacKinnon, D. W. (1962a). The nature and nurture of creative talent. *American Psychologist 17*, 484–95.

——— (1962b). The personality correlates of creativity: A study of American architects. In G. S. Nielsen (ed.), *Proceedings of the 14th international congress on applied psychology* (vol. 2) (pp. 11–39). Copenhagen: Munksgaard.

——— (1970). Creativity: A multifaceted phenomenon. In J. D. Roslansky (ed.), *Creativity: A discussion at the Nobel Conference*. Amsterdam: North Holland.

Maddi, S. R. (1965). Motivational aspects of creativity. *Journal of Personality 33*, 330–47.

Malkiel, B. G. (1985). *A random walk down Wall Street* (4th ed.). New York: W. W. Norton & Company. (Original published 1973.)

Mann, L. (1980). Cross-cultural studies of small groups. In H. C. Triandis & R. W. Brislin (eds.), *Handbook of cross-cultural psychology (vol. 5: Social Psychology)* (pp. 155–210). Boston, Mass.: Allyn & Bacon.

Markman, E. M. (1979). Realizing that you don't understand: Elementary school children's awareness of inconsistencies. *Child Development 50*, 643–55.

Maslow, A. (1970). *Motivation and personality* (2nd ed.). New York: Harper & Row.

Masten, W. G. & Caldwell-Colbert, A. T. (1987). Relationship of originality to Kirton's scale for innovators and adaptors. *Psychological Reports, 61*, 411–16.

May, R. (1975). *The courage to create*. New York: W. W. Norton & Company.

McClelland, D. C. (1962). On the psychodynamics of creative physical scientists. In H.E. Gruber, G. Terrell, & M. Wertheimer (eds.) *Contemporary approaches to creative thinking* (pp. 141–74). New York: Atherton Press.

McClelland, D. C., Atkinson, J. W., Clark, R. A., & Lowell, E. L. (1953). *The achievement motive*. New York: Appleton-Century-Crofts, Inc.

McCormack, M. H. (1984). *What they don't teach you at Harvard Business School*. New York: Bantam Books.

McCrae, R. R. (1987). Creativity, divergent thinking, and openness to experience. *Journal of Personality and Social Psychology 52*, 1258–65.

Mead, M. (1959). Creativity in cross-cultural perspective. In H. H. Anderson (ed.), *Creativity and its cultivation* (pp. 222–35). New York: Harper & Row.

Mednick, S. A. (1962). The associative basis of the creative process. *Psychological Review 69*, 220–32.

Melia, M. (1989). One tree might be worth a thousand ideas. *Marketing News 23*(23), 20.

Merton, R. K. (1968). The Matthew effect in science. *Science 159*, 56–63.

——— (1973). *The sociology of science*. Chicago: University of Chicago Press.

Mitgang, H. (1984, Jan. 3). Library displays the poet's search for perfection. *New York Times*, p. C-11.

Morgan, B. (1990, June). The man who invented Roger Rabbit. *TV Entertainment*, pp. 25–28.

Morgenstern, J. (1990, Apr. 29). Bart Simpson's real father. *Los Angeles Times*, p. 12.

Mulligan, G., & Martin, W. (1980). Adaptors, innovators, and the Kirton Adaptation-Innovation Inventory. *Psychological Reports 46*, 883–92.

Myers-Briggs type indicator, Form G report form. (1987). Palo Alto, Calif.: Consulting Psychologists Press.

Myers, I. B., & McCaulley, M. H. (1985). *Manual: A guide to use of the Myers-Briggs Type Indicator*. Palo Alto, Calif. Consulting Psychologists Press.

Myers, I. B., & Myers, P. B. (1980). *Gifts differing*. Palo Alto, Calif.: Consulting Psychologists Press.

Newell, A., & Simon, H. A. (1972). *Human problem solving*. Englewood Cliffs, N.J.: Prentice-Hall.

Newman, A. M. (1993, Feb. 28). A teacher tries to free intuitive spirits. *New York Times* (Connecticut, section 13CN), p. 19.

Ochse, R. (1990). *Before the gates of excellence: The determinants of creative genius*. New York: Cambridge University Press.

Okun, M. A., & Di Vesta, F. J. (1976). Cautiousness in adulthood as a function of age and instructions. *Journal of Gerontology 31*(5), 571–76.

Osborn, A. F. (1963). *Applied imagination* (3rd ed.). New York: Charles Scribner & Sons.

Parnes, S. J., & Harding, H. F. (1962). *A source book for creative thinking*. New York: Charles Scribner & Sons.

Pauling, L. (1980). Molecular basis of biological specificity. In J. D. Watson, *The double helix* (Norton Critical Edition, G. S. Stent, ed., pp. 146–53). New York: W. W. Norton and Company.

Planck, M. (1949). *Scientific autobiography and other papers* (trans. F. Gaynor). New York: Philosophical Library.

Plimpton, G. (ed.). (1986). *Writers at work: The Paris review interviews, seventh series*. New York: Viking.

Plimpton, G. (ed.). (1989). *Poets at work*. New York: Penguin.

Poincaré, H. (1921). *The foundations of science*. New York: Science Press.

Polya, G. (1973). *Mathematics and plausible reasoning* (vol. 1). Princeton, N.J.: Princeton University Press.

Raina, M. K. (1968). A study into the effect of competition on creativity. *Gifted Child Quarterly 12*, 217–20.

Ray, M., & Myers, R. (1986) *Creativity in business*. New York: Doubleday.

Renzulli, J. S. (1986). The three-ring conception of giftedness: A developmental model for creative productivity. In R. J. Sternberg & J. E. Davidson (eds.), *Conceptions of giftedness* (pp. 53–92). New York: Cambridge University Press.

Resnick, L. B., & Resnick, D. P. (1992). Assessing the thinking curriculum: New tools for educational reform. In B. R. Gifford & M. C. O'Connor (eds.), *Changing assessments: Alternative views of aptitude, achievement, and instruction* (pp. 37–75). Boston: Kluwer.

Richardson, L. (1994, Jan. 31). More teachers write textbooks out of the curriculum. *New York Times*, pp. B1–B2.

Roe, A. (1953). A psychological study of eminent psychologists and anthropologists, and a comparison with biological and physical scientists. *Psychological Monographs: General and Applied 67*, 352.

Rogers, C. R. (1976). Toward a theory of creativity. In A. Rothenberg & C. R. Hausman (eds.), *The creativity question* (pp. 296–305). Durham, N.C.: Duke University Press. (Originally published 1954)

Romaniuk, J. G., & Romaniuk, M. (1981). Creativity across the lifespan: A measurement perspective. *Human Development 24*, 366–81.

Rosenman, M. F. (1988). Serendipity and scientific discovery. *Journal of Creative Behavior 22*, 132–38.

Rosner, S., & Abt, L. E. (eds.). (1970). *The creative experience*. New York: Grossman Publishers.

Rossman, J. (1931). *The psychology of the inventor: A study of the patentee*. Washington: The Inventor's Publishing Company.

Rothstein, M. (1990, Feb. 16). A new show in and about a theater with a past. *New York Times*, pp. C1, C6.

Roweton, W. E. (1982). Creativity and competition. *Journal of Creative Behavior 16*(2), 89–96.

Rubenson, D. L., & Runco, M. A. (1992). The psychoeconomic approach to creativity. *New Ideas in Psychology 10*(2), 131–47.

Rubin, Z. (1970). Measurement of romantic love. *Journal of Personality and Social Psychology 16*, 265–73.

Runco, M. A. (1987). The generality of creative performance in gifted and nongifted children. *Gifted Child Quarterly 31*(3), 121–25.

Rutherford, F. J., Holton, G., & Watson, F. G. (1975). *Project Physics* (unit 2). New York: Holt, Rinehart, and Winston.

Sarnoff, D. P., & Cole, H. P. (1983). Creativity and personal growth. *Journal of Creative Behavior 17*, 95–102.

Schaeffer, C. E., Diggins, D. R., & Millman, H. L. (1976). Intercorrelations among measures of creativity, openness to experience, and sensation seeking in a college sample. *College Student Journal 10*(4), 332–39.

Schilpp, P. A. (ed.). (1951). *Albert Einstein.* New York: Tudor Publishing Co.

Scribner, S. (1984). Studying working intelligence. In B. Rogoff & J. Lave (eds.), *Everyday cognition* (pp. 9–40). Cambridge, Mass.: Harvard University Press.

Seal, M. (1990). Imagination, Inc. *American Way 23*(23), 54–60, 90–94.

Shahn, B. (1964). The biography of a painting. In V. Thomas (ed.), *Creativity in the Arts* (pp. 13–34). Englewood Cliffs, N.J.: Prentice Hall.

Shepard, R. N. (1978). Externalization of mental images and the act of creation. In B. S. Randhawa & W. E. Coffman (eds.), *Visual learning, thinking, and communication* (pp. 133–89). New York: Academic Press.

Silver, H. R. (1981). Calculating risks: The socioeconomic foundations of aesthetic innovation in an Ashanti carving community. *Ethnology 20*(2), 101–14.

Simon, H. A., & Chase, W. (1973). Skill in chess. *American Scientist 61*, 394–403.

Simonton, D. K. (1975). Sociocultural context of individual creativity: A transhistorical time-series analysis. *Journal of Personality and Social Psychology 32*, 1119–33.

——— (1984). *Genius, creativity, and leadership.* Cambridge, Mass.: Harvard University Press.

——— (1988a). Age and outstanding achievement: What do we know after a century of research? *Psychological Bulletin 104*, 251–67.

——— (1988b). *Scientific genius.* New York: Cambridge University Press.

——— (1991). Career landmarks in science: Individual differences and interdisciplinary contrasts. *Developmental Psychology 27*(1), 119–30.

Staff. (1991). "Guerrilla" marketer leaves Smartfood. *Food and Beverage Marketing 10*(3), p. 12.

Staff. (1994, Mar. 1). John James Audubon. *American Way 27*(5), pp. 92–100.

Stein, B. S. (1989). Memory and creativity. In J. A. Glover, R. R. Ronning, & C. R. Reynolds (eds.), *Handbook of Creativity* (pp. 163–76). New York: Plenum Press.

Stein, M. I. (1962). Creativity and the scientist. In B. Barber & W. Hirsch (eds)., *The sociology of science* (pp. 329–43). New York: Free Press.

―――― (1974). *Stimulating creativity: Vol. 1: individual procedures*. New York: Academic Press.

Sternberg, R. J. (1981). Intelligence and nonentrenchment. *Journal of Educational Psychology 73*, 1–16.

Sternberg, R. J. (ed.). (1982a). *Handbook of human intelligence*. New York: Cambridge University Press.

Sternberg, R. J. (1982b). Natural, unnatural, and supernatural concepts. *Cognitive Psychology 14*, 451–88.

―――― (1982c). Nonentrenchment in the assessment of intellectual giftedness. *Gifted Child Quarterly 26*, 63–67.

―――― (1985a). *Beyond IQ: A triarchic theory of human intelligence*. New York: Cambridge University Press.

―――― (1985b). Implicit theories of intelligence, creativity, and wisdom. *Journal of Personality and Social Psychology 49*, 607–27.

―――― (1986a). Inside intelligence. *American Scientist 74*, 137–43.

―――― (1986b). *Intelligence applied: Understanding and increasing your intellectual skills*. San Diego: Harcourt Brace Jovanovich.

―――― (1986c). A triangular theory of love. *Psychological Review 93*, 119–35.

―――― (1988a). Mental self-government: A theory of intellectual styles and their development. *Human Development 31*, 197–224.

Sternberg, R. J. (ed.). (1988b). *The nature of creativity: Contemporary psychological perspectives*. New York: Cambridge University Press.

Sternberg, R. J. (1988c). A three-facet theory of creativity. In R. J. Sternberg (ed.), *The nature of creativity* (pp. 125–47). New York: Cambridge University Press.

―――― (1988d). *The triangle of love*. New York: Basic Books.

―――― (1988e). *The triarchic mind: A theory of human intelligence*. New York: Viking.

―――― (1990a). *Metaphors of mind: Conceptions of the nature of intelligence*. New York: Cambridge University Press.

―――― (1990b). Thinking styles: Keys to understanding student performance. *Phi Delta Kappan 71*, 366–71.

―――― (1991). *Love the way you want it*. New York: Bantam.

―――― (1994). Thinking styles: Theory and assessment at the interface between intelligence and personality. In R. J. Sternberg and P. Ruzgis (eds.), *Intelligence and personality*. New York: Cambridge University Press.

———— (in press). Human intelligence: Its nature, use, and interaction with context. In D. K. Detterman (ed.), *Current topics in human intelligence* (vol. 4). Norwood, N.J.: Ablex.

Sternberg, R. J., & Davidson, J. E. (1982). The mind of the puzzler. *Psychology Today 16* (June), 37–44.

Sternberg, R. J., & Davidson, J. E. (eds.). (1995). *The nature of insight*. Cambridge, Mass.: MIT Press.

Sternberg, R. J., & Grigorenko, E. L. (1993). Thinking styles and the gifted. *Roeper Review 16* (2),122–30.

Sternberg, R. J., & Lubart, T. I. (1991a). Creating creative minds. *Phi Delta Kappan 72*, 608–14.

———— (1991b). An investment theory of creativity and its development. *Human Development 34*, 1–32.

———— (1992). Buy low and sell high: An investment approach to creativity. *Current Directions in Psychological Science 1*(1), 1–5.

———— (1993). Creative giftedness: A multivariate investment approach. *Gifted Child Quarterly 37*(1), 7–15.

Sternberg, R. J., & Wagner, R. K. (1991). *MSG Thinking Styles Inventory*. Unpublished questionnaire.

———— (1992). Tacit knowledge: An unspoken key to managerial success. *Creativity and Innovation Management 1*, 5–13.

Sternberg, R. J., Wagner, R. K., & Okagaki, L. (1993).Practical intelligence: The nature and role of tacit knowledge in work and at school. In H. Reese & J. Puckett (eds.), *Advances in life span development* (pp. 205–7). Hillsdale, N. J.: Larwrence E rlbaum.

Taylor, D. W. (1961, Oct.). Environment and creativity. In Conference on the creative person. Conference conducted by the Institute of Personality Assessment and Research at the University of California, Berkeley.

Taylor, I. A. (1972). The nature of creative process. In P. Smith (ed.), *Creativity: An examination of the creative process*. New York: Books for Libraries Press. (Original published 1959.)

Tetewsky, S. J., & Sternberg, R. J. (1986). Conceptual and lexical determinants of nonentrenched thinking. *Journal of Memory and Language 25*, 202–25.

Torrance, E. P. (1964). *Role of evaluation on creative thinking*. Minneapolis Minnesota: University of Minnesota, Bureau of Educational Research.

———— (1965). *Rewarding creative behavior: Experiments in classroom creativity*. Engelwood Cliffs, N.J.: Prentice Hall.

————— (1967). Nurture of creative talents. In R. L. Mooney & T. A. Rasik (eds.), *Explorations in creativity* (pp. 185–95). New York: Harper & Row.

————— (1974). *Torrance tests of creative thinking*. Lexington, Mass.: Personnel Press.

————— (1979). *The search for Satori and creativity*. New York: Creative Education Foundation.

————— (1988). The nature of creativity as manifest in its testing. In R. J. Sternberg (ed.), *The nature of creativity: Contemporary psychological perspectives* (pp. 43–75). New York: Cambridge University Press.

Torrance, E. P., & Horng, R. Y. (1980). Creativity and style of learning and thinking characteristics of adaptors and innovators. *Creative Child and Adult Quarterly* 5(2), 80–85.

Treffinger, D. J., Isaksen, S. G., & Firestien, R. L. (1982). *Handbook of creative learning*. New York: Center for Creativity Training.

Uhes, M. J., & Shaver, J. P. (1970). Dogmatism and divergent-convergent abilities. *Journal of Psychology* 75, 3–11.

Vernon, P. E. (ed.). (1970). *Creativity: Selected readings*. Middlesex, England: Penguin.

Wagner, R. K., & Sternberg, R. J. (1986). Tacit knowledge and intelligence in the everyday world. In R. J. Sternberg & R. K. Wagner (eds.), *Practical intelligence: Nature and origins of competence in the everyday world* (pp. 51–83). New York: Cambridge University Press.

————— (1991). Tacit knowledge: Its uses in identifying, assessing, and developing managerial talent. In J. Jones, B. Steffy, & D. Bray (eds.), *Applying psychology in business: The manager's handbook* (pp. 333–44). New York: Human Science Press.

Walberg, H. J. (1988). Creativity and talent as learning. In R. J. Sternberg (ed.), *The nature of creativity* (pp. 340–61). New York: Cambridge University Press.

Ward, W. C. (1969). Creativity and environmental cues in nursery school children. *Developmental Psychology* 1, 543–47.

Watanabe, T. (1990a, June 10). Toward creativity in Japan: "Steven Jobs of Japan" dispels old myths. *Los Angeles Times*, p. D-1.

————— (1990b, June 17). A Japanese rebel wins the respect of establishment. *Los Angeles Times*, p. D-1.

Watson, J. D. (1968). *The double helix*. New York: Atheneum.

Webster's Ninth New Collegiate Dictionary. (1983). Springfield, Mass.: Merriam-Webster.

Wechsler, D. (1944). *The measurement of adult intelligence* (3rd ed.). Baltimore: Williams & Wilkins.

Weisberg, R. (1986). *Creativity, genius, and other myths*. New York: W.H. Freeman Co.

Weiss, P. (1993, Dec. 26). Hollywood at a fever pitch. *New York Times Magazine*, pp. 20–27, 34, 40, 43, 45.

Whiting, B. G. (1988). Creativity and entrepreneurship: How do they relate? *Journal of Creative Behavior* 22(3), 178–83.

Williams, W. M., & Sternberg, R. J. (in press). *Success acts for managers*. New York: Harcourt Brace.

Winerip, M. (1994, Feb. 9). In school: A lifetime's worth of lessons from one stubborn but patient teacher of autistic children. *New York Times* section B, p. 20.

Wyatt-Brown, A. M. (1988). Late style in the novels of Barbara Pym and Penelope Mortimer. *The Gerontologist* 28(6), 835–39.

Zajonc, R. B. (1968). Attitudinal effects of mere exposure. *Journal of Personality and Social Psychology Monograph Supplement 9*, 1–27.

——— (1976). Family configuration and intelligence. *Science 192*, 227–36.

Ziv, A. (1976). Facilitating effects of humor on creativity. *Journal of Educational Psychology 68*(3), 318–22.

——— (1983). The influences of humorous atmosphere on divergent thinking. *Contemporary Educational Psychology 8*, 68–75.

Zuckerman, H. (1977). *Scientific elite: Nobel laureates in the United States*. New York: Free Press.

——— (1983). The scientific elite: Nobel laureates' mutual influences. In R. S. Albert (ed.), *Genius and eminence: The social psychology of creativity and exceptional achievement* (vol. 5, pp. 241–52). New York: Pergamon Press.

Index

317